A GUIDE TO
COLLEGE WRITING

A GUIDE TO
COLLEGE WRITING

Chris M. Anson
North Carolina State University

PEARSON

Boston   Columbus   Indianapolis   New York   San Francisco
Amsterdam   Cape Town   Dubai   London   Madrid   Milan   Munich
Paris   Montréal   Toronto   Delhi   Mexico City   São Paulo
Sydney   Hong Kong   Seoul   Singapore   Taipei   Tokyo

Vice President and Editor in Chief: Joseph Opiela
Program Lead: Lauren Finn
Development Editor: David Kear
Product Marketing Manager: Ali Arnold
Field Marketing Manager: Mark Robinson
Content Specialist: Laura Olson
Media Producer: Elizabeth Bravo
Project Manager: Shannon Kobran
Project Coordination, Text Design, and Electronic Page Makeup: Cenveo® Publisher Services

Program Design Lead: Beth Paquin
Cover Designer: Studio Montage
Cover Art: maxpixblue/123/RF
Senior Manufacturing Buyer: Roy L. Pickering, Jr.
Printer/Binder: Edwards Brothers Malloy
Cover Printer: Lehigh-Phoenix Color/ Hagerstown

Acknowledgments of third-party content appear below appear on the appropriate page or on pages 353-355 which constitute an extension of this copyright page.

PEARSON, ALWAYS LEARNING, and MYWRITINGLAB are exclusive trademarks owned by Pearson Education, Inc. or its affiliates in the United States and/or other countries.

Unless otherwise indicated herein, any third-party trademarks that may appear in this work are the property of their respective owners and any references to third-party trademarks, logos, or other trade dress are for demonstrative or descriptive purposes only. Such references are not intended to imply any sponsorship, endorsement, authorization, or promotion of Pearson's products by the owners of such marks, or any relationship between the owner and Pearson Education, Inc., or its affiliates, authors, licensees, or distributors.

Cataloging-in-Publication Data on file at the Library of Congress

1 2 3 4 5 6 7 8 9 10—EB—19 18 17 16

Student ISBN-10: 0-13-418644-3
Student ISBN-13: 978-0-13-418644-3
A la Carte ISBN-10: 0-13-418650-8
A la Carte ISBN-13: 978-0-13-418650-4

PEARSON

www.pearsonhighered.com

Contents

7 The Comparative Anatomy of Texts *233*

A Guide to College Writing is intended to foster what is probably the single most constructive movement in American college education in the past several decades: *Writing across the Curriculum* (or WAC). In every discipline, in hundreds of colleges and universities, teachers are discovering that writing teaches the writer. History students can write in order to learn history, not just to become better writers or to be tested on their knowledge. Chemistry students can grasp the logic and significance of an experiment by explaining it in prose. Math students are being asked to discuss in writing the application of various formulas to different situations as a means of deepening their comprehension. Even students of dance or studio arts are using writing to keep track of their progress, to reflect on their artistry, and to analyze other people's performances and works. What was once the peculiar domain of departments of English and composition programs has become the responsibility of all college instructors. As an English teacher and lifelong supporter and researcher of writing across the curriculum, I wholeheartedly rejoice in this development and hope that, supported by this book, it will continue to expand.

In spite of the heavy emphasis on writing across the college curriculum today, there exist very few textbooks that help students to understand the variety of, and expectations for, such writing. Busy trying to teach the complex content of their courses, faculty across the curriculum don't always have time or knowledge to help students to write; instead, they may believe that students come into their courses already prepared to write effectively. Research shows that transferring abilities across such contexts represents a serious challenge for students, and they need the knowledge and perspective to understand what to do in unfamiliar assignments and genres.

A Guide to College Writing helps students to navigate the challenges of writing in all college-level courses. Designed both as a guide to be assigned in any college course and as an excellent introduction to college writing for use in a foundational or first-year course, *A Guide to College Writing* takes students through the processes of using writing as a learning tool; understanding and unpacking short, one-draft microtheme assignments that are designed to enhance reading and critical thinking; putting together high-stakes, formal assignments and projects from start to finish (including an entire chapter on drafting and revising); conducting primary or secondary research, including source work and the integration of outside material into a research project; and conducting an "anatomy" of texts in order to understand how particular forms of writing work across a diverse range of contexts.

Unlike books aimed at writing in one specific discipline, *A Guide to College Writing* works at a level of abstraction to make it uniformly useful in all disciplines. The student who uses the book for a writing-intensive History course will not have to return to the bookstore when he or she signs up for a course in Microbiology that requires a hefty term paper. The strategies for developing ideas, refining and testing a thesis, organizing material, drafting, and revising remain largely constant, regardless of content. However, plentiful examples appear throughout the book to show how writing may vary across the disciplines in terms of genre, organization, and style. The final chapter, "The Comparative Anatomy of Texts," leads students to observe and analyze for themselves the distinctive characteristics of any text type—whether it's a movie review, a lab report in a Heat-Transfer course, a mathematical proof, a report of a social-psychological experiment, or a paper in public history—in order to present their own discoveries in the language and forms of the intellectual community of practice that the discipline represents. This book doesn't teach any one form; it teaches how to observe, analyze, and reproduce the forms and concomitant intellectual strategies of whatever texts the students might be asked to read and write.

Features of *A Guide to College Writing*

A Guide to College Writing includes a number of features that are designed to support student understanding and mastery of the concepts, and to apply the concepts that they are learning. These features include the following:

- **What's the Point?** These introductory questions frame the concepts of the chapter and identify for students the skills that they will learn in the chapter.

- **Give It a Try.** Each chapter includes a number of opportunities to practice and apply the skills that are presented in the chapter in a low-stakes fashion, in ways that will directly impact the writing they are doing in other classes.

- **Key Concepts.** Important, foundational ideas *about* writing that students should take with them beyond the course and use in other settings are called out for students in each chapter. Longer explanations of them appear in the glossary of Key Concepts at the end of the book.

- **Putting It into Practice.** This chapter-ending feature provides a summary of the key concepts covered in the chapter and lists broader ways in which students can begin to apply the concepts and skills throughout their courses.

- **Sample Assignments.** Unpacking assignments is an important skill that will help students better develop their writing skills. Throughout the book, sample assignments are included to help students better understand the goals of their writing and the rhetorical situation of their assignments.

- **Sample Student Texts.** Analyzing student texts is a valuable tool for students to use in order to assess their own writing. At various points, sample student texts are included to demonstrate the concepts discussed and are analyzed to demonstrate their strengths and weaknesses.

- **Professional Texts.** Chapter 7 presents and analyzes in detail three sample professional texts (from the sciences, social sciences, and humanities) as a way to bring all of the concepts from the book together and demonstrate how they can produce a successful essay.

How This Book Is Organized

Although *A Guide to College Writing* is designed primarily as a textbook that provides support to students in both entry-level courses with a cross-curricular emphasis and courses in any and all disciplines in which writing is assigned, it also echoes many of the principles and methods that teachers use to weave writing into their courses. In this way, there is symmetry between what teachers do in their instruction and the support and advice that students need, which are often difficult to include instructionally because so much significant content must be covered.

Especially when they first enter college, students are not always acquainted with the way in which writing varies across different courses and disciplines. Chapter 1 introduces students to foundational principles of writing in all disciplines, explaining how writing works in college courses across the disciplines. It offers students strategies for what to do when they enter new contexts in which the writing requirements and genres may be unfamiliar. At the center of those strategies is activating prior knowledge and analyzing situations using metacognitive strategies. Chapter 1 also introduces a model of writing in academic courses that is often used by teachers, starting with learning goals that lead to specific assignment designs, then moving to supporting activities, and finally ending with the role of evaluation and how it can be used productively during the writing process.

Chapter 2 introduces the concept of writing to learn and the distinction between low-stakes and high-stakes writing. It then introduces students to academic journals and learning (b)logs as a highly effective strategy for understanding course material more deeply and thoroughly. Varieties of learning blogs include collaborative forums and dialogues in which students work with each other to strengthen their explorations of course material. Chapter 2 also describes the process of reflection, which is central to a deeper learning of all subject matters and is made more effective through writing.

Chapter 3 describes a type of focused low-stakes writing called the microtheme. Microthemes are brief, unrevised papers that are assigned for the purpose of helping students to practice and learn various intellectual processes, especially those common to different disciplines. Students are shown how to unpack microtheme assignments in order to understand their form, purpose or goal, level of formality, and audience. Beneath microthemes (and all writing assignments) is a *structure of activity*—a set of underlying processes that students need to engage in to learn most fully. The chapter includes explanations and examples of structures of activity from actual assignments. Finally, Chapter 3 explains the concept of critical thinking, using microthemes to demonstrate the processes of description, analysis, synthesis, and interpretation. Plentiful examples of microthemes from many disciplines are included.

Chapter 4 provides support for larger, high-stakes, and more formal writing projects. It begins with a discussion of "transfer": the process of deploying skills and knowledge of writing across different contexts. It then turns to strategies for exploring a subject thoroughly before and while writing a high-stakes paper, including methods of invention. A section on the thesis provides advice and examples for creating and supporting a well-defined, compelling thesis statement. This discussion is followed by a section on organizational strategies, focusing on how to structure a piece of writing based on its goals.

Chapter 5 is devoted entirely to drafting and revising a high-stakes writing project. The chapter begins with strategies for producing a full rough draft of a writing project and then includes a thorough treatment of revision. Three resources for prompting revision are explored: the writer's own resources, such as self-evaluation strategies; peer response; and the resources of a writing center or tutorial service. The chapter focuses predominantly on the broader structural, content-based, stylistic, and genre-conforming aspects of revision, as distinct from editing and proofreading.

Chapter 6 explores the purposes, varieties, and nature of research in undergraduate education. It begins by distinguishing between primary and secondary research, and orients research in the context of discipline-based inquiry. Students are then led through strategies for designing a compelling, manageable research question and for beginning to find information related to that question. A section on developing a search strategy is followed by helpful advice about how to put the project or paper together. The chapter ends with a section on source use and documentation, showing students the importance of understanding and practicing specific documentation styles that are common to specific disciplines.

Chapter 7 leads students through the process of analyzing—that is, "anatomizing"—texts in specific fields. Each part of the anatomy is explained with examples while students are also working through their own chosen example from a discipline in which they intend to major or specialize. Following the description of the process are anatomies of three sample articles: one from the hard sciences, one from the social sciences, and one from the humanities.

A glossary gathers together all of the Key Concept sidebars in one place and provides extended definitions, elaborations, and examples.

Instructor's Manual

Closely matching the structure of *A Guide to College Writing*, the Instructor's Manual provides expert advice and strategies for teachers of first-year composition as well as teachers of any discipline who are incorporating writing into their courses. Chapter 1 provides background on writing across the curriculum from a professional and pedagogical perspective, offering insights from the literature on this important movement. Chapter 2 lays out a rationale for low-stakes writing to learn, and includes tips for responding to and evaluating students' work and tying prompts to course content. Chapter 3 turns to the creation and integration of microthemes and other focused, brief writing assignments designed to encourage critical analysis, problem solving, and dialogism. Plentiful examples of assignments and student work from across the curriculum are included. Chapter 4 leads instructors through the process of designing, supporting, and evaluating higher-stakes, formal projects. Material includes suggestions for linking assignment design to course goals, creating evaluation criteria or rubrics, and building opportunities for students to practice important processes before tackling a paper. Chapter 5 focuses on tools for teaching drafting and revising, including a major section on how to make peer-group revision conferences really work, through preparation, modeling, accountability, and assessment. Chapter 6 offers suggestions for teaching and supporting the research process, with plentiful attention to helping students develop compelling research questions, choose appropriate methods if they are conducting primary research, and writing and documenting a research paper (whether based on primary or secondary research). Chapter 7 provides support for leading students through an "anatomy" of a sample text, especially one in their discipline. The Instructor's Manual also has material on how to use the

Key Concepts in the book, how to design a writing-intensive course that incorporates the material in the book, and how to provide response on students' work through different modes such as screencast technology and the use of text expanders.

Pearson Writer and *A Guide to College Writing*

Good writing is an important skill that opens doors for students, whether in school or in the workplace. **Pearson Writer** offers writing support for anyone, regardless of skill level, subject, or discipline. It's affordable, built for mobile devices, and easy to use, so rather than spending time learning new software, students can just focus on their ideas. **Pearson Writer** takes care of the labor-intensive details of writing—gathering and citing sources, proofreading for grammar and usage, and staying organized—so that students can concentrate on what matters. Students' grades will improve, their thoughts will be clearer, and they will become better writers.

The *Disciplines* section of **Pearson Writer** provides guidance on writing in a number of disciplines, both for the classroom and for a student's career. Each discipline includes *Strategies for Writing* in that discipline, including common types of writing, strategies for success, and expectations and conventions. Numerous examples of the types of writing in each discipline are also available, with annotations focusing on organizational strategies, style, format, and research. Combining the discipline-specific instruction with the coverage in this text will help students develop writing skills in both their chosen disciplines and across the curriculum.

Additional features of Pearson Writer include the following:

- **Writing, Grammar & Research Guide** is a student's go-to resource anytime the student has a question or needs help.

- **Automatic Writing Review** checks papers for possible spelling, grammar, and style errors, while offering grammar lessons and suggestions for revising and editing.

- **Citation Generator** keeps track of every source throughout a student's research and builds the student's bibliography in the background, taking care of formatting details.

- **Research Database** finds relevant, reputable academic sources for research papers.
- **Project and Task Manager** helps the student stay on top of multiple projects and make sure deadlines are not missed.

See more at: http://www.pearsonhighered.com/writer.

Acknowledgments

I am indebted first to my wife, Gean Anson, for enduring yet another book project that often took my time away from our other activities; and to my sons, Ian and Graham Anson, for their continuing support of my work. Joe Opiela at Pearson had a vision for this book from the start and faith that I could complete it in record time, and I am grateful for his organized way of making that happen. I also wish to thank the reviewers: Laura Brady, West Virginia University; Pamela B. Childers, Lesley University and University of Phoenix; Virginia Crank, University of Wisconsin—La Crosse; Tajsha N. Eaves, Cleveland Community College; Kathleen Gonso, Northeastern University; Sherry Hart, Appalachian State University; Melissa Ianetta, University of Delaware; Rita Malenczyk, Eastern Connecticut State University; Dan Melzer, University of California—Davis; Tracy Ann Morse, East Carolina University; Tim Peeples, Elon University; K. L. Redfield, Forsyth Technical Community College; Erika Scheurer, University of St. Thomas; Stacey Sheriff, Colby College; Julie M. Thompson, Metropolitan State University; Terry Myers Zawacki, George Mason University and to the many faculty at North Carolina State and across the country, especially those at the University of St. Thomas in St. Paul, Minnesota, who have given me a smorgasbord of ideas about teaching writing in the disciplines from their excellent work. Many of those ideas and examples appear in this book. David Kear, Development Editor, provided excellent advice from start to finish, and his words of encouragement were much appreciated. Thanks also to the fine team at Pearson who shepherded this book through its production: Shannon Kobran, Project Manager; Ali Arnold, Marketing Manager; and Emily Brower, Editorial Assistant.

Chris Anson

Introduction

Writing to Learn, Learning to Write

Imagine that someone asks you for your opinion on, say, why, according to world statistics, the United States isn't Number 1 in the educational achievement of students by the time they finish high school. You might offer the first thought that comes to mind—for example, that American kids have too many distractions to study hard (sports, watching TV, playing video games, hanging out at the mall). Now imagine that you're asked to *write* about this question informally. At first you might just write down your initial response, but then, as you reread and think about that idea—as it loops back into your mind from the screen or page—it generates new thoughts. Are all video games "anti-learning? What skills are practiced by playing video games? Is free time, such as being with friends, a bad thing? Don't most children around the world have some free time? What else might account for this fact? Are some of the higher-achieving countries smaller, with fewer problems such as poverty that can affect schooling? What percentage of the U.S. gross domestic product (GDP) is spent on education compared with higher-achieving countries? How well trained are the countries' teachers? How well paid are they? How respected are they? Maybe we don't emphasize the importance of education strongly enough. Is education just a "bitter pill" to swallow on the way to getting a job? Maybe youth culture negatively stereotypes being "smart." What about disproportionate school funding? And what about the "fact" itself? Is it a *good* fact? Where did it come from, who generated it, and with what tools?

Even a little writing opens up new ideas and new possible interpretations that might not have occurred to you at first. Writing *inscribes* and *makes visible* your thoughts, which then come back at you and generate more thoughts. Notice the questions, too; writing expresses what you already know and what you don't know. If you were asked to look into this question in more detail, you'd want to know what percentage of the highest-achieving countries' GDP is spent on education and how much the United States spends, or what survey results say about kids' motivation to be in school (yes, there are surveys on that), or what percentage of their time kids watch TV or play video games. Your quick, initial writing might seem unpolished and haphazard, but there's no question that your *thinking* will be more complex, more detailed, and more sophisticated now. What happened?

The first time you thought about the question, the response flickered briefly in your mind and probably vanished. As you wrote, though, you didn't just give a knee-jerk response; you actively examined the question. You had to, in order to write something. You had to turn the question over, considering it from different angles and perspectives, extending its reach and complexity. Writing about the question forced you to explore it more carefully than before and drove it deeper into your consciousness.

Writing about anything invites you—actually, almost forces you—to think more deeply about a subject than you have before. By putting your thoughts into words and making them "stick" to a screen or page, your notes act like a sort of external memory, allowing you to preserve more questions, hunches, and intuitions than you could ever remember on your own. By pressing you to find the right words to capture your thoughts, writing also demands a certain concentration, solidity, and definition in your thinking. The wispy, half-formulated thought, instead of dissolving into a mist, gains body and firmness when you force yourself to find the words to record it. (Go back to a Facebook post you made a year or two ago, and see how it awakens the memory of an event that's become just a blur.) Your idea comes out of the shadows and into the daylight, where you can then *do* something with it: affirm it, question it, share it, test it, research it, discredit it, prove it, modify it, and/or develop it. Any of these will lead to more thought and maybe even more writing. By now, you've gone well past simple memorization of details or a knee-jerk response and into the development of genuinely new knowledge and new understanding.

Why This Book?

A Guide to College Writing will show you ways to use writing in order to explore your own thinking, to teach yourself, and to teach others. As you read and follow the suggestions in this book, you will write to learn, write to demonstrate learning, and write to inform others. You'll soon be surprised by how much more fully you can understand, recall, manipulate, and use the information you confront. A substantial body of research bears out this observation. Exercise builds muscle; writing builds intellect. It's a pretty reliable finding.

This simple discovery is what has driven the *writing across the curriculum* movement for decades (or WAC for short). Professors from all disciplines know that *writing teaches the writer*. Writing about history teaches the student history; writing about philosophy leads to deeper thinking about philosophical issues; writing about chemistry helps you to think like a chemist. Even in math departments, professors ask students to write in plain English about complicated equations and proofs, with the result that students become better mathematicians (and better writers as well).

One important discovery about this movement concerns reading. Students and teachers have long known that there's reading, and then there's *Reading*. It's one thing to let your eyes drift listlessly over a column of prose and then walk away, with the content dribbling out your ears. It's another to read an article, then try to state on-screen just what the author's point is, and what you have made of it. Suddenly, a vague impression seems vaguer still. What *is* the author's point? And *why* is it important? Then you're back to the article, getting to the real heart of the matter. By comparing your attempted summary to the original source, you can refine your understanding of what the author actually said. A bit more writing and thinking then leads you to an understanding of the significance of the author's ideas *for you*.

As a result, your reading sticks. You understand, you remember, and you have a clearer notion of what you think of it all. By exploring that simple fact about educational achievement, you have learned to see it, and you are able to raise some questions about its broader significance. By writing about a book, an article, a lecture, or an observation of an experiment, you actually read or see or listen in a more searching and thoughtful way.

For all these reasons, today's students can expect to be writing *a lot*, no matter what their major and specialty. If you're a student, this probably doesn't strike you as great news. After all, writing is work. Few tasks take as much time and energy—sheer intellectual muscle—as thinking through a problem, organizing an answer, and stringing it across the screen, word by word, paragraph by paragraph.

It can also be unsettling. When you write, you're forced to take a stand, to put your ideas on the line. You're exposed in an essay in a way that you never are in working out an equation. Seeing that exposure, line for line, can make writing slow and painful. Many people sit at their keyboard and think, "I'm no good at this. I'm not a writer. Every time I do this, it's hard and it looks crappy." Writing is tough work, and it can be nerve-racking, especially under a deadline. I know this. As a writer myself, I live with it daily. Having studied, taught, and practiced writing for many years, though, I've learned helpful ways of going about it. Writing can be useful, satisfying, intriguing, and profitable—especially in how strongly good writing is related to career advancement. To realize these benefits, I'd like you to try a few of the approaches that have worked for countless writers.

What's in This Book

A Guide to College Writing is designed to help you use writing as effectively as possible as a way to *learn the material of your courses*, *communicate your ideas*, and *develop your thinking*. The book isn't tailored to any specific subject. Anything that can be talked about can be written about, and anything that can be written about can be thought about more deeply and learned more fully as a result. This book can be as useful to a biochemistry major as to a history major, and as useful to an engineer as to a musicologist. Further, in Introductory Composition courses, it offers you a preview of how writing will work in all your college courses. Some principles and methods in the book can be used across all majors, all disciplines, and maybe even all writing situations. Others you will have to adapt and repurpose to fit the specific context in which you're writing.

Chapter 1 offers an overview of how writing works in college and university settings. It explains the difference between the writing you'll usually find in Introductory Composition courses and the kinds of writing you will be assigned in other "content" courses, such as Biology, History, or Physics. It also shows you the importance of developing a higher level of knowledge *about* writing, and describes an assignment design model that many teachers use to structure and evaluate students' writing.

Chapter 2 first explains the difference between low-stakes, informal writing and high-stakes, formal writing. The first kind then becomes the focus of the chapter as it makes a case for using informal writing as a way to strengthen learning. Keeping a learning log or an academic journal is an excellent way to deepen your understanding of course material and to explore its significance. More importantly, when you write a lot *about* the material you are learning, your *reading* and *understanding* will improve, and you'll likely perform better on tests of your knowledge, take more from each course, and earn higher grades. This chapter also shows you the value of carrying on academic dialogues with your peers.

Chapter 3 helps you to understand the purpose and value of "microthemes," short, one-draft assignments that are geared toward certain kinds of problem solving, the practice of various intellectual skills, or stronger and more insightful reading. Microthemes can be unique, creative, and even fun, because they don't have to be restricted to the forms that are common to the discipline. This chapter shows you how to "unpack" a microtheme assignment and consider its underlying "structure of activity," or the kinds of thinking it requires. A section on critical thinking helps you to understand what's behind this all-purpose term and shows you ways to practice analysis, synthesis, evaluation, and interpretation—four mental activities at the heart of much college learning and many writing assignments.

Chapters 4 and 5 shift the focus to higher-stakes, larger, and more formal assignments. Chapter 4 shows you strategies for coming up with ideas for a longer paper, considering your audience(s), and finding a clear, logical structure for presenting your information. Drafting and revising, because they're so important to good writing and to learning how to write more effectively, get their own coverage in Chapter 5. Here you'll learn strategies for producing a full rough draft of your material; how to use self-evaluation strategies to work back through your drafts; how to make the most of peer feedback (and provide it in turn); and how to make the best use of a writing center or tutorial service.

Chapter 6 is all about *research*. No one escapes the need to engage in research in college, whether it's researching what others have found out about a topic or conducting your own research (such as administering a survey, running an experiment, or writing an ethnography of some human context). This chapter shows you how to ask good questions for research, how to collect and analyze sources that are relevant to your topic, and how to assemble all of your information into a compelling, readable paper.

Finally, Chapter 7 introduces you to the process of "anatomizing" the writing or discourse of a particular field. As the early chapters point out, it's often difficult to "transfer" what you learn from one context to a new one. How can you use what you learned in first-year Composition as you tackle a challenging assignment in a Social Psychology course using a type of writing that you've never done? This chapter shows you how you can begin "reading" new contexts, especially different disciplines, in order to understand how writing works in them. The strategies you learn here will stand you in good stead, not only as you move across the landscape of higher education, but also as you eventually move into work settings where some or many types of writing will be unfamiliar.

Along the way, you'll find several features included in the book. At the start of each chapter is a list, titled "What's the Point?," that tells you what you'll be encountering in the chapter and why. Throughout each chapter you'll also see "Key Concept" sidebars.

These are important, foundational ideas *about* writing that you should take with you beyond the course into other contexts. (Longer explanations of these appear in the Glossary of Key Terms at the end of the book.) Periodic sections, called "Give It a Try," offer you a chance to practice various strategies or to explore concepts more fully, either on your own or by the invitation of your instructor. Finally, at the end of each chapter, you'll find activities called "Putting It into Practice." These outline broader ways that you can implement the strategies and advice in the chapter as you work on your projects and assignments.

Admittedly, that's a lot to cover, but if you hold this book up edgewise, you'll see how compact it is. If you're like most people, you're busy. The book moves quickly and offers its advice succinctly. Other help will come from your instructor along the way, from the growing resources online, and, at times, from your peers. But you have to pitch in as well.

Learning to write is like learning to play the piano (or tennis, or chess). It takes just a minute to explain a good forehand, a difficult key change, or a strategic board move, but it takes lots of practice to master it. The book can give you great advice, but to learn it, you need to try it out, experiment with it, and give it your best shot. Write about what you hear, what you read, and what you think. Write *in order to* think. It really will make you smarter. And it can be very interesting.

1

Writing across the Curriculum—and Why You Should Care

After you read, think about, and put this chapter into practice, you will be able to:

- Explain why there's a lot of writing in college
- Differentiate between writing in foundational courses and writing in other disciplines
- Understand the importance of "metaknowledge" for writing successfully in different contexts
- Recognize the term *genre* and know how genres are defined in different contexts, called *communities of practice*
- Use an assignment design model to understand how teachers build assignments into their courses and how that can help you know how best to complete them

Writing in College

Imagine this. You're enrolled in a Geography course focusing on global migrations and are attending the first class session. When Professor Werner projects the online syllabus on the screen in the classroom, you find that there are six writing assignments: two "migration in the news" reports, a data and mapping paper, a gapminder exercise, a country migration report, and a report of an interview (see Figure 1.1). The interview paper at least sounds familiar, but what about the others? What are they? What are they supposed to look like? What should their content be? What style is appropriate? Do they need research and references?

Course activities:
> Since learning is best done using all parts of the brain, we will read, discuss, report, write, see videos, use case studies, do research, have debates, listen to community leaders, and have field experiences.

Grades (% of total):

Migration in the news reports (2)	10
Data and mapping exercise	5
Gapminder exercise	5
Country migration report	20
Class exercises	20
Interview and report	20
Field trips (4)	20
TOTAL	**100**

If you are keen to investigate some specific topic, just let me know and we can factor it into your grade. For example, if you are motivated to research women and migration, human trafficking, or Russians in our city, and want to write a term-paper length paper and make a class presentation, we can figure out a way to do that.

FIGURE 1.1 A Section of the Online Syllabus from Geography 231

As Professor Werner talks more about the course, you learn that some of the assignments are weightier than others—at least in their length and in the percentage of the grade that they earn. The country migration report and the interview and report paper are the most substantial. Each counts for 20 percent of the final grade, or nearly half the course together. For the country migration report, you need to choose a country and then research its migration issues, providing an objective description and some analysis of the trends. For the interview and report paper, you need to find and interview a migrant from another country, and then write a paper discussing not just the "facts" of the person's history but also what Professor Werner calls the "nuances" of the person's experience as a migrant.

Alongside these larger projects are short assignments, such as two "migration in the news" reports, each worth 5 percent of your grade. In these papers, you must research a migration issue being covered in the media, write up a brief report of the issue, and make a "micropresentation" to the class about it. The "gapminder" exercise, also worth 5 percent, requires you to use an online program that shows the gaps between economically developed and underdeveloped countries. You need to study one of the variables (income, employment, health, education, etc.) between the United States and a country where people are migrating from, and then reflect on the results. By the time Professor Werner has finished introducing the course, you realize that *writing* is going to play a leading role. But why? After all, this is a geography course. Shouldn't writing be taught in the English Department? What does a geography expert know about writing?

In fact, Professor Werner is doing what thousands of teachers are doing in colleges and universities of every kind: carefully integrating writing into their courses, supporting its development, and using it to make up a significant portion of students' grades. Consider the parallel between writing and speaking. Why wouldn't a professor of, say, Genetics who is untrained in the discipline of Communication Studies lead a class discussion in which students *speak* to learn the subject matter? Every teacher, no matter what the discipline, uses reading, writing, speaking, listening, and visual and digital literacy not only in their own work but also in order to help students to learn. Today, you're as likely to write a lot in Introduction to Soil Science, Principles of Anthropology, Advanced Calculus, Explorations in Musicology, and Genetics 101 as you are in Basic Composition. Here's why:

- *Writing about what you are learning enhances your learning.* When you try to express your knowledge in a course, you discover gaps that tell you what you need to review or learn anew. When you write to go over what you have learned, you solidify and strengthen it in your memory. When you write *about* themes, information, opinions, and research, you explore the material more deeply and learn it more fully. *Writing* extends your knowledge and helps you to perform better on tests.

- *Writing in all your courses improves your writing.* Writing is one of the most "developmental" of all abilities, meaning that it improves slowly over many years. You can't write for just fifteen weeks in a composition course and expect to be done "learning how to write." Writing takes *constant* practice—years of it. Ask any person over the age of fifty (or sixty, or seventy) whether they are still learning to write, and almost always they'll say yes. If you write in every course you take, your writing ability strengthens and prepares you for many situations, especially in the workplace, where people usually sink or swim depending on how well they can write.

- *Writing about material in different courses helps you learn to adapt to new situations as a writer.* If all you know is dancing at raves and you're invited to a ballroom dance, you'll feel bewildered ("Where am I supposed to put my feet?" "Why is everyone moving in the same way?"). If all you know are five-paragraph themes and you're asked to write an in-depth historical analysis of a battle from the perspective of both warring factions, your lack of experience with different kinds of writing will not allow you to adapt quickly. Writing in many contexts gives you experience with different forms, styles, and purposes for writing.

Writing across the Curriculum and in the Disciplines

Before we begin exploring how an understanding of writing in all disciplines can help you to succeed, let's consider the place of writing across most of higher education.

It's very likely that your college or university requires you to take an introductory composition course in your first year. That course gives you *foundational knowledge and experience*. The course is there to get you started writing at a college level by teaching you new perspectives and skills. But many students make the mistake of thinking it's a be-all and end-all—that it's like learning to swim or to ride a bike. Once you learn it, you're done. In fact, many students make an even more serious mistake of assuming that they "got" writing in *high school* and shouldn't have to keep taking courses in it.

Nothing could be further from the truth. The term *foundational course* brings to mind a building. The foundation of a building is useless until a structure gets created on top of it. In writing, the structure comes from all sorts of other writing experiences in courses like Sociology 300 or Elements of Particle Physics or Principles of Nursing. Some of the courses may be ones that you take as part of general-education requirements, but, eventually, all of your upper-level courses will be in (or in some way relate to) your major field of study. In upper-level courses, you learn specialized kinds of writing used in the higher reaches of academic research or in the occupations that your major prepares you for.

As Figure 1.2 suggests, you begin your college education with one or more courses focusing strongly or exclusively on becoming a more skilled writer. These are designed to prepare you for the kinds of writing you will encounter in your other courses, first in general courses you take in various areas and then in specialized courses you take in your major. The writing in those courses will be

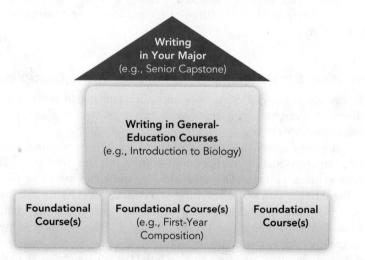

Writing in Your Major
(e.g., Senior Capstone)

Writing in General-Education Courses
(e.g., Introduction to Biology)

Foundational Course(s)

Foundational Course(s)
(e.g., First-Year Composition)

Foundational Course(s)

FIGURE 1.2 The Place of Writing in the College Curriculum

more strongly focused on the particular *content* or *knowledge* being taught. And there will be a lot of writing: the National Survey of Student Engagement, which is administered to tens of thousands of students at hundreds of colleges and universities across the United States, reports that on average students write approximately 100 pages in their first year of college and 150 pages as seniors. And that doesn't include a lot more informal writing, as we'll explore in Chapter 2.

Encountering New Writing Contexts

The first thing you'll notice about writing in a college setting is its diversity. Yes, there are lots of assignments with familiar labels: *term paper, summary, lab report, essay*. But it's important to recognize that alongside these common forms of writing in college are many *discipline-based* forms as well—writing that relates to the kinds of thinking, research, and activities that people within academic and professional fields engage in. If you were to do an inventory of writing assignments across your college or university curriculum, you would probably find a lot of strange-sounding names:

- phase report
- crit
- script cover
- integration project
- provided-data paper
- company obituary
- object condition report
- evidentiary historical analysis
- "damned lies" analysis
- literacy biography
- antipaper
- society argument
- violation of social norms analysis

- scheduled reinforcement report
- case analysis

(Not to mention a country migration report or a gapminder exercise!)

Second, many college-level writing assignments that may sound familiar will involve entirely different kinds of thinking and writing. Consider the word *analysis*. You've probably been asked to analyze something dozens of times in your education. But look at how analysis is described in just three different disciplines:

Sociology: Society is really a process, made up of ongoing interactions at multiple levels of size and complexity, and to turn it into a monolithic thing is to lose all that complexity. People make decisions and choices. Some groups and individuals benefit, whereas others do not. Identifying these intermediate levels is the basis of sociological analysis.

Chemistry: Quantitative chemical analysis is a branch of chemistry that deals with the determination of the amount or percentage of one or more constituents of a sample. A variety of methods is employed for quantitative analyses, which for convenience may be broadly classified as chemical or physical, depending upon which properties are utilized.

Art History: [The formal analysis] requires a detailed description of the "formal" qualities of the art object (*formal* here means "related to the form," not "fancy" or "elegant"). In other words, you're looking at the individual design elements, such as composition (arrangement of parts of the work or parts in the work), color, line, texture, scale, proportion, balance, contrast, and rhythm. Your primary concern … is to attempt to explain how the artist arranges and uses these various elements.

Further, even the *same fields* may use different kinds of "analysis" to discover new knowledge. For example, in political science, quantitative scholars rely on statistics, while political theorists favor careful interpretation and historical study:

Political theory differs from other subfields in political science in that it deals primarily with historical and normative, rather than empirical, analysis. In other words, political theorists are less concerned with the scientific measurement of political phenomena than with understanding how important political ideas develop over time. And they are less concerned with evaluating how things are than with debating how they should be.

As you'll see in later chapters, certain very general properties of "analysis" are common across fields, but as these explanations suggest, specific objects, processes, and goals of analysis will differ. This is just one example of the kinds of context-specific interpretations you'll have to make when you encounter new tasks. Terms such as *observe, collect, organize, process, distill, summarize, synthesize,* and *reflect* will take on certain meanings when they refer to different phenomena across disciplines.

The third thing you'll notice about writing in a college setting is that your teachers will assign papers that are unique to their specific course. These papers can be hybrids of different assignments, such as a personal interpretation of an art object that then morphs into a formal analysis following some research into the artist or the context of the work. Or they can be staged or sequenced assignments that involve different kinds of papers linked together around a specific subject. Or they can be one-of-a-kind assignments that require creativity in the midst of analysis, such as asking students to pretend they are a gram-positive bacterium that has infected a human being and then write a series of blog posts (from the perspective of the bacterium) chronicling what happens to them until the infection is resolved.

So, how can you do well if you keep wandering into new and unfamiliar places where the writing isn't what you are used to? First, don't worry. You don't have to learn all of these and many other types and uses of writing—no one does. But at the same time, you do need to learn at least some new forms, styles, and contexts for writing. As you move into courses within your major, you'll find that what you've learned to do in your introductory writing courses and some of your general-education courses won't just effortlessly apply to the new kinds of writing and thinking in your major. You'll need to study and practice these new forms, with the help of your instructors and mentors. This process is sometimes called *enculturation* into a discipline. If you think that sounds anthropological or sociological, it is: it's about becoming a *member* of a group tied together by the

> **KEY CONCEPT** *Enculturation* refers to the process of becoming a member of a group (a discipline, a laboratory, a church, etc.) and learning how it communicates among its members and with others. See Key Concept Glossary.

goals and objects of their inquiry, by the way they explore those objects, and by the forms of communication they use among themselves to communicate it.

In essence, that's the subject of this book, and further chapters will help to prepare you to figure out what to do when you write in courses as different as economics, philosophy, and entomology. But before we launch into the specifics, let's review a few fundamental concepts.

Metaknowledge

One emphasis of this book is on developing and using what's called *metaknowledge*, a way of thinking about how thinking is done (and, in this case, how writing is done). For example, if you've ever practiced some kind of activity, such as playing an instrument or creating something artistic, your metaknowledge is activated when you stand back from *doing* the activity and reflect on it. Coaches and teachers often help you do this by giving you conscious strategies to reflect on before, during, and after the activity:

> **KEY CONCEPT** *Metaknowledge* is knowledge about knowledge—what knowledge is and how it's created. It's a way of standing back from what you're doing and thinking consciously about it. See Key Concept Glossary.

Yoga instructor to yoga student: OK, let's walk through how to do the half-standing forward bend. As I explain this, make a mental map of these motions to remember and focus on. First, make sure that your hands are at the middle of your shins. Now lift your upper body so that your shoulders are about on the same plane as your hips. Move your spine forward and push your thighs back. You should feel your spinal muscles engage at this point. Now try it.

Guitar lesson on YouTube: OK, so the song's in D minor. So we're going to be in this D minor pentatonic shape, first position to start with.

And the beginning is in harmony. Most of the solo is in harmony. So we're going to start here on fret 12 on the D string to 10 on the G.

When we're concentrating on an activity we already know something about, we alternate between just *doing* the activity and then applying our conscious, "stand-back-from-it" knowledge, often during periods between the activity (e.g., you might spend an hour just playing your guitar along to some tunes, but then you might consciously practice some chords because you noticed you had some trouble during some of the songs). When we find ourselves in a place where actions and behaviors are unfamiliar, we scan our own prior experience to see if anything we know "fits" the situation— something we can "transfer" from the known to the unknown. We'll consider the concept of *transfer* in more detail in Chapter 4.

Consider this example. If we were not raised in Japan, the first time we go to a sushi restaurant, we may not know what to do with the green paste piled in a little mound on one side of the plate, or what the pinkish slices are next to the green paste, or what to do with the little bowl of soy sauce, or how to hold the chopsticks. Our prior experience tells us that sauce in a little bowl is usually for putting on the food—so far so good. But we're not sure whether to pour the sauce onto the sushi pieces or dip the pieces into it. Again, we apply reasoning and prior knowledge, figuring that a small, somewhat flat bowl would not be a good receptacle to pour something from, and we remember that, in Chinese restaurants, the bowl of similar shape that contains sweet and sour sauce is there to dip our egg roll into. We would also probably glance around to see what other diners are doing with the paste, the soy sauce, and the little sliced pieces of radish, in a process called *modeling.* We might experiment, too—and that's OK, even if we do it wrong. Eventually, we would learn how it's done, especially

> **KEY CONCEPT** In writing, *modeling* is a process of looking at the behaviors and products of writers in a specific context in order to acquire knowledge and produce texts that adhere to the conventions that define the community's expectations. For example, if you've never taken minutes at a meeting, it would help you a lot to see what a set of meeting minutes looks like and how someone writes them. See Key Concept Glossary.

if we get help and advice. When we become aware of this process (of mapping existing information onto the new situation), we are using a higher-level, "meta" kind of thinking. We're consciously standing back from the situation and analyzing it in order to know how to act.

Notice that, in the sushi situation, you need *prior knowledge* about *what* to do: the soy sauce is there to dip the sushi in, the pickled ginger slices are there to cleanse your palate between bites, the green paste (called *wasabi*) adds flavor (and some spiciness) to the sushi, and only a little is placed on top of a piece of sushi, although some Americans mix it into the soy sauce, and so on. You also need to know "how." You might know *that* you hold chopsticks in one hand and pick up the sushi pieces with them, but you need to know *how* to do that (a skill only learned with time, patience, and practice). It's essential to have "*that*-knowledge" in writing—that, for example, an object condition report is used by curators in museums for a number of different purposes, including displaying or storing the object. But to write an object condition report you also need "*how*-knowledge": how to organize the information, how to write in the appropriate style, and how to include references to authorities about what humidity levels might damage the object. Similarly, you might know *about* lab reports—that they describe the procedures and outcomes of experiments—but until you've tried to create one, you may lack "*how*-knowledge."

> **KEY CONCEPT** *Prior knowledge* refers to what you already know or have experienced and can use in a new situation. See Key Concept Glossary.

In new and unfamiliar contexts for writing, having tools for "going meta" will be highly valuable for more quickly figuring out how writing works in those contexts. Developing skills to analyze your audience(s) and purpose(s) will give you "*that*-knowledge" which then greatly helps as you figure out *how*: how to make decisions about your style, structure, and other features of your writing. Modeling will also do this. There will always be some trial and error, which is what all learning involves. But you'll begin to "get it" more quickly, through less trial and, most important, less error, than if you just keep plugging away without reflecting on writing and your experience doing it. We'll explore this process of analyzing the writing of different disciplines in Chapter 7.

Working in Different Communities of Practice

One more note about the term *transfer*. The term itself is a little misleading because it implies a simple deployment of skill. In fact, when you learn to write in a new community, you also become "socialized" into the community. You talk the talk. Think of some group you belong to, such as a bunch of gamers, a soccer team, a hiking club, or a rock band. When you are with the group, it's not likely that you talk the same way as you talk in your Business Principles course or with your family. Consider the following text. A football coach is in a meeting room with his team, and he's explaining a play called a "Spider Two Wide Banana" (popularized by announcer John Gruden):

> Ok, so this is play action, OK? First you gotta know that the thing's in code. We're talking slide protection, capital S and capital P, and that makes spider. So you got halfback, tight end, two wide receivers and the fullback set up like a usual under-center play with the WRs wide on one side and the tight end is over on the other side. We get the snap, fullback is rolling out, QB fakes a handoff and can hit the fullback while the TE is running the banana, which is a post-route downfield, the route indicated by the 2, to the right of the field, or the QB can hit the TE who is a secondary passing option. Usually there are two WRs and the TE is on the other side. The WRs are a third passing option. So there's a diversion here with the fullback catching the defense off-guard. OK?

If you're not part of the "community" of football aficionados or players—even if you watch football and know a little about it—this kind of conversation may be baffling.

In writing, every specialized community uses its own terminology, its own style, its own way of organizing a text, its own reference system, and its own role for authors. So, when you join such a community, it's going to take a while to become a member; there's no avoiding this fact. But learning to "read" the community and its ways of communicating will be of great help.

> **KEY CONCEPT** *Community of practice* is a term often used to describe a group of people who use language (and writing) in a particular way based on their needs and interests. Unless you know how knowledge is created and conveyed in that community, you may feel and behave like an outsider. See Key Concept Glossary.

Here's a snippet from the paper of a student in a psychology course who is examining theories of human behavior based on choice:

Simply understood, the dominance principle argues that individuals ought to prefer those actions that always provide at least as much utility as any other alternative, and occasionally provide more. More formally, an action, s_i, is weakly dominant to any other action, s_i', as long as the utility derived from s_i is greater than or equal to the utility derived from s_i' for all possible strategies of one's opponents, S_{-i}, or equivalently: $u_i(s_i, s_{-i}) \geq u_i(s_i', s_{-i})$ for all $s_{-i} \in S_{-i}$.

Now, compare another snippet from the paper of a student in a Political Science course who is examining electoral politics in Brazil:

Hagopian completes the picture with her finding that Rice Index scores of party discipline in Brazil's National Congress rose from 62 to 80 between 1986 and 1999, with especially dramatic increases in the cohesiveness of the Social Democrats, currently Brazil's main opposition party. She describes these changes as part of a broader shift away from delivering patronage goods to pursuing ideological programs. In her opinion, the shift means that party scholarship must focus less on the incentives (usually perverse) created by the electoral system and work to better understand the incentives now pushing politicians toward party loyalty and programmatic appeals.

In both of these examples, it's clear that the students are mirroring the writing practices of their respective communities (psychology and political science, respectively). They're reproducing the language, terminology, concepts, arguments, and research practices of their fields. Notice also that in the first example, the student includes material that looks like it comes from the philosophy of formal logic (there's even a formula). This suggests that even within disciplines, there will be *interdisciplinarity*, or overlap between and among disciplines.

> **KEY CONCEPT** *Interdisciplinarity* refers to the joining together of different disciplines, or specific approaches, theories, or research from different disciplines, in order to enrich a particular inquiry or to form a new path of investigation. A good example is what happened when computer science came together with medicine to create the human genome project. See Key Concept Glossary.

You may be wondering why there's all this specialized writing and communication found in different communities. It's a vital part of disciplines, because underneath what seems like jargon and gobbledygook are concepts already understood by specialized readers and writers as a function of their work. In addition to the different information or knowledge conveyed in different disciplines are different forms or types of writing. These are called *genres*. You already know dozens of genres and can identify them. An e-mail is a genre. So is a letter to the editor, a post to Reddit, a tweet, a birth certificate, and the assembly instructions you just pulled from the Ikea box that your bookshelf came in. If you haven't seen or written a genre, though, its characteristics will be unfamiliar. What does an amicus brief for a Supreme Court hearing look like? What about an executor's deed or a letter of probate? A white paper in the research division of a pharmaceutical company? A patient log entry in the nursing station of a hospital ward? A gas lamp fantasy or a piece of steampunk? Genres are also only "stable for now" and continue to evolve within their communities of practice. For example, over time,

> **KEY CONCEPT** *Genre* refers to a specific *type* of writing that can be recognized by a combination of its characteristics and the uses to which it is put. Like genres of music (country, metal, ska, zydeco, blues, reggae, etc.), there are hundreds of written genres. See Key Concept Glossary.

various rules or norms were formed for contributions to different kinds of social media, such as Facebook and Twitter. Knowing a genre involves keeping up with changes in the way its community understands and uses that form of discourse in the community.

Genres, then, help to define how a community creates and shares knowledge and information. But what about the need to communicate this complex knowledge and information to ordinary people? Here's where *flexibility* is crucial—being able to translate specialized knowledge into language that is understandable by those outside the field. Too often, for example, scientists can't translate their writing to reach broad, public audiences. The result can be misunderstandings on a national level (as is the case with many people's resistance to overwhelming technical research showing the negative results of climate change). Writing well is not just about joining the community that relates to your major, such as sociologists, molecular biologists, art historians, architects, business managers, or nanotechnologists. It's also about moving *between* that community and other communities, especially more general publics. In a busy computer start-up company, for example, highly technical people will need to explain to other employees who will be marketing the product how their innovations work. Dumping a bunch of specialized language on the marketing team will be of no use. Explaining the innovations in language that the marketing team can understand will let them begin formulating a plan for selling the product. In turn, the marketing team needs to translate what they make of the specialists' innovations into even more general language in order to reach a broad range of possible buyers.

GIVE IT A TRY

Make a list of *genres* that you are familiar with (either because you have read them or have created them). For example, a high school yearbook is a genre. So is the legal document that you are supposed to approve (but that almost no one actually reads) by clicking "OK" or "Agree" after updating an application or a computer program. Now choose a genre, and make a list of all the characteristics that define or describe it, such as its style, length, organization, and purpose(s). Has it changed at all over time, to your knowledge?

Using an Assignment Design Model

In addition to your "going meta," you will also often get help from your instructors, who are aware that you may be learning types of writing you haven't encountered before. But what form does that help take? Let's take a moment to understand the role of writing from *their* perspective. How do they think about and integrate writing into their courses? What assumptions can you and your teachers share about that writing? Figure 1.3 shows a model of what many teachers think about when they assign writing and what they hope you pay attention to as you respond to their assignments. Knowing how this model works will help you think about future writing assignments and develop strategies to effectively complete them.

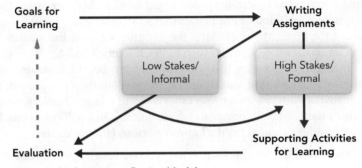

FIGURE 1.3 An Assignment Design Model

First, all assignments have implicit or explicit *goals* for learning. Those goals could relate to something in your course (such as helping you to understand a theory, creating a lively discussion, or causing you to read something with great care); to the improvement of your writing (such as learning how to support a claim with appropriate evidence); or to your exposure to writing in your field (such as practicing business memos or research proposals). Take a look at the goals a professor of management developed for a major writing assignment on organizational behavior:

The purpose of this project is to help you

- create a personal and comprehensive guide of the essentials for successful leadership of organizational behavior;
- identify themes that you will use in leading organizational behavior;
- demonstrate a deep understanding of the course concepts; and
- discern your personal leadership insights and challenges.

As you can see, these are large, ambitious goals that relate strongly to the overall goals of the course itself. The goals determine the nature and scope of the assignment, which in this case will need to be large, comprehensive, and formal. They can also help to guide how you plan, draft, and revise your writing.

In some cases, the goals for your writing assignment may be included in the assignment, to help you understand why you're doing it and what you're supposed to get from it. At other times, the goals may be missing or implicit. If that's the case, you'll need to figure out the goals by "unpacking the assignment" and the teacher's expectations, a subject we'll return to in Chapters 3 and 4.

In Figure 1.3, notice that assignments can be "high stakes" or "low stakes," meaning that based on the goal(s), they can require a lot of sustained work on a project that's worth a large chunk of your grade or they can be informal and done quickly, and will count much less. Consider this goal from a Latin American History course:

The goal of this assignment is to help you read the material on confrontation and conquest carefully so that you learn it and can discuss it with authority.

Unlike the goal in the management course shown on the previous page, this one does not require a long, formal paper. Instead, the teacher asks students to write a brief dialogue:

Imagine that you were present at a meeting where Fernando Cortés and Motecuzoma Xocoyotl sat down to discuss what each thought of the other's civilization. What do you think they would have said? Write a dialogue (of at least one page in length) between the two men, discussing what they admired and disliked about each other's culture. Keep in mind what each might have considered "civilized" and "uncivilized" about the other.

Clearly, this is an assignment that doesn't carry a lot of risk or weight—it's a "low-stakes" assignment (even though it inspires some careful reading and thinking!). As we'll see in Chapters 2 and 3, it's important for you to understand the expectations for all of the assignments in a course, based on their scope and degree of formality.

Informal, low-stakes assignments are usually done in one draft between classes. They don't really need support because their purpose is to bolster your learning or to create some thinking that can lead to good discussion. But the larger and more formal an assignment is—the higher its stakes—the greater will be the need for support, as shown on the bottom right side of Figure 1.3. This is when your instructor may include activities that will help you create or improve the paper, such as practicing certain kinds of analysis or setting up a peer-group conference in which you'll read and provide feedback on the rough drafts of a couple of other class members. For example, a professor in a Political Science course gives a major assignment that asks students to analyze statistics that different stakeholders manipulate (sometimes deceptively) in order to support various positions on public policy. Before students work on their own chosen statistics, they receive a set of sample statistics to analyze and then discuss in class. This gives them practice with a skill that they will then use in their own papers.

Many teachers use low-stakes writing assignments simply to help students think about the course material; they're self-contained and don't "go anywhere" except into your knowledge. But notice the little arrow in Figure 1.3 that loops from low-stakes writing to high-stakes writing. Informal, low-stakes writing can also be an excellent way to produce a high-stakes project. In fact, very few people write perfect prose that flows out of their heads and onto a screen or a page. The vast majority of people work toward a formal text through a series of jottings, false starts, notes, drafts, and revisions. Their writing is *shaped* over time. When you lower the stakes for yourself, you also allow your mind to focus more freely on what you're trying to say, without the constraints of creating perfect, elegant, compelling prose.

When you feel that you're about as finished as you can possibly be on a piece of writing (which is usually determined by a deadline), you'll submit it for evaluation. In informal, low-stakes writing, evaluation will also be informal and advisory—more about helping you to continue thinking and learning than judging the paper against a set of standards (after all, you haven't "finished" learning; your writing is used *to* learn, a point we'll come back to in the next chapter). The professor's feedback might be to the entire class ("here's what I'm seeing in your paragraphs reflecting on this concept") or a quick note at the end of your paper. Or you might be asked to share your writing to get ideas from your peers. But when your instructor evaluates more formal, polished writing, he or she will not tolerate half-baked thoughts, poor editing, or a lousy, uneven style. The good news is that evaluation doesn't have to remain a mystery to you. Even though the process is controlled by a teacher or someone giving a judgment on your performance, you can learn a lot about the evaluative process or expectations for your work that is useful *before* you submit the final draft. Your teacher will also be looking for how well learning goals are reflected in the text you submit, as shown by the dotted vertical arrow on the left side of Figure 1.3. Keeping your own focus on those goals will take you a long way toward figuring out how to do well.

KEY CONCEPT A *rubric* refers to a set of criteria or expectations for a product—in this case, a piece of writing. It's designed to help guide the evaluation of the product, but it is also a very useful device for the creator of the product, who can use it to gauge success throughout the process. See Key Concept Glossary.

Many teachers use *rubrics* or descriptions of criteria to evaluate your writing. Very often, they include these rubrics as part of their assignments. But why would they do this, if it helps to guide how *they* look at your work? In part, they want you to have access to the criteria so that *you* can use them productively when you write. The rubrics become a kind of litmus test, a set of questions you can ask yourself about your developing (or finished) paper.

Consider the following rubric from a course taught by Economics professor Saavedra. Students were asked to analyze alternative economic policies for dealing with the problem of illegal drugs.

An above-average paper (A to A-) will
- clearly explain the different impacts that each policy might have in the market equilibrium for illegal drugs;
- discuss the market situations that illustrate the different impacts that the policies might have;
- discuss the economic concepts used to explain the different effects of the policies; and
- contain the student's own words (i.e., it will not be a copy of the material from the book).

An average paper (B+ to B-) will
- address each of the points suggested in the description of the assignment. However, it will not provide enough discussion of the different policy effects, and it will not explain why the two policies might produce different market outcomes.
- not be an exact copy of the material from the book.

A below-average paper (below C+) will
- not be specific about the different impacts that the two policy approaches might have;
- provide a summary of the concepts without explaining well how they are applied to the understanding of the impact of the supply vs. the demand side of policies in the assignment; and
- be a copy of the material from the book, with no significant contribution from the student.

KEY CONCEPT *Formative evaluation* refers to a kind of evaluative commentary or feedback designed mainly for improvement, not to judge a final product or performance. For example, a theatrical director uses formative evaluation during rehearsals of a play to help the actors improve. In contrast, *summative evaluation* measures a final product or performance against some criteria, as a theater critic will do for the opening performance of the same play. See Key Concept Glossary.

Notice how Professor Saavedra has included specific characteristics of papers that meet different evaluation standards. As she grades students' final submissions, she uses this rubric to make judgments about their quality. She gives herself a little elbow room to fine-tune her judgments within the general categories, based on students' handling of the different theories and the quality of their writing. But, just as important, she makes this rubric available to her students so that they can use it *formatively*, as they think about and write their papers.

GIVE IT A TRY

Pick a writing assignment from one of your courses, and try to map it to the assignment design model in Figure 1.3. Identify and write down the learning goals, the writing assignment requirements, the support provided, and how the assignment will be evaluated. Is each of the stages clear to you? Is the assignment low stakes or high stakes?

Putting It into Practice

This chapter has introduced some important principles that drive this book. First is the understanding that *all* teachers, regardless of their discipline, want to assign writing both to help you learn and to enhance your skills of written expression. That's not going away, and you'll be deluding yourself if you think that some professions don't need good writers or that you won't need to write during your career. Second is the usefulness of "going meta," of thinking deliberately and consciously about the kinds of texts you need to produce in certain contexts and how to figure out how people in that context create and use texts. Finally, teachers know that they need to support your learning, and many follow a process of defining learning goals; choosing a kind of writing that's best suited to those goals; supporting the development of larger, more formal texts; and carefully evaluating the results (making as much of that evaluative process available to you as possible so that you can use it *before* and *while* you write). Knowing that process and matching your own work to it can help you to be "in sync" with your instructor and not feel bewildered by their purposes or have to ask them incessantly, "What do you want in this paper?"

Here are some things you can be doing now to put these principles into practice in all of your courses:

- Make a list of the kinds of writing you're expected to do in each of your courses. List what they have in common and how they differ.

- Create a log for yourself of the conventions you see in the writing for each of your courses. For now, just note general contrasts (we'll come back to a much fuller analysis in Chapter 7). Note the specialized terminology you encounter in each course. Note the kinds of sources the instructors use and how the instructors document them. Pay attention to the tone and style of the writing in each subject.

- For each writing assignment that you receive, try explaining to yourself what the goals are, what the assignment is asking, what forms of support will be included (or what you can do yourself to prepare for writing), and how the final product will be evaluated (look for criteria). When you don't have a clear understanding of a step, ask your instructor for help (see Chapter 4 for more detail).

2

Low-Stakes Writing and Why You Should Take It Seriously

WHAT'S THE POINT?

After you read, think about, and put this chapter into practice, you will be able to:

- Explain the purpose of writing to learn
- Identify assignments as low stakes/writing to learn or high stakes/writing to perform and communicate
- Use academic journals or learning blogs as a *way in* to enhance learning and understanding
- Use forums and dialogues to engage in reflection and discussion
- Understand different types of reflection and use them in learning and thinking about course material and working toward formal papers and projects

What Is Writing to Learn?

Think about it. When students hear the words *writing assignment*, they're likely to imagine something like "a test." It's a little different than circling true/false or multiple-choice options, but you're still writing down what you know so that your instructor can figure out whether or not you do know it. Even when you learn something in the process of writing a paper—say, through research—the paper is the *outcome* of your learning, and your teacher weighs and measures it, asking "does this student know her stuff, and can she explain it?"

Try flipping this around. Imagine that you're asked to use writing as a *way in* to knowledge. Now certain aspects of the writing no longer matter. You don't fully understand a concept? That's fine, because the writing will help you figure out why you don't understand the concept or will show gaps in your knowledge. You don't have a thesis that drives your thoughts about some challenging material? Of course you don't! You don't know enough yet to formulate a thesis. What if your sentences sometimes are incomplete or have missing articles? Or you write quickly and use abbreviations? Or you make some mistakes in punctuation? Don't worry. All people who write quickly without revising, even those who have a PhD in English, make mistakes.

Take a look at this piece of writing that Paul, a student in an Embryology course, did:

> The really neat thing I liked about the Thursday lecture was she told us the mechanisms of epiboly. I was wondering how sheets of cells move. Well, it seems that the octodermal cells put out little pilipodia which attach to the vitelline membrane and then contract. This continues until the ectoderm completely covers the yolk. Aha! Then one of the layers is the ectoderm. Dumb-de-dumb-dumb! Okay, so what's the second layer? Possibly mesoderm? Yeah. How about endoderm? I don't think so because the endoderm is the first to form from invagination at the primitive streak. The endoderm displaces the hypoblast according to Abbott (although the book doesn't take his point of view—it says that the endoderm is formed on top of the hypoblast). Regardless, the endoderm is completely formed by the time the mesoderm is invaginated. Therefore, it's probably mesoderm and ectoderm!

In this course, students were required to keep an online learning blog (sometimes called a *course journal* or *academic journal*) where they were asked to write about what they were learning. Notice that the writer uses a lot of informal language ("Well," "Aha!," "Dumb-de-dumb-dumb," "Okay," "Yeah," etc.). If you were to include this sort of language in a formal assignment, your teacher would quickly circle it and comment on it, and maybe even take off points from the paper's grade. Here, however, *this language is perfectly appropriate*. This is a good example of *low-stakes writing*, which is done quickly and informally for the main purpose of *strengthening learning* (as displayed in Figure 1.2 in the previous chapter). Notice how the writer has a literal "aha"

> **KEY CONCEPT** *Low-stakes writing* is writing that is informal, is done quickly (without much, if any, revision), is worth a small percentage of a grade (or none at all), and is not concerned about refined style, perfect grammar, or other characteristics of polished writing that is directed to an audience. See Key Concept Glossary.

moment, figuring out something that might have remained confused—right up until test time.

Many teachers across the curriculum now assign low-stakes writing because they know about its potential to help students study and learn challenging material in their courses. Using this kind of informal, low-stakes writing is part of a movement—an offshoot of writing across the curriculum—known as *writing to learn.*

Now consider a brief excerpt from one of Charles Darwin's journals:

> Marsupials at Australia. — Will this apply to whole organic kingdom when our planet first cooled. — Countries longest separated greatest differences — if separated from immense ages possibly two distinct type, but each having its representatives — as in Australia. This presupposes time when no Mammalia existed; Australian Mamm. were produced from propagation from different set, as the rest of the world. — This view supposes that in course of ages, & therefore changes every animal has tendency to change. — This difficult to prove cats, &c., from Egypt. no answer because time short & no great change has happened. I look at two ostriches as strong argument of possibility of such change, as we see them in space, so might they in time.

Notice again the abbreviations, the partial sentences, the missing pronouns and articles. In light of Darwin's immense contributions to knowledge and his obvious brilliance, we don't fault him for not writing highly stylized or even "correct" prose here (as he did in his formal papers and addresses), because his *purpose* was to use writing as a way to think and learn (and record that thinking and learning)

Low-Stakes and High-Stakes Writing

Your teacher may explicitly refer to the difference between high-stakes papers designed to test your knowledge and writing ability (as output), and low-stakes papers designed to help you learn (as input). When your teacher gives a writing-to-learn assignment, the teacher's main goal is to enhance your learning and understanding of the course material (ideas, concepts, arguments, data, etc.). The assignment emphasizes more engaged, higher-order thinking. Because writing is your "way into" learning, it may look informal, unstructured, or directed to yourself as a learner. In contrast, formal, polished writing—the kind you do for longer papers that are worth a significant portion of your grade—will be structured, written in an appropriate style, and grammatically correct; will adhere to the conventions of the discipline; and will be sensitive to the needs of its intended audience(s). Figure 2.1 shows these differences along a continuum, from the most informal and learning-centered on the left to the most formal and audience-centered on the right.

Writing to Learn	Writing to Perform/Communicate
Goal: mastering content	**Goal:** mastering form/type of text
Types of writing: varied	**Types of writing:** limited
Input: Practice/learning based	**Output:** Performance based
Stakes: low	**Stakes:** high
Style: informal	**Style:** formal
Purpose: "way into" knowledge	**Purpose:** "display" of knowledge

FIGURE 2.1 Some Differences Between Learning-Based and Performance-Based Writing

The difference between writing to learn and writing to perform or communicate is a matter of *orientation,* based on your purposes. Of course, these two kinds of writing are not mutually exclusive. Instead, think about them in terms of their features: when you are writing to learn, you're less concerned about "getting the text right" than about "getting the thinking done," so the writing is informal. Take a look at Figure 2.2, which lists some types of writing along a similar continuum, from the most informal, quickly done writing at one end to the high-stakes, often longest and most polished writing at the other end.

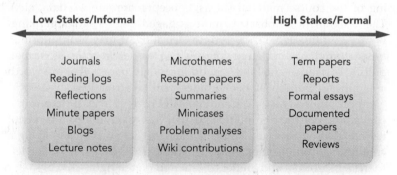

Low Stakes/Informal   **High Stakes/Formal**

Journals	Microthemes	Term papers
Reading logs	Response papers	Reports
Reflections	Summaries	Formal essays
Minute papers	Minicases	Documented papers
Blogs	Problem analyses	
Lecture notes	Wiki contributions	Reviews

FIGURE 2.2 A Continuum of Formality and Stakes

At the left-most side of the continuum, we can put occasions for writing that are fleeting, informal, and nonconsequential (in the sense that there's no judgment of their *textual* quality): lecture notes, for example. In some courses, at the end of class you may be asked to write "minute papers" (or "exit slips"), maybe focusing on what you least understood from a lecture or what you found most interesting about the lecture. Your instructor might use these "minute papers" as a window into your class's learning. The papers may even be anonymous, so the stakes are very low. Some kinds of journals or blog writing may also be informal but may be just a little farther to the right on the continuum—maybe because you need to write a certain amount or you need to write in a specific way.

At the right-most end of the continuum, we find the usual formal papers and projects. Term papers that count for a large chunk of a final grade are found here; they're expected to be carefully organized, well researched, stylistically appropriate, and error-free. Senior capstone projects appear at the tip of the arrow. Even further to the right, probably off the edge of the figure, are master's theses and doctoral dissertations. The stakes for them are extremely high because most master's and doctoral candidates' entire futures depend on them.

In the middle of the continuum are assignments that tend to be short—a page or two. Like those on the left, they are written in *one* draft (whereas everything on the right usually requires multiple drafts, with careful revision, ideally with plentiful responses from helpful readers). But as we'll see in Chapter 3, they may require more specific kinds of thinking or response than, say, a free-association journal entry. This chapter focuses on the lowest-stakes writing— writing that appears on the left side of the continuum.

Academic Journals and Learning Blogs

Many teachers require students to keep an academic journal, and many such journals now take the form of an online "learning blog" or "learning forum." In some cases, teachers may want to see your informal writing so that they can judge their own coverage of the material and the class's understanding of it. There may be minimum page or word requirements for such material as well. Be sure to read any guidelines for informal writing carefully.

> **KEY CONCEPT** A *learning (b)log or academic journal* is a paper notebook, a file on your computer, or a space online where you write about course material very informally in order to learn the material better and to prepare for exams and formal papers. See Key Concept Glossary.

Consider Maria Gonzalez, a junior majoring in architecture. It's nearly midterms, and she has been worrying about an upcoming test in her History of Modern Architecture course. The test will cover a lot of material on nineteenth-century and twentieth-century architecture: major figures, famous structures, important theories, and principles of design. She's nervous because her teacher has given the class few clues about what specific information will be covered on the exam. All she knows is that it will include an objective section and a brief essay section.

It's Sunday evening, and the test will be given the following Friday. Maria wants to get a head start on her studying, so she sits back on her bed, with her lecture notes, some articles, her textbook, and her laptop scattered around her. Soon she is flipping back and forth between her notes and the articles, comparing terms, and checking her textbook for ideas raised in class.

After a while, she locates her loose-leaf notebook labeled "Learning Log—Arch." She opens it to a blank page and begins jotting down questions and ideas, filling the pages with terms, brief paragraphs, circled words, and lists; for example, "When did the Bauhaus movement really get started?" She writes "Bauhaus" and lists four names, and then circles Mies van der Rohe and adds, "father of the movement? 1910, 1920?" Then she draws a line down the middle of the page, writes "Bauhaus" on the left, and, without stopping, fills the right side with a running commentary about what she knows. Then she writes "Romanesque" and more commentary:

> Good ex. Is Trinity Church in Boston—1872—Henry Hobb Richardson, style of great prestige, used for churches, gov. buildings, business blocks. Richardsonian Romanesque—1885—1905? Characteristics: weight and mass, medieval qualities, minimal elements, rough masonry walls. Arches and towers? How related to Chateauesque Revival style of same period?

Each night, Maria returns to her notebook, reads what she has written, and continues to scribble more notes and ideas. She tests her understanding by trying to define major concepts in her own words, and then she turns back to her textbook to compare its definitions with her own. One evening she draws a time line and places various styles and developments along it as best she can. A day later, she studies photographs of buildings in her textbook, writes down the features she sees, and decides what these tell her about when the buildings were built and by whom. In all of these sessions, she moves from her journal to her textbook and back again, and with each attempt to reproduce her knowledge on paper, she is getting a firmer grasp of the material.

When Maria walks into her History of Modern Architecture course on the day of the exam, she notices the buzz of activity. Other students are nervously comparing notes, flipping through pages of their textbooks, and showing each other screens of information on their laptops and iPads. Maria takes a seat, sits back, and composes her thoughts. Her course log, where she has written and learned for the past five days, sits on her desk at home, no longer needed. The writing in it has served its purpose. She has written her way into knowledge.

In her own way, Maria is a successful writer and learner. "Successful writer" doesn't mean that Maria finds writing easy, quick, or painless. It means that instead of groaning with dread each time she thinks about opening a blank document on-screen, she uses her work and writing to her advantage. "Successful learner" doesn't mean that Maria was born with knowledge, but, rather, that she has discovered ways to explore and become expert in whatever courses she takes.

Maria keeps a journal of her learning in a notebook so that she can learn more effectively—she's doing this on her own, in what's called "self-sponsored writing." (You can just as easily do the same thing on a computer, or even write by hand on a tablet.) When you write on social media, such as Facebook or Reddit, or contribute to forums or blogs that are dedicated to your specific areas of interest, or when you write fiction or poetry or letters to relatives, you're engaging in self-sponsored writing. No one is making you write; you're doing it for your own pleasure or self-improvement.

> **KEY CONCEPT** *Self-sponsored writing* is writing that you are motivated to do on your own, rather than as an assignment or work-related task. Most writing done in social media is self-sponsored. See Key Concept Glossary.

How to Use Academic Journals or Learning Blogs

Some teachers recognize the power of an academic journal or learning blog and require you to keep one. If this is the case, take it seriously. Each entry may be worth only a half a point or less of your final grade, but it's worth far more in the way it can bolster your learning and help you write better formal papers and take high-stakes exams. If you're not assigned such a blog, *then keep one anyway.* Following are eight specific uses for learning blogs and academic journals; each will be explained fully.

1. Make the most of lectures.
2. Explain the harder concepts to yourself.
3. Apply new knowledge; connect to other learning.
4. Pin down exactly what an author is saying.
5. Compare two or more contrasting positions.
6. Explore problems in your learning.
7. Prepare for an exam.
8. Extract information for a formal paper.

MAKE THE MOST OF LECTURES. In many courses, especially ones with higher enrollments, it's too easy to become a passive learner, sitting like an empty bucket waiting to be filled with information. Your mind can be elsewhere—on your smartphone, on Facebook,

● ● ●

Lincoln—early moves as President. After outbreak of war. Invited Robert E. Lee to be general of Union Army. [Why Lee of all people?] Lee turns Lincoln down, stays with South. [Why did he do that? What happens if Lee goes with North?] Lincoln, string of generals after that, none satisfactory. McClelland—"got the slows"—[McC's side of the story? Lincoln got "fasts"?]

or even turned off completely. Don't tune out. Instead, write what you're hearing, but at the same time, try to raise questions and make connections in your mind as you listen and watch. You might put these thoughts inside square brackets or highlight them to set them off from the lecturer's information, as shown on the previous page.

Once you have taken your notes, don't stop there. Can you state in three or four pithy sentences the main points of the lecture? Try it—on-screen. This will help you to grasp the significance of the entire lecture. The same is true for any presentation that you might watch online, only now you can stop to write or even replay certain parts.

GIVE IT A TRY

Look back at your notes from a lecture for a class that you're taking. Read through the notes, and jot down five questions about the material that you might want to explore further or understand better.

EXPLAIN THE HARDER CONCEPTS TO YOURSELF. Every discipline has its own terminology and its own special, often highly useful, jargon, but it's useful to you only if you understand it. When you encounter new terms or specialized uses for old terms, try to define them in your learning blog, using your own words. For example, Avon wrestles with the term *mass* in an Introductory Physics course for nonscience majors:

If one rock weighs one kg and the other 10 kg, why does Dr. Lawrence keep insisting that "mass" isn't "weight"? It weighs 1 kg, what's the problem? Idea—it does here, but on the moon or mars or the sun would weigh something else. That is, its pounds would change, but it would still be 1 kg??? Or if floating in space, doesn't weigh anything. How could you tell a heavy rock from a light one, same size, in space? Is this what resistance to acceleration mean? How far—fast—can you throw it? Is that what "mass" means?

If Avon double-checks his hunch, he'll discover that he's on the right track.

For another of your classes, make a list of five terms or concepts that are new to you. Pick one of those terms or concepts, and write a short paragraph explaining it to yourself. Now reflect on the results. What happened? Did you experience any new thinking or perspectives? Did you identify any gaps in your knowledge that you need to fill?

APPLY NEW KNOWLEDGE; CONNECT TO OTHER LEARNING. Knowledge out of context is useless. If you can't apply new concepts to something real and concrete, the concepts won't stay with you, and you may be wasting your time. A learning blog is an excellent place to connect your new academic learning to other events and situations in your life. What does the headline story in the *Huffington Post* have to do with your Introduction to Ethics course? How does the recent thread in your sub-Reddit group about a clear-air turbulence crash of a major airline relate to your aerodynamics class?

PIN DOWN EXACTLY WHAT AN AUTHOR IS SAYING. Do you know what instructors, across all higher education, say they constantly worry about? They worry that you—their students—aren't reading assigned material carefully, thoughtfully, and critically (or even at all). Instructors come to class ready to lead a stimulating discussion, and their students often sit there and wait for them to tell them what to think. Is this true? If so, then a lot of potential learning is lost (like getting cheated out of half your take-out order). Writing not only helps you think but also can help you read. And reading is *essential— central, crucial, indispensible, of utmost importance!*—to learning and to virtually all of your education. You can't learn, and you won't learn, without reading the assigned material, but it takes an investment of your time. Thankfully, a large amount of research shows that when you write about what you're reading, you read more incisively, insightfully, carefully, and critically. Here are a few ways to use writing to improve your reading.

1. Glance over the chapter or article quickly just to get a sense of its organization. What subtitles or divisions do you see? Can you get a sense of the general argument? Try sketching a rough preliminary skeleton of the piece before diving in, or even just highlight the subheadings if you're reading online.

2. Instead of highlighting in a text, try writing abbreviated notes capturing the "Most Important Ideas" in the text on an index card or in a word document on-screen. For each "Most Important Idea" that you write down, now write two or three subsidiary ideas beneath it. If you were doing this for the material that you're reading right now, you might put down "Writing enhances reading" as your "Most Important Idea," and then beneath it, "sketch skeleton of reading beforehand," "do Most Important Idea cards," and so on.

3. Try to summarize the gist of the work in one pithy sentence. A professor at a large East Coast university has her students write tweets capturing the essence of peer-reviewed journal articles. Sound easy? Try it. In figuring out what the gist of the article is and rendering it into 140 characters, you'll know the contents in detail and remember them more clearly.

4. Use a forum, as described earlier, to discuss readings with classmates or others. The result can be very helpful.

5. See if you can find commentaries or responses to the reading (these will be more easily available for books than articles or chapters). Ask yourself if you agree with the comments and interpretations.

6. Paraphrase the work in a page or a paragraph, trying to capture as much of the author's argument as possible. Once you're able to formulate such a paraphrase, you can feel confident that you understand the work you have read.

7. Try creating a brief dialogue between yourself and the reading. (There will be more on dialogues later in this chapter.) You can make this sound as cheesy as you want—after all, you're writing

for yourself: "Author: If you write about your reading, your reading will be enhanced. Me: Seems like extra work when I can just read. Author: A lot of research shows that writing about what you read makes you read more carefully. Me: Hmmm. . . ." Chelsea, for example, started asking questions of the author of an article on cattle grazing in her Land Management course:

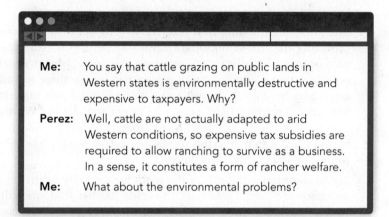

Me: You say that cattle grazing on public lands in Western states is environmentally destructive and expensive to taxpayers. Why?

Perez: Well, cattle are not actually adapted to arid Western conditions, so expensive tax subsidies are required to allow ranching to survive as a business. In a sense, it constitutes a form of rancher welfare.

Me: What about the environmental problems?

GIVE IT A TRY

For a reading in one of your classes, choose one of the strategies noted in the preceding list, and apply it to the reading. If you're not sure which one to choose, try writing a tweet about the article. As you do so, think about your process. How did you consult or use the reading? What happened to your understanding of the reading and its specifics? Did your knowledge of the reading change?

COMPARE TWO OR MORE CONTRASTING POSITIONS. When you read one author's work at a time, it's easy to find yourself in agreement. The writer presents a convincing case, suppresses contrary arguments, and seems reasonable. Unless you're an aggressive, critical reader, you'll find yourself sucked into the argument, nodding in assent. Avoid doing this. When you have a chance, use your learning blog to put two authors' points together, and let them speak to each other. Create sentences that have the structure, "Author 1 argues X, but Author 2 points out Y," or "Although Author 1 believes X and Author 2 agrees, Author 2 also argues that Y." This strategy will help you to dig deeply into each author's points so that you know you'll be able to talk or write about each one confidently.

EXPLORE PROBLEMS IN YOUR LEARNING. Writing about your frustrations when trying to understand challenging or confusing material can often show you the source of your confusion. Here's an example from Latoya, a student in an English Linguistics course, who is having trouble with phonetic transcription:

> This is my second reading of this chapter, yet there are some things that still seem contradictory. In the section on glides on p. 46, the following sentence is written about y's and w's: "When occurring in a word, they must always be either preceded or followed directly by a vowel." But in the word "merry" no vowel comes before or after the y. Or how about the name Myra. The "y" isn't preceded or followed by a vowel. Maybe these examples are unfair since the "y" in "merry" is an "ee" sound, not a "y" sound. And the "y" in Myra is an "aii" sound, a dipthong, not a glide. So "y" isn't a vowel. Just checked on that, it's the English spelling problem again! I get it!

Halfway through her blog entry, Latoya discovered why she was confused, because her writing *caused her to express and focus on* her confusion.

PREPARE FOR AN EXAM. As the story of Maria Gonzalez earlier in this chapter shows, writing informally can be an excellent way to prepare for an exam. Several short sessions over a week or two can be far more useful than an eye-burning all-nighter in which you try to cram information into your exhausted brain.

EXTRACT INFORMATION FOR A FORMAL PAPER. If you know you'll have a formal paper to write later in the term and you can pick the topic, start thinking about it early on. Remember the curved line in Figure 1.3 that loops from low-stakes writing back to high-stakes writing? Almost all high-stakes writing begins in an informal way, through various notes, jottings, and semidrafting. So use your learning blog to write your way toward a formal paper. As you begin the paper, use the blog or journal space to create notes, ask questions, think up possible leads, and record URLs and tags. For example, one of the most effective methods for beginning a writing task is called *freewriting*. You may have learned freewriting as a brainstorming tool to help you write essays in your composition course. But freewriting is something you can use in all your courses.

> **KEY CONCEPT** *Freewriting* is a method of fast, nonstop writing, designed to open up your thinking while removing the usual constraints of formal composing. See Key Concept Glossary.

In freewriting, you write as fast as you can for a fixed period of time (usually ten minutes). During that time, don't stop—keep writing or typing, even if nothing comes to mind. Eventually it will, and you'll end up in places you hadn't imagined. Take a look at some of the freewriting of Scott, who was enrolled in a psychology course

> The Morrow reflex is kind of interesting. Seems to be an innate reflex related to monkeys clutching their mothers, but it's a startle reflex in humans. Lots of infantile reflexes seem very primitive and basic. Makes it seem as if most basic characteristics of infants are the closest to our primitive ancestry, more then develop as humans the farther they go away from those. Possible thesis? Earliest reflexes most monkey-like? What would it take to prove or how would I know if wrong?

and was feeling his way toward a term paper on research into the reflex responses of infants.

GIVE IT A TRY

Pick a topic from a course that you're currently taking, like Biology or Management, and freewrite on that topic for five minutes. What insights did you gain?

Writing in a Learning Blog

It will seem like heresy coming from an English professor and a writing expert, but when you're writing at the left-most side of the continuum in Figure 2.2, you'll use a very relaxed style, *textually* speaking (and as seen in the examples in this chapter). The point is not to worry about composing perfect sentences; if you do, you'll spend your intellectual resources fretting about little details of language instead of about ideas and concepts (e.g., "Should I put a comma here?"). Of course, this doesn't mean that you should toss out precision—say, in the words you use to describe an idea. It means that you don't obsess over creating the most polished, elegant prose. Here are some tips for writing to learn.

USE A COMFORTABLE STYLE. Entries in learning blogs are often messy, associative, and exploratory. This is as it should be. In the journals of famous scholars and scientists, we find all sorts of personal abbreviations and shortcuts—even errors. Charles Darwin's extensive journals are filled with them (but, of course, not his formal papers and books). Sometimes a blog entry might ramble on for several screens, and at other times you might skip through an idea more quickly than you would in a formal paper. But who cares? This leads to a profoundly important point: if writing in your academic journal or learning blog is helping you to clarify your thinking—*your* thinking, not your reader's—you're doing it right.

CHOOSE A MEDIUM APPROPRIATE TO YOUR PURPOSES. Some people do their best work when they can use visual cues—diagrams, circles, and so forth—alongside their written text. This can be difficult on computers (unless you have a tablet that allows handwriting). There's nothing wrong with using a spiral-bound or loose-leaf notebook. If you would rather store your material online (or if your instructor requires you to use a particular space in a learning management system or course blog), then try to adapt your writing to that space.

WRITE REGULARLY. You may be assigned to write on specific topics or on specific days, or you may be asked to write a certain amount. Regardless, don't put a learning blog aside for long. To keep your mind actively focused on the material in your course, keep your blog healthy by "feeding" it often.

START WITH THE OBVIOUS, AND WAIT FOR THE BRILLIANT. Some students have trouble with learning blogs because they're trying to be too insightful too soon and are not letting the information sink in a bit. The blog isn't a place to capture your most dazzling insights. Instead, think of yourself as growing crystals. Write down simple, unflashy, ordinary facts and ideas about your subject, and see what they combine to form. Write, and keep going. What we call insight, after all, isn't usually *sight* into anything; it's a perception of pattern, order, and form.

Forums and Dialogues

Another common type of low-stakes writing to learn involves carrying on a *dialogue* with one or more students in your class. Today, most dialogue journaling takes place online, through various forums or other social media for digital exchange. Such digital exchanges are likely to be second nature to you because almost all social media uses them, from Facebook to the response options at the bottom of YouTube videos to the forums on Reddit. In this case, you're using a similar interactivity to work through and discuss the complex material in your courses.

To get a sense of what a typical dialogue forum might look like, consider the excerpts below from a course in Criminal Justice. The students have been reading about proposals in a couple of states that would allow women who have been convicted of non-child-abuse-related crimes to live with their children in minimum-security detention facilities. Here we see Karla expressing her interest in such programs and arguing that they might be helpful in the process of the women's rehabilitation.

On the topic of incarcerated women allowed to live with their young children if their (woman's) crime was not child abuse related. In a way this seems humane to me, esp. because women who have young children shouldn't be denied the right to nurture them (we talk about rehabilitation!), plus the children have a right to be with their mothers.

Brea, who is interacting with Karla in an online space in their course management system, then writes back:

Karla,
      I agree that it is really hard on kids to be taken from their mothers but if their mothers aren't a role model for them they should be in foster care. Plus the kids are also in a kind of prison and that is not a good environment to live in. The gov. also has to pay more and where is that money going to come from? People may be angry that money is going to help out women who have committed crimes. But maybe in less high security prisons it could work if there was a way to fund it.

Notice that both students use an informal style, with abbreviations. But consider the thought processes beneath the words. Karla gently pushes back at Brea's post, raising questions about whether it's good for kids to live in a detention facility, what sorts of role models they will encounter there, and who will pay for the additional costs of feeding and caring for them. Their dialogue is helping Karla and Brea to *explore* and *think about* their course material—without a teacher.

Unless your class is very small, your instructor will probably assign you to a forum that is populated by just a handful of students— usually three to five—sometimes using a content management system like Moodle or Blackboard. This makes your interactions manageable and gives you a chance to respond individually to other members of the forum. But, unlike many social media sites such as Facebook, inter-active academic forums will require something more than just random chit-chat or posts about your cat or dog, friends, and social activities. Most teachers will be looking for *engaged thinking* about the course material. Sometimes you'll be expected to write whatever comes to mind about the material, and at other times you may be given prompts, scenarios, or other focuses for your interactions. In a course on literacy in the United States, for example, students were asked to dialogue about a fictitious farming community that has no written literacy but has passed on its highly successful farming practices for generations. Should it matter that the community doesn't have writ-ten literacy? (Students had been reading about different orientations to literacy, one of which argues that literacy isn't essential but is used according to its needs within specific societies). Here is what Cheryl wrote to the other members of her forum:

> **KEY CONCEPT** *Engaged thinking*, which is highly favored by teachers in all disciplines, requires something more than just a description of an event or a phenomenon. It requires "going deeper," seeing connections, relationships, and patterns among different ideas or concepts. See Key Concept Glossary.

Here, Cheryl makes a focused assertion about the topic.

In a situation where there is no inherent need for literacy, it would be false to say that literacy is entirely useless. This is because, for example, even if a farming community has their own ways of doing things that are achieved without literacy, they could always become literate and use that ability and technology to record—in a more permanent way—their use

You can see how Cheryl thoughtfully explores the reason for her assertion.

of tools and methods of farming. However, even though literacy is not completely useless to the community that lacks it, it is also not a necessity and they should not be seen as second-rate cultures simply because of their lack of literacy. I believe that the minds of people who are illiterate are not any less cognitively challenged than the minds of those who are literate. [Cheryl's entry continues for another long paragraph.]

Here, Cheryl reflects on the perception of the value of literacy.

Notice that Cheryl is *focused, reflective,* and *thoughtful* in her post. Now another member of her forum, Gunther, responds to what Cheryl has written:

Cheryl, I agree with you in the sense that the farmers don't inherently need literacy in the same sense that others might. For instance, according to the Western or Eurocentric understanding, literacy is considered a by-product of and connected to formal schooling. An individual's illiteracy or literacy contributes to how they are viewed within Western society and seems connected to some extent to an individual's expected degree of success within the modern world. Given that the farmers are already very successful year after year, it does not appear as though the farmers would need literacy in the conventional sense. Nor, based on Scribner's study of the Vai people, would literacy generate significant "cognitive consequences" in the sense that it would not improve the farmers' abilities to handle complex situations. If anything, their firsthand experience with farming would continue to provide them with that ability. However, if, as Wiley argues, understanding literacy is a "social, collective enterprise," developing literacy could be beneficial to the farmers as it would give them a means to preserve their way of life for future generations (54). [Gunther's entry continues for another paragraph]

Gunther agrees with Cheryl and extends the discussion with additional support.

Gunther links the discussion to a reading from the class on cognitive ability.

Gunther links to another reading on the value of literacy

Notice how Gunther agrees with much of what Cheryl has written but *extends* it and links it to the course readings. You can easily see how this interaction is both strengthening the students' understanding of the material and pushing them to think "around" a complex issue raised in the course.

If your instructor sets up a forum for low-stakes dialogue, he or she will give you specific guidelines about how often you need to write, how long your entries should be, and what you might or should focus on. First, it seems pretty obvious that you need to *interact*. Yet, often students forget that they're supposed to write as a group. This requires reading your other group members' posts and then thinking about them alongside your own ideas. Remember also that you need to be willing to have your ideas critiqued (this is especially important if you're the first to post to a forum about a specific topic). All of this is good—a sign that your partners are carrying on a conversation. You can always respond in turn, fine-tuning what you originally wrote, digging up more evidence for a claim, or acknowledging the wisdom in your partners' newly expressed ideas. Whatever you do, don't get angry or take responses personally. Keep your focus on the material.

Also, consider how much to write. Initial posts and initial responses need to have some substance—you can't explore something very well if you just write a line or two. Your instructor may have requirements for the amount you write. Thereafter, your interactions might vary in length. For example, you might write "agreed, Gunther, though I still maintain that literacy isn't important to this group if they really do effectively pass their methods on orally" as a rejoinder to a longer exchange. That's fine—its purpose is to maintain a kind of social order in your interaction. But don't rely on "sound bites" when you need to think fully and write more extensively about a subject. At the same time, remember that the group members may have a tolerance threshold for the length of your posts. Instead of writing six screens of text, write one screen and hold back your other ideas for later as the interaction proceeds.

GIVE IT A TRY

Pair up with someone in your class. Then, agree to discuss a topic, question, controversy, or excerpt from a reading. Write one or two exchanges to each other about your choice. See if you can recognize instances of learning in your exchanges with each other.

The Importance of Reflection

Even though we've been considering very informal, learning-based writing, your teacher is still expecting you to do something more than describe what you read or chronicle your experience ("I thought this reading was boring" or "I attended the guest lecture, and it was OK"). Most teachers prize a certain kind of thinking, often called *reflection*. Reflective thinking involves "standing back" from an idea or experience and considering it from different angles. In certain contexts, such as courses that involve service-learning activities, reflection can be very personal, focusing heavily on your own experiences, feelings, and growth. In more typical academic

> **KEY CONCEPT** *Reflection* refers to a kind of thinking that considers ideas, phenomena, and experience from multiple perspectives, generating new learning. See Key Concept Glossary.

work that's the focus of this book, we're going to think of it as a kind of *thoughtful exploration* of ideas, concepts, presentations, readings, discussions, observations, experiments, data, and other material or activities found across college curriculums. More specifically, reflection encourages you to

- review something more carefully and critically, seeing it from different angles and trying to understand it beyond first impressions or thoughts;
- create a hypothesis about some phenomenon and then mentally test the hypothesis, especially with further information;
- ask yourself "what else" might explain, account for, or disambiguate something, in order to go beyond an initial explanation; and
- push back against sets of assumptions that seem to be made too easily (in a reading, a discussion, etc.) and bring a healthy skepticism to conclusions.

If Cheryl had written about the farming scenario, "This scenario is about a group of farmers who don't have literacy but still farm well. They pass their farming knowledge down orally to the next generation," this would not be reflective but descriptive, like a diary entry. Instead, she and Gunther *explore* the implications of the group's illiteracy, *reflecting* on its implications. As Ken Bain, author of *What the Best College Students Do,* has written,

> highly productive and creative individuals think about their own thinking while they are thinking. This process, called *metacognition*, allows people to engage in a valuable conversation with themselves, exploring their background, questioning and correcting their thinking in the process, and pursuing the dynamic power of their minds.

Scholars have proposed various models or cycles of reflection. Let's consider one that's especially useful for academic work because it focuses on writing (Figure 2.3).

Descriptive writing is just that: writing that simply *describes* some experience, phenomenon, or information. Consider Brianna's descriptive account of what happened to her as she drove to school:

> Today I was in a car accident. A man in his late 80s ran a stop sign and crashed into the right rear of my car. It caused a lot of damage but no one was hurt and thankfully the car wasn't totaled.

In the movement toward reflection, the writer begins speculating beyond just what happened and toward what it says, implies, or means. It requires asking "so what" about the event, but not

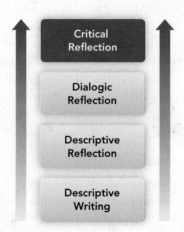

FIGURE 2.3

TABLE 2.1 Types of Reflective Writing

Type of Reflective Writing	Explanation
Descriptive writing	Describes (a reading, phenomenon, observation, experience, etc.), with no evidence of reflection. Useful for getting the facts and details down, but doesn't really go anywhere—doesn't think *about* what's being described. Think diary entry: "Today this happened, and then this happened." Or plot summary: "This book is about this, and then this happens."
Descriptive reflection	Goes somewhat beyond description, demonstrating something deeper, such as a different perspective or reasons for some action. Think simple explanation or connection: "Today this happened, and it reminded me of this." Or simple exploration: "This article seemed slanted toward one side of the issue."
Dialogic reflection	A more advanced kind of reflection, involving some greater distance from the event, idea, phenomenon, and so forth, with more attention to multiple perspectives. It can also critically explore the self: "Why do I feel this way?" "Why did I see this or interpret this in what I read (saw, etc.)?" Think internal dialogue: "I think this, but I can also see that." Or conversation: "What about …? I don't entirely agree. …"
Critical reflection	Builds on dialogic reflection by considering even broader contexts beyond multiple perspectives of interpretation, such as the historical or the sociopolitical. Considers structural and institutional aspects of a phenomenon, idea, concept, or action. Think critique: "Underneath this is an implication that. …" Or challenge: "We don't see this injustice because we are programmed to believe. …"

answering the "so what" with more description, such as "So I was angry" or "So I was late to class." Here, Brianna extends the details a little while speculating about the age and ability of the man who hit her car, and then brings in societal obligations. You can see that the incident becomes a springboard for deeper issues beyond the one Brianna writes about (e.g., as usually happens in the media after a mass shooting, prompting renewed discussion about gun control).

> Clearly, this older gentleman, with his thick glasses and hearing aids, and his difficulty getting out of the car, was not fit to drive. He seemed bewildered and unable to think. Our society needs to pay more attention to the loss of faculties in the aging population when it issues driver licenses.

As you move toward dialogic reflection, you expand on the perspectives opened up in descriptive reflection, considering your ideas from different angles and positions. There's clearly a movement outward, away from the "heat" of the incident or phenomenon itself, toward a more dispassionate, exploratory stance. Notice how, as Brianna continues her reflection, she considers some further thoughts about older drivers and imagines different *kinds* of drivers in different situations and living conditions.

> One problem associated with denying driver licenses to older people who have lost some of their abilities to drive well is what happens to those in places that lack public transportation. An older poor person might not have the resources to take cabs, or there might be no cabs in their rural area, or they might not have friends and relatives to help them shop or get their medicines. At the same time, if there is a tangible risk to the public, not just in cars but pedestrians and bicyclists, or to people's personal property, then those risks might outweigh the concerns for the elderly poor, and some other solutions would need to be found for their transportation.

Finally, *critical reflection* is sometimes the most difficult kind of reflection to do because it requires seeing the phenomenon (incident, reading, etc.) from a *systemic* perspective, involving large forces (political, institutional, and the like). For this reason, it sometimes reveals social injustices, forms of discrimination or oppression, or major societal problems that are not easily or quickly solved. Brianna's writing begins moving toward critical reflection as she considers the broader implications of the accident.

Overall, society tends to sweep the aging population under the rug, for-getting their contributions and the fact that they were once young. How can an old man like this get around without risking injuring someone? Our legislature has repeatedly voted against putting in any mass transporta-tion, even light rail, so if this man is denied his driving privileges, he has almost no options. It's another case of how neglected and oppressed the aged are in our culture. In some other cultures, the old are revered, or there are strong family networks to care for them. We just want to put them into nursing homes, but poor people end up in nursing homes that are substandard and are sometimes even guilty of negligence or criminally inhumane treatment.

Here, Brianna has opened up even higher levels of thinking and spec-ulation. In this case, her reflection doesn't yet move toward resolu-tion or action, but it does begin exploring what started as a simple experience in much deeper and more meaningful ways.

Later in this book, when we focus on high-stakes writing such as essays and research papers, it will become clear that engaging in critical reflection through informal writing is an excellent strategy for exploring ideas in ways that your teachers will strongly encour-age and reward. This is because "making knowledge" in virtually all fields doesn't happen through simple description or even descriptive reflection; it involves deeper and more complex forms of analysis. By way of conclusion, consider this brief excerpt from the paper of Nisha, a student in a composition course, focusing on the use of accents in Disney films. Notice how Nisha has moved into higher levels of critique as she explores the social implications of Disney's choice of accents for some of its animated movies' characters. This paper had its origins in the process of *critical reflection*:

There are many noticeable patterns in Disney's use of accents, and these point toward a series of stereotypes that reinforce unhealthy attitudes toward people of different cultures. In Aladdin, all of the "good" characters speak with a standard American accent even though the film is set in a non-descript Arab country. Good characters, even living in non-U.S. countries, speak standard American English. And when good characters are grouped together, the "best" characters have the most standard, Midwest American accents (compare Mulan, who is from China yet speaks American English, with Mushu, who is "less good" or somewhat flawed and has an African

American accent, and Yao, also inferior to Mulan, who has a nonstandard Brooklyn accent). In several movies, the American accents of the heroes or heroines are set against the British accents of the evil characters (Snow White vs. the Evil Queen, Cinderella vs. her stepmother, etc.).

Putting It into Practice

This chapter has introduced the concept of *writing to learn*, with a focus on low-stakes writing—writing that is done quickly, in one draft, as input to learning—as a *way in* to stronger thinking, memory of the material, and analysis. Solo learning blogs can be an excellent medium for exploring concepts and ideas or rehearsing what you know. Dialogue journaling, through blogs and electronic forums, provide an excellent interactive way to test your thinking and get alternate opinions and ideas from your classmates. If your instructor doesn't assign or set up such opportunities, *take them seriously* and engage with them on your own. Write to and for yourself. If you can find one or more students in your class to partner with, create a forum and use it to study and explore the material. Only good things can result, including more engagement in your coursework, more effective learning, and higher grades.

Here are some things you can do now to put these principles into practice in all of your courses:

- See writing to learn as a way to further your understanding, and find ways in each of your courses to use the skills from this chapter.

- Identify the types of assignments you receive in your classes as low-stakes or high-stakes assignments, and try to focus more on the content or meaning in your low-stakes writing and less on its style or linguistic perfection.

- Start an academic journal or learning blog for one or all of your courses. This can be either a file on your computer that you update or a separate paper notebook for each class.

- Join a forum for one of your classes. If such as forum doesn't already exist, find some students in your class and start one on your own, or ask your instructor to set one up.

3

Microthemes and Why They're So Powerful as Tools for Learning

WHAT'S THE POINT?

After you read, think about, and put this chapter into practice, you will be able to:

- Understand the nature of short, focused assignments (microthemes)
- "Unpack" the purposes and forms of microthemes
- Analyze the "structure of activity" within microthemes
- Understand and apply critical thinking to your microtheme responses
- Recognize some common types of microthemes that are assigned in various disciplines

What's a Microtheme?

You probably weren't in college more than a few days—long enough to get the syllabus from your first course—before you realized what a lot of written work you could expect between then and graduation. If you could pull together all the pages you can expect to write in college, they would add up at least to a full-length book manuscript.

Whenever you see a human effort on this scale, it's fair to ask the question, "Why?" Why are you assigned all this written work? What's all this writing intended to achieve? Such questions are not only fair; they're also useful. The better you understand the purpose of any activity, the more likely you are going to fulfill it. The more clearly you perceive the role of written assignments in college, the more you'll get out of doing them. Your work will be both more rewarding and more successful.

KEY CONCEPT A *micro-theme* is a short writing assignment that is usually done in one draft but requires certain kinds of analysis or problem solving, or focused preparation for a class session, such as rereading through a particular analytical lens. See Key Concept Glossary.

This chapter looks in detail at the role that short, focused writing assignments play in college and offers suggestions for how to understand and approach them. Although these kinds of assignments have all sorts of names, for convenience we'll call them "microthemes" throughout this chapter and the rest of this book. If your assignment is longer than two or three pages, is worth a significant portion of your grade, and/or is more about seeing how much you have learned than about providing a way *to* learn, Chapters 4 and 5 will help by offering some useful strategies for coming up with ideas, structuring and drafting your more formal paper, and revising it for ideas, clarity, and expression.

In Chapter 2, we looked at how different kinds of writing can be placed on a continuum from very informal and low-stakes to very formal and high-stakes. When you do self-sponsored writing or use your writing to explore the subject of your learning, it doesn't have major consequences, like a passing or failing grade in a course, a reflection of your abilities for a job promotion, or a score on an entrance examination. The consequences are mostly about how useful the writing is to *you*, not to someone else. Your teacher may assign this kind of low-stakes writing to ensure that you learn more thoroughly and may assign some points to it, but usually it won't figure into your grade in a significant way. It *will* figure into your grade in a significant way if you take it seriously and use it productively—for example, by helping you to learn better, prepare for exams, or generate ideas for a high-stakes paper.

Your teacher might move a few notches along the continuum, though, by framing assignments that are still relatively brief but that strategically ask you to do some kind of analysis or problem solving within the content and discipline of the course. The stakes increase slightly because you need to show some evidence of your learning process, but you'll still usually do this kind of writing in a single draft, often between classes or online sessions. In this sense, these "middle-of-the-continuum" assignments differ from formal, high-stakes writing assignments, which almost always need several drafts and lots of attention given to revision and editing.

Microthemes are designed to open up your thinking by asking you to apply a concept, explore an idea, analyze a phenomenon or some data, think up a possible solution to a problem, or extend a theory. They may also play a role in the class itself, by getting you to put down ideas for a stimulating in-class or online discussion or a small-group activity, such as role-playing. Even a brief assignment of several paragraphs can force you to mold, shape, and distill your original hazy impressions into sharp, precise conceptions or to turn new ideas over in your mind, seeing their implications in more sophisticated ways.

Microthemes are designed to help you practice important skills of careful reading and critical thinking found in specific disciplines. Some kinds of microthemes are very creative and unique (e.g., scenarios or dialogues). Others may be more formulaic, such as summaries of readings. Here's a partial list of the kinds of microthemes that many teachers are now creating to benefit their students' learning, along with brief descriptions. If any look strange, don't worry: we'll be considering some examples as we go along.

Minicases and scenarios	Real(istic) situations that pose a problem or ask you to enter a fictitious world and respond to something relating to your subject matter that happens in it.
Provided-data microthemes	Papers requiring the analysis or synthesis of data or factual information (often presented randomly)
"Join the Conversation" microthemes	Fictitious statements about a reading or other course material to which you need to "respond back"
Dialogues	Brief papers requiring you to create an imagined dialogue between two or more people (theorists, characters, politicians, etc.); may also include your own voice

(continued)

(continued)

Proposition microthemes	Short papers that ask you to agree or disagree with one of two opposing propositions or statements that often have gray areas between them ("Violent videogames do/do not lead to violent behavior in children")
Thesis/support microthemes	Papers in which you must briefly create and defend a thesis about a topic in the course
Summaries	Brief papers that synthesize articles, chapters, or even books in a concise way that captures the main ideas or gist of the text
"Teach It" microthemes	Papers that explain ideas, theories, processes, research studies, or other information to audiences who are deliberately defined as nonexperts
Lens microthemes	Papers that view a reading, artifact, or phenomenon through a specific assigned lens or perspective, such as gender
Applications	Papers that apply something from a course or reading to one's personal life or to a social context
In–the–news microthemes	Papers that ask students to explore a problem, concept, or other idea in a course in the context of contemporary events (as reported in the news)
Quandary-posing microthemes	Papers in which students present and solve a puzzle relating to the course material
Wiki contributions	Brief, informative posts to a wiki on specific subjects

"Unpacking" the Microtheme and Other Short Assignments

It almost goes without saying that the first thing you should do after getting any writing assignment is to think about what it's asking. Launching right into writing, unless you're very familiar with the type of assignment you have been given, would be like trying to create a good lasagna without studying the recipe or checking your spice rack for oregano.

How, then, can you "unpack" short, learning-based writing assignments? After all, why *isn't* this all intuitive—like making the same lasagna that you prepared in your mother's kitchen? You've been responding to writing assignments for years. But think of this as a tennis coach might, if you were suddenly to make the varsity squad. Even realizing that you had been playing tennis for several years, the coach would be expecting you to train for a higher level of play by spending even more time consciously studying each part of your game: serve, backhand, lob, volley, and so forth. Glancing at an assignment and then just writing is like listening with one ear to your coach's suggestions about rushing the net and then just playing as usual.

What's the Form?

Assignments will come to you in a variety of forms. Each gives you different opportunities to clarify what's expected of you.

- *The written assignment:* Most assignments will come to you as written texts, sometimes within an online or paper syllabus but more often as links from the syllabus or as separate paper handouts. This is done for a simple reason: to ensure that the entire class understands exactly what's expected and will follow through systematically. Written assignments also allow the teacher to make certain specifications that otherwise would take up valuable class time to explain. Whenever you get a written assignment, *takes notes on it*, either by hand on a paper copy or using a markup system if it's in digital form (such as Insert Comments in Microsoft Word). This is especially important if your teacher adds any oral commentary in class.

- *The oral assignment:* Sometimes a teacher will give you a writing assignment in class by describing it only orally, or perhaps with some accompanied notes on a whiteboard. Although this method is rarely used for larger assignments, microthemes can sometimes take this form. Whatever you do, take careful notes when an assignment is given orally, and *ask for clarification*. For example, Professor Grant says this in his Introductory Physics course:

  "For next class, I'd like you to try explaining the concept of momentum to a group of young boy scouts who are trying to earn a merit badge."

  Here are some questions you might ask:

  "What's the goal of the assignment?"

  "Can we include any visuals, such as diagrams, or describe props that we might bring to the scout meeting?"

  "What are the approximate ages of the scouts?"

  "How much detail is needed?"

  "How long should the presentation be?"

  In addition to learning a lot more about Professor Grant's expectations, you're also helping him to think about what additional details he can include in the assignment for the next group of students in Introductory Physics. Notice that these questions are *specific*. Avoid asking, "What do you want in this paper?" Such a question shows that you haven't thought at all about the assignment, since there are plenty of clues already embedded in it.

- *The textbook assignment:* If your textbook or online resource includes writing assignments, your teacher may simply ask you, as an example, to "complete Exercise 4.6 on page 219." In this case, everything you need should be contained in the textbook, since the assignment is linked to its contents. Before launching into the assignment, go back through the preceding material, looking for key ideas and principles to use in your response. If your teacher gives the textbook assignment orally, listen carefully and add any notes of elaboration, since teachers sometimes repurpose textbook assignments in unique ways, in which case you will want to capture all of it for later use. The last thing you want to do is "compare the views of Descartes and Locke on the existence of matter" (the textbook assignment) if your instructor has told you to substitute "Hume" for "Locke."

What's the Purpose or Goal?

Many students run into trouble in their writing because they have little or no sense that their papers should *do* anything. They think of writing as vaguely "informative," with "informative" meaning simply to "write stuff down." A study at the University of Hawaii compared teachers' descriptions of what they wanted from their assignments with how students interpreted those assignments. Take a look at one (of many) mismatches:

The teacher's intention: "For the short paper on a video, I wanted students to make connections among the archeologist's questions, the methods used to get answers, and principles from their reading."

A student's interpretation: "This assignment was like writing a high school movie review. I wanted to give my own personal understanding about the video, so I was going to write a narrative."

Of course, most conscientious teachers will include an explicit goal at the start of each writing assignment, as we saw in Figure 1.1. Consider these examples (the goals are highlighted):

Economics: The goal of this short writing assignment is to help you to understand the implications of the concept of the "Invisible Hand" in an economic context.

Anthropology: This assignment is designed to help you read the assigned article by Clifford Geertz on shadow plays carefully and critically.

Landscape Design: You should be "seeing" landscape design everywhere you go. This assignment asks you to begin practicing that process and making it a habit.

Political Science: This "think piece" is designed to support Course Goal #3: to be able to describe and analyze emerging issues in developing

nations, such as financial reform, liberalization, adjustment and stabiliza-
tion strategies, foreign debt, the new political economy, and sustainable
development. The assignment goal supports the course goal by helping
you to practice identifying, describing, justifying, and testing a hypothesis concerning a growth-related issue in developing nations.

Notice how each of the goals in these short assignments focuses
on the *course material*—more so than the writing. It would be odd
for an instructor of, say, musicology to have as the *main* goal of a
microtheme something only writing related, such as creating error-
free sentences. As you consider explicit goals, try jotting down
some notes about what domain of knowledge is at stake, such as a
"growth-related issue in developing nations" or "the concept of the
Invisible Hand." Where is that information found? What are its lim-
its? How are you supposed to work with it?

Notice also how the political science goal is deliberately linked
to a larger goal for the entire course. This high-impact practice shows
you not only the point of the microtheme but also how it helps to
achieve broader learning goals and outcomes.

If your instructor doesn't include explicit goals in a short assignment, either ask for them directly—and don't be shy about this, as
every teacher knows what an assignment is supposed to accomplish—
or try creating the goals yourself, based on the information in the
assignment. Here, Emily, a student in a course on Gender and Psychology taught by Professor Scott, jots down the learning goals that she
thinks underlie a microtheme that her teacher has assigned:

Professor Scott's Assignment: For this microtheme, in a page or two,
explain to your grandmother what is meant by the phrase "doing
gender" and how this differs from the idea of "having gender." In your
description, use an example of how *you* have "done gender" since
getting out of bed this morning.

Emily's Goal Clarification: I think Professor Scott is asking us to review the
material in the chapter on the distinction between biological sex and the
social and psychological construction of gender. Plus, she wants to see us
not just working with the concepts in a sort of abstract way but also how
they apply to our own lives and our conceptions of gender.

Wisely, Emily has figured out exactly what her teacher wants students to think about and learn, simply by looking carefully at the assignment.

What's the Level of Formality?

Even though microthemes do exist somewhere toward the middle of our continuum and are admittedly done quickly, usually in a single draft, teachers may have different expectations about their formality. Your teacher in your Cultural Anthropology course may be expecting nothing more formal than focused freewriting in response to his assignment, "What specific freedoms and constraints do you think characterized the status of women in nineteenth-century Japan?," while your sociolinguistics teacher may want a more careful or methodical explanation of her assignment, "Compare the way that Labov and Wolfram define the term *dialect*."

Many teachers will ask you to write a microtheme in a particular *genre*, such as a letter to the editor, an imaginary dialogue, a tweet, a fictitious diary entry by a character, or a wiki entry (as we explored in Chapter 1). They do this for different reasons, occasionally to help you practice writing in that genre, but more often to put a frame or context around your work with the information or to engage and interest you more fully. Compare, for example, writing a summary of the role of Boxer, the overworked horse in *Animal Farm*, with an imaginary journal entry that Boxer might have written about the farm and the roles of its animals, especially the pigs. Either way, the microtheme is designed to get you thinking about the book and its themes, but the journal entry is potentially more interesting, pushes your thinking and imagination more fully, and its more pleasant to write and share.

Usually when you are asked to write a microtheme in a particular *genre*, your teacher will expect you to adhere to at least some aspects of that genre. Take a look at this microtheme assignment from a course in World History:

> Calicut, May 1498. You are a Hindu merchant operating on the Malabar coast (now in India) and in Calicut (now Kozhikode). You write a letter to your brother in another city with various news, including the arrival of Da Gama. What do you tell him?

Now, the form of the writing—a letter from the imagined perspective of a Hindu merchant written to his brother—becomes slightly more important (in contrast to the learning blog entries we looked at in Chapter 2). For this reason, the writing in this kind of microtheme may feel just a little more constrained. But your teacher also recognizes that you are writing microthemes more quickly than full-fledged formal papers and will not expect highly stylized prose or "completed" learning; after all, microthemes are designed to help you learn.

Whenever you're in doubt, ask your teacher for clarification or just err on the side of formality, unless you see something in the assignment that *strategically* asks you to be informal or chatty. It's less likely that your teacher will look negatively on a microtheme response that's a little too formal for the assignment than one that's not formal enough for it.

GIVE IT A TRY

Compare the following two microtheme assignments. Try defining and describing their expected level of formality.

Sample Assignment #1
Take a look at the statistics on how many people were living in large and small Italian cities in the years before and after the plague. Do you notice any patterns? In a half a page or so, jot down your thoughts about the reasons, drawing on the data, and bring your writing to class.

Sample Assignment #2
Examine the statistics for density of population and urban index for large and small Italian cities in the years preceding and following the plague. Then analyze the patterns discernible from the statistics, paying special attention to the relationship between urban areas and the low-country regions. In one to two pages, create a hypothesis, and defend it with reference to the data.

Who's the Audience?

We've already seen some interesting microtheme assignments that gave students an imaginative scene to write about and/or an imagined reader to address. Doing so gave the microtheme a little more rhetorical complexity and also could lead to stronger learning because the students needed to "translate" what they knew for someone who might not share their knowledge (e.g., a grandmother, a scout troop, the brother of a Hindu merchant). Remember that the teacher is creating these audiences deliberately and strategically. It helps, then, to put yourself into the scene as fully as possible and write *to* the person or persons identified in the assignment, but also to pay attention to the ideas at its heart. In microthemes, furthermore, your teacher will usually tolerate or even encourage some degree of creativity. Go ahead and try to use some seventeenth-century language. Have some fun with the back-and-forth that comes from creating a dialogue with a theorist or character. Your writing skills can only benefit.

If no audience is defined or implied in your writing, then in most cases you will be writing *for* a professor but *to* an audience that is more or less fictional: the "educated reader" or maybe the "average American"—an "invoked" audience. Because microthemes are used so often as a springboard for class discussion and activity, your responses might also address members of your class. (As explained in Chapter 2, you might even address specific students enrolled in your course if you are part of a forum or blog group, or even *yourself* if you are explaining or exploring course material on the way to learning it.) Whatever the case may be, it's important to think consciously about your intended or imagined reader when you respond

> **KEY CONCEPT** An *addressed audience* is a predefined audience whom you write to directly, such as a senator, an imaginary character in a scenario, or a member of your small-group forum in your class. An *implied* or *invoked audience* is an audience that you construct from the way you write. If you imagine an audience of people completely opposed to an argument you are making, they aren't actual people, but your writing is invoking them as if they are. See Key Concept Glossary.

to microtheme assignments—just as you will, even more importantly, in longer formal projects.

GIVE IT A TRY

Try describing the audiences you are expected to address or invoke
in the following microtheme assignment. Then explain what strategy you would use in responding to the assignment in light of this
audience.

Sample Microtheme Assignment (Accounting):
You are an accountant in the tax department of Kubiak, Kartcher,
and Elway, certified public accountants. Saturday morning you are
in Winchell's Donuts, as usual. Just as you finish reading the com-
ics and start on your second apple fritter, a gentleman sits down
beside you. He introduces himself as Fred O. McDonald, a farmer
from up in the valley. He says he recognizes you as "that CPA who
frequents the donut shop." Fred has a problem and asks tax advice
from you. Here's Fred's problem:

Last Tuesday, farmer McDonald planned to remove stumps
from a pasture. So he drove out to the pasture, lit a stick of dynamite, and tossed it near the base of a stump. Fred's playful dog,
Boomer, saw his master throw the "stick" and scampered to fetch
it. Boomer picked up the stick. Fred yelled at the dog. Boomer,
thinking he was going to be punished, ran under Fred's pickup
truck. Boomer dropped the dynamite stick. The dog escaped harm
just as the truck was totally destroyed by the blast. Fred wonders if
he can deduct the loss of the truck for tax purposes. Write a letter
to Fred O. McDonald to answer his question.

The "Structure of Activity"

So far we've been analyzing the general nature of microthemes and
short writing assignments. Doing so will give you a framework for
understanding the assignment and its parameters. But it's like figuring
out how to open a complicated box. Now that it's open, what's really
inside? What is the assignment asking you to do? Inside the box are

various activities: reading, analyzing and interpreting, comparing, gathering data, observing, interviewing, and imagining. We're going to call everything that the assignment asks you to *do* its "structure of activity."

Take a look at the following assignment from a course in medical ethics. In this assignment, students have read a survey study that asked

women and their partners what they think should happen to extra frozen embryos that they now no longer need for in vitro fertilization because they have successfully given birth to a child. The embryos are "prehumans"; from one perspective, they represent potential human life, but from another perspective, they're just cellular matter. They can't be kept forever, so, what should be done?

Assignment goals: To help you read, understand, and think critically about an article that reports on a study of an important ethical issue concerning women's views on what should become of their frozen embryos.

While reading and reviewing the Lyerly and Faden article, you find yourself in the company of several people who have read this study and are talking about it. The conversation is wide-ranging and, as is typical in discussions about complicated ethical issues, gets a little tense. At one point, Paul, who has been quietly listening, blurts out this response:

"This study is bogus! The authors totally twist their results to support an anti-embryo-protection stance. The fact that 42 percent of patients can't be located after five years to say what they want to do with their embryos indicates that they want them cryogenically preserved forever, that is, never destroyed. The authors report that a significant percentage (82 percent) of those who said they *didn't* want their

(continued)

(continued)

> embryos donated to other couples wanted to save them for
> themselves or keep them forever frozen. The authors never
> talk about these results! Nor do they talk about the fact that
> more "partners" felt it was OK to donate the embryos than
> the infertile women who produced the eggs from which the
> embryos were created. Totally biased!"
>
> In two to three paragraphs, respond back to Paul as if
> you're part of the conversation. Is he right about the bias?
> How do you know?

Notice that the teacher has included explicit *goals* for the assignment: to help you *read* more fully and carefully and *think about* the
ethical implications of the study. She has invented a situation: a person (Paul) has interpreted the reading in a particular way. Students
need to think about whether this seemingly objective study, which
does report that a significant number of women do not object to their
embryos being used for scientific study, is "biased" or not. (Although
students don't usually know it at first, the teacher has also included
both accurate and inaccurate numbers—82 percent and 42 percent—which causes students to reread the article very carefully.) In
completing such an assignment, you need to do at least the following, which is part of the assignment's clever design and makes up its
structure of activity:

- read the article;
- read and carefully consider Paul's account of the article, which
  could be wrong, sensible, erroneous, biased, or accurate;
- reread the article, seeing if any details support Paul's interpretation (which requires thinking about the study's methods as well
  as how the results are presented—and, along the way, discovering Paul's factual errors);
- choose a way to respond to Paul, including agreeing or disagree-
  ing with his points and correcting anything he has said that is
  inaccurate or that misinterprets the article; and

- put all this into language that sounds realistic, as if you were actually talking to Paul (a process that also helps you to practice various writing skills of persuasion and conversation).

Although it may seem almost intuitive to create this bulleted list (something you might "do in your head"), it's very common for students to skim through an assignment and then begin writing immediately. Two bad things can happen as a result. First, the response may not really accomplish the learning goals that your teacher planned for it to accomplish, with the result that your teacher will think, "Did this student even read the assignment?" Second, and more important, you will probably have lost an opportunity to think and learn as fully as the assignment intended. Over time, such lost opportunities squander your college experience and weaken the strength of your degree.

Here's a process for figuring out the structure of activity beneath a microtheme or other short assignment:

- First, describe the *form* or *genre* that the writing will take (a letter, a dialogue, a report, a tweet, etc.), and describe in as much detail as you can what form the writing should take, based on the assignment. If a form is given, such as "write a *dialogue*," explain what the dialogue would look like.
- Describe the *level of formality* that the writing will take.
- Describe the intended or imagined *audience* for the text.
- Now carefully consider the assignment's *goals*. If no goals are provided, make a list of goals from the assignment's details, as illustrated in Emily's example earlier in this chapter.
- Create a list of every process you need to go through in order to complete the assignment. Use as much detail as possible.
- Within each process, specify the *information* required and what you need to do with it, using verbs such as *compare, describe, list, find,* and the like.

Juan, a student in a course titled Geography of the Southwest, worked out the structure of activity beneath one of the very creative and engaging microthemes created by his teacher. Here's the teacher's assignment:

> Imagine that you are one of the sheep living in a Diné-controlled flock sometime around the year 1900. In about seven hundred words, provide a description of what your life is like AND how it compares to the lives of some of your sheep ancestors who came to the Southwest in Spanish-controlled herds. Since you are writing for an audience of humans who have never experienced life as a sheep, be as explicit as possible about your relationship with the land-scape and with the Diné community (or the Spanish colonial community, in the case of your ancestors).

Juan noticed that the assignment didn't have an explicit goal. So, first Juan described the genre and audience for the assignment, and then he described what he thought was the purpose of the assignment:

The genre of the assignment isn't specified—a description to humans—so it could be a letter or just a narrative. The audience is humans, generally.

She wants us to be aware of how land is used differently by different populations (settlers, migrants, etc.). By making us see this through the eyes of sheep, she asks us to describe how open grazing changed toward the more restricted use of land on reservations.

Juan then created the following structure of activity implied in the assignment:

1. Read the material about land use of the Diné community and Spanish settlers.
2. Focus on the content relating specifically to land use.
3. Compare information about land use between cultures.
4. Hypothesize differences in the use of land.

5. Put an account of land use into the experiences of sheep herds living in the different periods.

6. Create a narrative from a sheep to a human that describes its experience on the land and compares it with information from its past (ancestors).

7. Figure out a way or a style to put the sheep's words in.

Here, Juan creates a road map of the processes that the assignment implies. If he passes over any of these processes or doesn't engage in them fully (such as reading the material about land use or comparing the land use between the two cultures), his response will suffer. Creating the structure of activity obliges him to pay attention to each step.

Another way to figure out the structure of activity within an assignment is to annotate it based on the process described above. Here's an example of an annotation that Hunter, a student enrolled in a Human Nutrition course, created for an assignment involving food choices at a local school.

The goal of this microtheme is to support one of our course outcomes by giving you practice evaluating the nutritional quality of food served to stakeholders in various kinds of institutions such as day-care centers, schools, retirement homes, and prisons. At the following link, you will find the choices in the cafeteria of Caswell Elementary School that were available on Oct. 16. Each choice includes some data (serving size, calories, fats, sodium, etc.). First, imagine you are a child moving through the lunch line and making selections from each food category (main course, dessert, drink, etc.). Using the tools from our course so far, do a quick analysis of the nutritional value of the food your fictitious child chose. Now take on the role of a consulting nutritionist. On the basis of your analysis, write a letter to the school principle, *evaluating* the nutritional quality of the lunch program. Bring your microtheme to class.

- sets goals for learning
- narrows assignment to "provided data" analysis
- requires process of analysis
- specifies form or genre of writing
- identifies specific audience to address
- further specifies thinking process that asks for criteria to be developed

You can see how Hunter's annotations take him a long way toward understanding the assignment and mapping out his process for completing it.

GIVE IT A TRY

Here's a particular type of short assignment, a "provided-data" microtheme, from a course in American History. Using the process described above, try describing this microtheme's structure of activity. Since no explicit learning goals are included in this microtheme, start there—by trying to figure out what the assignment is designed to help students practice or learn. (Students have bought a packet of course readings at the bookstore that contain some maps.)

Using the maps in the front of the packet, compare the distribution of churches within Anglo-America east of the Mississippi River in 1750 with the distribution in 1850 and, in one sentence *not exceeding* fifty words, hypothesize the reasons for the difference. Write your response on a 5" x 8" card.

How Microthemes Encourage Critical Thinking

We have seen so far that "unpacking" assignments and exposing their processes can reveal underlying expectations that will help you to practice essential academic skills. But there's an even deeper level to those skills, a core set of thinking processes that teachers in virtually all disciplines expect you to use and refine. These processes often get lumped into the catchall term *critical thinking*. And, although the nature of critical thinking will vary a lot across different areas of knowledge and study, it shares some common intellectual activities that are worth understanding fully. It's also *crucial* in all formal, high-stakes writing, as we'll see in Chapters 4–6. Here, we focus on how microthemes are designed to encourage, even guarantee, the kind of critical thinking prized in all academic settings.

Teachers in all disciplines express a common concern—one that reveals the goodwill of the teachers themselves (they want their students to learn) and a little anxiety as well (the sense that students don't learn as well as they might). The concern is often expressed in the phrase, "I want my students to think critically." What this suggests is that teachers aren't looking for students merely to absorb information and parrot it back. They want students to analyze and evaluate what they study, to take it apart, to examine it piece by piece, to weigh it, judge it, and perhaps (who knows?) to doubt or reject it, or even to improve on it, add to it, develop it further. Teachers want students to be *active* in their pursuit of knowledge while at the same time exercising a little healthy skepticism. They want students to go after knowledge with a pick and shovel and then put everything they unearth to the acid test—not to be cynical or distrustful, but to constantly search for "true gold."

> **KEY CONCEPT** *Critical thinking* is an all-purpose term that refers to the careful and thoughtful analysis of information or phenomena. It requires a kind of positive skepticism that doesn't take everything at face value but tries to weigh it, reflect on it, and reach a fuller understanding of it and its implications. See Key Concept Glossary.

Thinking critically takes a lot of work. Memorizing and replaying information is easy. Critical thinking demands effort, active questioning, a sharp eye, a deeply ingrained restlessness, and a refusal to be easily satisfied. It also demands some sort of method. Where do you begin? How do you gain entrance? Which nuts and screws do you have to remove first?

The major intellectual operations of critical thinking are like the basic moves in dance: whatever you perform (classical ballet, swing, popping, flamenco, hip hop) will be built on some combination of basic moves. Don't confuse these basic moves with the commands in the assignment (trace, argue, choose), even though they sometimes carry the same labels. The operations represent a deeper structure, a more fundamental activity of the mind. They have less to do with the actual final form of your work than with the thinking that is necessary to develop your material. All five of the operations discussed here—*fact-finding, analysis, synthesis, evaluation,* and *interpretation*—may be involved in a single assignment (as in, "Trace the development of the effectiveness of programming languages, and speculate about what this development suggests for the future"). Let's take a look at each of these operations in detail.

It All Starts with Details: Fact-Finding
Not much critical thinking can happen until you know what you're talking (or writing) about. Probably the simplest of the mental

operations, "to explain the facts," just means to record the details of some phenomenon, to produce an accurate picture or account of it. You don't need to explain anything—yet. For now you are just logging facts and collecting raw data. It takes time, patience, and meticulous observation. (Remember how Sherlock Holmes keeps chiding his companion: "You *see*, Watson, but you do not *observe*.")

Look around you (and listen). Everywhere people are not thinking critically because they are not basing assertions or arguments on *enough facts and evidence*. A politician votes against a bill that would provide help for veterans suffering from post-traumatic stress disorder. The opposing party uses that to criticize the politician during an election cycle. But the politician voted against the bill because it *also* included a section inserted by the opposing party (and irrelevant to the veteran issue) that would have defunded pre-K educational support for children in poor families. Knowing all the facts casts a totally different light on the reason for the politician's vote: she wasn't against the veteran part of the bill; she just wasn't also going to vote for defunding the pre-K program. Having enough facts—enough details or description of what's true—makes up much of the activity of the law. You can't prosecute a case by saying, "Well, we don't know anything, but we think this man is guilty."

Teachers often assign microthemes that require fact-finding to help students develop their powers of observation. In the health sciences, for example, one of the most important processes for clinical practice is looking carefully, noticing unusual characteristics or symptoms. A doctor, nurse, dentist, or other clinician will wait to begin a formal diagnosis of a patient's problem until she's made a full description, which may come from notes taken during the observation. A historian or biographer won't reach conclusions about a person's life until he's ferreted out and sorted through all the facts. A newspaper reporter can't park near a political rally and take notes from her car; she has to get in close, read the signs, and listen to the chants—that is, observe events.

Many assignments will ask you to do more than explain details or describe, but that "what else" may depend crucially on observation and a cataloging of facts. It can be tempting to rush right into that "what else," but don't. An excellent way to begin a microtheme—or any assignment, for that matter—is to describe, as fully as possible, exactly what you see or what's happening in the painting, cadaver, tribal community, microscope lens, YouTube video, or Shakespearean sonnet that you'll be analyzing.

From a course in Education that involves student teaching, here's an example of a microtheme designed to help students hone their skills of description.

> The purpose of this short assignment is to help you practice close observation of the interaction of children in your assigned classroom in preparation for analysis of their behaviors. For a period of thirty minutes *during a lesson by your site teacher*, carefully watch what all the students are doing. Take specific, descriptive notes (using abbreviations to capture as much as possible). Then, within four hours of your observation (so that your memory doesn't fade), write a one-page description, based on your notes, of exactly what was happening in the classroom during the lesson.

It's easy to see the importance of description in this assignment. If a student doesn't really *look at* what's going on in the classroom, she can't fully *describe* the children's interactions and behaviors, and that would ruin any higher-level analysis later on—a subject to which we'll now turn.

Taking Things Apart: Analysis
From the Greek word for loosening up, *analysis* means, strictly speaking, taking something apart for the purpose of looking at its different elements. In chemistry, this "something" is a substance whose parts are measured in amounts and proportions: "What element makes up this compound?" In cultural anthropology, this "something" might be a community of people, and your analysis might involve sorting out and examining separately their familial, political, commercial, and religious activities and structures.

Take Sigmund Freud, for example. He strove for decades to arrive at the useful division of the mind into its major components (remember that he was engaging in psycho-*analysis*.) In his early model, he divided the mind into the unconscious, the preconscious, and the conscious. Not satisfied, he later reanalyzed the psyche and created three divisions for it: the ego, the id, and the superego. Since then, these theories have been further refined or critiqued and rejected. (*Analysis* at the level of a discipline doesn't just stop when something has been analyzed.)

Given any topic, you can search for several ways to subdivide it or break it into its components, and assess what results you get from each division. Imagine that a professor (don't worry about the discipline for now) hands you a letter written by Benjamin Disraeli, prime minister of England under Queen Victoria, and says, "analyze this." How many options can you imagine for ways to analyze the letter? Following are some of them:

1. You could analyze the letter *rhetorically* (by author, audience, topic, and rhetorical strategy). Who was Disraeli? Who was he addressing, and why? What was he discussing, and how? How was his argument structured?

2. You could analyze the letter as a political act. What was the situation? What did Disraeli want to achieve? How was he using the letter to do this?

3. Knowing that Disraeli was a novelist as well as a politician, you could analyze the letter as a literary artifact. How would you describe Disraeli's style? What images or metaphors does he use? Are there examples of parody? What elements in the letter can also be seen in his creative work?

4. If you had the actual document, you could even subject it to a physical analysis. What kind of paper and ink were used? Where did he get them? Is it possible that the letter is a forgery? Could an analysis of the paper tell us this?

Like description, analysis is more often assumed or implied in the way a microtheme assignment is presented than stated outright. When it *is* used explicitly, it will also refer to somewhat different practices based on the discipline and the kind of information you're working with. Like description, analysis is often a kind of prelude to synthesis, interpretation, or evaluation. You analyze a play (as in breaking it down into its different elements) in order to assess the artistic contributions of each: script, direction, acting, lighting, score, and so on. You anatomize an Amazonian apple snail in order to understand how the parts work.

In the second stage of the Education microtheme assignment above, students are asked to move from their descriptions of the behaviors and actions of the children in their assigned classroom to an *analysis* of those behaviors and actions. That will involve taking the entire phenomenon—half an hour of an elementary classroom lesson—and pulling it apart to look for patterns. The description gives you the raw data, but now you need to work with the data. For example, you might have noticed that students on the left side of the room, near the windows, were less likely to be looking at the teacher during the lesson than students on the right side of the room. Or you might have noticed that every time the teacher turned his back on the class, some of the students interacted with each other by passing things or whispering. These may be captured in your observations ("T turns to board; S2 whispers to S3; S6 passes object to S7"), but your *analysis* reviews all of the data, separating random, one-time occurrences from repeated ones. By pulling the entire session apart to examine its components, you're on your way to a deeper understanding of what's going on in the classroom.

GIVE IT A TRY

Choose something—an object, a concept, an activity—that is amenable to analysis. For now, just try to break what you choose into subcomponents. For example, how would you analyze the structure of a play? Or the components of a flatworm? Or the instruments that contribute to a song by your favorite band? Although this may seem like a very simple kind of analysis, it demonstrates the fundamental principles behind this kind of thinking.

Putting It All Together: Synthesis

If analysis involves taking something apart, *synthesis* means putting things together—combining elements of entities to form a whole. At some level, for example, all fields build theories about their objects of study. A theory is a set of more elaborate generalizations based on a large-scale synthesis of what a field has observed about its subject. A synthesis may follow an analysis: you've examined all the pieces carefully, considering their relationships to each other, and now you want to assemble what you've examined into a more complex view of the object being studied. Microthemes, as well as high-stakes papers, often ask you to bring together disparate information, opinions, observations, and the like into a fuller understanding of the object of study.

Charles Darwin constructed his theory of evolution from a lifetime of careful observations and analyses. As he drew on more observations about various animal species and their behaviors, habitats, and biological characteristics, he was led, finally, to *synthesize* his findings into a model of genetic variation, differential reproduction, and speciation that had an enormous impact on how we think about our natural world. By contrast, Tycho Brahe put years into making meticulous observations of the movements of the stars and planets, but he got no further. It was left to Johannes Kepler to *synthesize* Brahe's data into his three laws of planetary motion, which in turn paved the way for Sir Isaac Newton's still broader synthesis, resulting in his formulation of the law of universal gravitation.

The point here is that by itself, *collection* isn't *synthesis*. Fact-finding and description don't automatically yield more than a heap of givens ("data" in Latin). Synthesis entails finding the *connections*, or *linkages*, between various facts before you. To synthesize means not just to add one thing to another and to another, but to see what new entity they form among them and what patterns hold the givens together. It's also important to note that *synthesis* requires or presupposes a preliminary *analysis* of the data—a sorting of the data into its major categories. These processes can sometimes happen at the same time. For example, as Jesse takes notes to analyze the composition of a website, he instantly categorizes them into sections on "layout," "white space," "images," "text and font," and "color." He can then apply principles from his course to think about each component (such as the Golden

Ratio, which describes how the sizes of the parts of a web page should relate to each other so as to be most pleasing to the viewer).

Consider the following assignment, another "provided-data microtheme," from a course in Invertebrate Zoology. Students are asked to look at an assortment of statements and then *synthesize* them into a coherent theory about the relationship between two organisms:

> Arrange the propositions below in a logical order, connect the individual statements with appropriate transitions, and arrive at a conclusion that is supported by your argument. Using all of the points supplied below, write a two-page essay on the topic, "The relationship between coral and zooxanthellae."
>
> - Coral reefs are formed by scleractinian corals that typically occur in shallow (<60 m) water.
> - Hermatypic corals contain photosynthetic algae (zooxanthellae) in special membrane-bound cavities inside the cells of the gastrodermis.
> - Reef corals are limited to clear water because suspended material interferes with the transmission of light.
> - Over two-thirds of the metabolic requirements of corals are provided by zooxanthellae.

In this expertly designed assignment, created by Professor Gerald Summers at the University of Missouri, the factual data—what you would get from description—and some level of analysis are all given to students prepackaged. Now the students must put them all together into a coherent view of a complex relationship, practicing skills of crucial importance in the field of zoology.

Reaching Informed Judgments: Evaluation

If you analyze the root of the word *evaluation*, you get e-valu-ation: that is, the act of drawing out the value of something, of determining its worth. If a microtheme or a more formal assignment calls for evaluation, then it's no longer enough to describe or to explain whatever you are discussing; you're now called upon to say *how good it is*, according to specific criteria. (This is what professors do all the time: they reach decisions about the value of students' work, as well as work in their professions, using a set of criteria or standards.)

The range of things you can evaluate in an academic setting is extensive. In high-stakes projects, you can write a *review* of a movie, play, or concert. You can evaluate the success of Washington's military tactics in the Revolutionary War. You can evaluate the design of a research project in biochemistry or the layout and usability of a website. You evaluate can the performance of a football team in a specific game or of just its quarterback. In low-stakes writing, you can evaluate the nutritional worth of the food in a school lunch program, as demonstrated in the earlier microtheme we examined. Or you can briefly evaluate a claim made in an online article. Even evaluations can themselves be evaluated, which becomes a higher level of critical thinking: why did the pundits think the president's performance in his State of the Union address was so bad (or so good) when you had an entirely different impression? How could the top critics on rottentomatoes.com have given this film an average score of 12 out of 100 when you found it so entertaining?

To evaluate anything, you need to understand what the "anything" is; you need to formulate criteria for your evaluation, measure the object against those criteria, and draw your various measurements together into one general assessment. That is, you need to

- *analyze* the entity into its different components and decide on standards for the assessment of each;
- *observe* and *describe* the object itself, to see how it measures up against each criterion; and
- *synthesize* your assessments into one coherent, evaluative conclusion.

Notice that you're *starting* with analysis—that is, you're deciding on the parts or categories of what you want to evaluate, but you're also specifying what values should be associated with each category. Then you're fact-finding details through the lens of each of those parts or categories. And *then* you're pulling together your observations into an overall assessment.

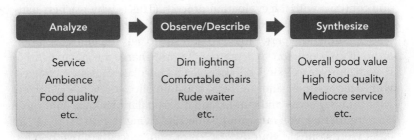

FIGURE 3.1 Sample Evaluation Process for a Restaurant

Figure 3.1 shows how this process might work in evaluating a restaurant. To evaluate a restaurant (the "anything"), you will analyze it for its components (such as service, ambience, food quality, and value); decide on the standards for those components (e.g., lighting should be well placed and at an appropriate luminosity for a romantic restaurant; volume level and type of background music, if any, should set a positive mood and not intrude on conversation); observe and describe each component against the criteria ("lighting is so dim that it is almost impossible to read the menu"; "chairs are very comfortable for a long meal"; etc.); and synthesize the assessments ("Overall, Chez Jacque provides excellent continental cuisine at a good value in spite of. . . . ").

Just setting up the evaluative criteria can be a big part of the intellectual challenge. How do you assess the action of a particular political leader in the past? By how it served the interests of the political leader's own nation? By how fairly it dealt with all concerned parties? By how it strengthened or weakened the leader's political power? By whether it resulted in the greatest good for the greatest number of people, even if it destroyed a few lives in the process? By how consistent it was with the leader's campaign promises? You can't judge anything unless you have a *lens* through which to see it; every measurement implies a tape measure, and sometimes you will need to evaluate the criteria themselves in turn!

Establishing criteria for evaluation can be challenging, but it's far better to set up the criteria in advance than to make them up as you continue with the evaluation process. (This is why teachers usually spend a lot of time creating evaluative criteria *before* they begin reading student papers.) To do so, it helps to ask yourself how much of your own opinion and preferences are shared by other people. If you happen to like a breakfast of a chocolate croissant covered with peanut butter and ketchup, and thin slices of salmon, topped with caraway seeds and cumin, and a particular breakfast joint can't prepare that for you, are you justified in giving it a poor rating? In other words, should your own needs or preferences be a criterion for judgment? However, if a restaurant refuses to modify anything on its menu (like leaving the cheese off a made-to-order sandwich), that problem might affect many people.

Once you're in the mind-set of a particular "target" audience or public that is most relevant to the thing or activity you are evaluating, then you can begin thinking about evaluative criteria. Given this intended audience or user, what are the major features, components, or elements that must work effectively both alone and with others to make what you are evaluating a "good one"? How do people know a good one when they see it? Also, each feature needs to be observable and describable, or able to be experienced, in order for it to be a good criterion, and those observations and experiences need to be shared by different people who are the "audience" for the thing or phenomenon. If you're evaluating the performance of a crust punk band, you'll see your criteria through the lens of crust punk fans (not classical music aficionados or people who would attend a Jimmy Buffet concert).

Figure 3.2 encapsulates the process of formulating criteria. First you define the "target" audience for the evaluation. Some audiences will be very large and general, such as when you're evaluating the design of a web page. Others may be much narrower, as is likely if you're evaluating the quality of horses at an equestrian show. Some audiences may be broadly "public," and others may be specialized— for example, if you're evaluating all-electric general aviation vehicle prototypes at an aerospace engineering competition.

Finally, spell out the features within each category that can be observed or experienced. This part will take some work because you're making explicit (in words) what can often be implicit ("felt").

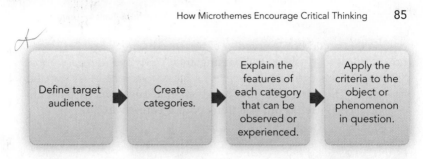

FIGURE 3.2 A Process for Creating Evaluative Criteria

In evaluating the quality of a particular hiking trail, for example, "well rated" (for difficulty) begs for more features: "vertical ascent (feet per mile), terrain (obstacles, grading of path, washout), and total length of hike are appropriate to stated level of difficulty." As you work out these features, it helps greatly to discuss them with others who are members of the target audience; they, too, experience what you're evaluating and can give you additional perspectives. Finally, try it out! If you can't reach any clear judgments on any categories of features, go back to the drawing board.

Caretta, a student in a Consumer Behavior course, was assigned a microtheme to sketch out an evaluation of local car washes that she could turn into a live survey instrument. Her obvious target audience was her teacher and peers (who would share their criteria), but she was asked to imagine that her evaluation might be published in a report for the general public. Because the imagined goal was to interview people in order to get information about their satisfaction, Caretta had to create evaluative categories that would make sense to them. She chose "speed," "attention to detail," "courteousness," "value," and "final outcome." Note that in doing so, she broke down, or analyzed, the car wash experience into separate parts or components. For each one, she had to list specific features that could be observed (this was important because she had to imagine that these features would be used in consumers' evaluations). For example, under "speed," she created a simple, objectively observable scale: under 10 minutes, 11–15 minutes, 16–20 minutes, and over 21 minutes. Under "courteousness," which is more subjective, she created

criteria that could be observed or experienced: "greeting," "explanation of process," "ushering to waiting area," "payment process," and
"parting." She could easily create a scale for each of these specific
aspects of "courteousness" and turn them into questions ("On a scale
of 1–5, how courteous did you think your greeting was?").

GIVE IT A TRY

Choose something general to evaluate, such as a song, an airline
trip, a lecture, a visit to a museum, or a novel (you don't have to
have experienced it). First define the likely target audience, user,
or "experiencer" of the thing or activity you are evaluating. Then
create a set of categories or features that will be part of your evaluation (for a pizza, you might include the crust, the quality of specific
toppings and of the sauce, the amount of each component, etc.).
Now, based on more specific features in each category, try to sketch
the criteria that you or others would use to reach a judgment about
each component. This part is hard. What makes a good crust? If you
were evaluating a specific pizza, you would then pull together your
judgments of all the components into a general conclusion about
the quality of the entire pizza: "The pizza at Luigi's is baked to perfection, with a crust that. ..."

Again, remember that to evaluate something means going
beyond expressing whether or not you like it. You're trying to assess
some quality in the thing itself, not just what you're seeing. (An
example is that travel guide writers can't just report that a hotel is
lousy because *they* prefer hard beds and the beds are not rock hard;
they have to think more objectively about the experience of other
travelers.) Observing and recording your rough impressions of the
object gives you a good starting point—but that's all. A raw opinion
isn't an evaluation. For that you need to ask yourself what it is about
the particular book, biopic, speech, theory, policy, website, experimental design, work of art, classmate's paper or presentation, or
poster, that strikes you as good, bad, or indifferent. Even more challenging, you need to consider whether your original impressions are

actually well founded, based on a careful analysis using the criteria that you have established.

Suppose you're taking British History from Queen Elizabeth to Queen Victoria and you begin reading about the British treatment of the American colonies in the early 1700s. As an American with years of July 4 celebrations in your past, you may feel that the British policies were brutal and uncalled for. But were they, really? Once you have examined the facts and evidence more closely, and once you have developed criteria for assessing foreign policy, the British policies may look more restrained and fair than you had supposed—or they may look worse. You will no longer be registering gut feelings but, rather, a careful, responsible assessment.

Interpretation: What Does It Mean?

The term *interpretation*, like *evaluation*, turns up as a command in some microthemes as well as in more formal assignments. Also like *evaluation*, it tends to be defined as an intellectual operation. To *interpret* anything means to *say what the entity means or points to beyond itself.*

- What do the results of this physics experiment *mean*? What do they tell us about the hypothesis being tested or about the broader theory from which it was derived?

- What does a particular sonnet *mean*? What does it say about love, truth, beauty, and longing?

- What do recent fluctuations in the Dow Jones average *mean*—or tell us—about the odds of another economic recession?

- What does a bit of body language *mean*? Does an interviewee's crossed arms on his chest suggest displeasure or defensiveness at the interviewer's questions?

- What does it *mean* that this particular animal species never crosses a particular geographical boundary?

All of these are questions of interpretation, of "reading," in a sense, the meaning of some phenomenon. To interpret anything is to view it not just as itself, but as a symbol for something else, as a sign indicating a reality in some other context. Consider the Constitution.

What does it say about the right to privacy? The actual phrase occurs nowhere in the Constitution, but does the document as a whole actually mean or intend to guarantee some such right to American citizens? And if it does, what would such a right to privacy *mean* for women seeking abortions, for the terminally ill seeking to be released from life support, for confidentiality of psychiatric records (e.g., when buying a gun)? Actual wars have been fought over some questions of interpretation—and may well be again.

Any object can also be read in light of multiple contexts or language. Konrad Lorenz began his famous studies of animal aggression when he noticed how intense and varied the colors of his tropical fish were. They were beautiful, but he went beyond their aesthetic appeal ("so beautiful!") to wonder if their colors *meant* anything. Did they serve a purpose, or point to some reality or system beyond themselves? Years of observation and thought eventually convinced him (and others) that the colors of the fish were essential in determining social behavior (and therefore survival) in their natural environment. To a biologist, the colors *meant* this. But you could also imagine how fish colors might show up as symbols in a literary work. Or in dreams. Or as something significant to a specific culture (blue fish = sacred, hands-off; other colors = edible). Or as an index of water quality and pollution.

Here is an example of a microtheme that requires interpretation:

Choose one of the pieces of modern art at this link. First, jot down some notes about the work you chose. Consider its title. Look *carefully* at it, studying the features that we have been discussing in class. Next, write a brief interpretation of the work: what do you think it means? What is the significance of the features that stood out for you? Finally, go to this page, find your work in the list, click on it, and read the professional interpretation there. Now write a one-page response comparing your interpretation with the professional interpretation. How were they similar or different? Do you "see" what the professional art critic sees?

Finally, it's also important to recognize that critical thinking often leads to contesting the status quo through interpretation. Take the example of statistics on race or class. As a percentage of the population, African American males are far more likely to spend time in prison than white males. Without thinking critically about this issue, many Americans erroneously and ignorantly jump to the racist conclusion that African American males are more criminally minded or "bad" than white American males. Interpreting the statistics means asking more sophisticated, broader questions about the reasons, such as higher levels of police profiling and arrests among African Americans, unfair and race-based prosecution or sentencing, the effects of repression or poverty (including the ability to hire counsel), and the systematic denial of equal opportunities because of racism. Don't take everything at face value! And don't think that just because something is published in a journal or a book, it must be "right." Bring a critical perspective to the information—and *especially* to opinions. (We'll return to the critical evaluation of information and courses in Chapter 5.)

GIVE IT A TRY

Take a look at the following microtheme assignment from an Education course focusing on theories and practices of literacy. Then try to figure out which of the five processes of critical thinking will be required in the assignment.

Imagine that you have the authority to set policy for access to literacy in a prison. Sketch and defend that policy in a two-page microtheme. Here are some questions to get you thinking: What "good" comes from access to literate materials (books, magazines, etc.)? Should all inmates have access to these materials? What about inmates who are serving life sentences with no chance of parole? Are the functions of literacy the same for them? What about inmates on death row? Since these criminals have taken lives, do you think access to literacy should be granted to them, or is denying access part of their punishment? If you believe the latter, should they be denied access to all texts (including religious ones)? If not, how would we decide which texts are acceptable? Who would decide? If there's a positive purpose to reading religious texts (even pleasure?), why not offer positive purposes through other texts? What's the difference?

Putting It into Practice

This chapter has explored short, focused assignments, often called *microthemes*, and has provided strategies for understanding and working with their learning goals, their expectations, and their underlying "structures of activity"—the kinds of thinking, problem solving, and analysis they require.

Here are some things you can be doing now to put these principles into practice in all of your courses:

- Describe the general nature of the assignment: its form, purpose or goal, level of formality, and audience.

- Now, figure out the structure of activity beneath the microtheme: what will you need to do, step by step? What is the assignment expecting of you in terms of your learning processes?

- To uncover the expectations for critical thinking underneath microthemes, go back over the structure of activity you created for the assignment: form/genre, formality, audience, goals, and steps or stages in the process (including information or content and specific activities). Then dig deeper: of the five processes in critical thinking, which will it be necessary to deploy, and why? What specific mental operations will you need to conduct to perform successfully?

4

Higher-Stakes Projects: Getting from Ideas to Text

After you read, think about, and put this chapter into practice, you will be able to:

- Understand what's expected in higher-stakes writing projects
- Be more conscious of how to transfer what you already know and can do into new writing situations
- Use several strategies to explore your knowledge about a subject and begin organizing that knowledge into possible chunks or sections of text
- Know exactly what a "thesis" is and how to create one

What Changes with Larger and Higher-Stakes Projects?

We're now going to move further along the continuum that we considered in Chapter 2, toward the formal end (see Figure 4.1). On this part of the continuum, papers and projects

- are *larger and more extensive*;

- are usually *worth a higher percentage of your grade* or factor more heavily into whatever assessment is used to judge your work; and

- are more *formal*, requiring more attention to style, a more careful structure, an adherence to the conventions of the course's discipline, a sharp focus on the logic of your ideas and support for them, careful and copious revision, and a lot of attention to smaller details, including grammar, punctuation, and format.

91

Low Stakes/Informal		High Stakes/Formal
Journals	Microthemes	Term papers
Reading logs	Response papers	Reports
Reflections	Summaries	Formal essays
Minute papers	Minicases	Documented papers
Blogs	Problem analyses	Reviews
Lecture notes	Wiki contributions	

FIGURE 4.1 A Continuum of Formality and Stakes

Clearly, the game changes at this end of the continuum. Now it's less about using writing as a "way in" to your learning and more about an evaluation of how well you have learned and can convey that learning to other readers. It's formal, it's academic, and it takes time and effort, but with practice and by applying the principles in this chapter, it's a skill that you'll be able to develop.

From your reading of Chapter 3, you will have learned processes for understanding what's beneath microthemes and shorter assignments: how to see the structure of activity that they require and how to figure out what sorts of critical-thinking processes they encourage you to use. All of those processes also will apply to larger, higher-stakes papers and projects, except that now you'll be working in stages to draft and revise them. Each stage may require specific kinds of activities, and these activities may not look the same. Critical thinking, which microthemes and other short assignments get you to practice in order to learn, will now become even more important as an outcome of your process. In fact, all your teachers will be looking *especially* at how your writing reflects your mind at work. Unconsidered ideas, unexplored statements, unsupported generalizations, assertions that everyone already knows—these are dead giveaways of flabby, *un*critical thinking and rushed, careless writing.

Because of the greater depth and complexity of longer papers and the careful thinking that they reflect, your approach to writing them will differ in important ways from your approach to writing a short microtheme. Longer papers require more reflection, reading, and thought. The question you answer tends to be more complex, with various perspectives needing attention and more sophisticated relationships needing to be understood and assessed. You also have more freedom to present your ideas about the question, which means that you have to carefully consider how to organize and compose your response.

Because longer assignments are more complex, you will usually have a week or more—sometimes an entire semester—to write them. If you use this time well, you'll be able to work up, write, revise, and polish a fine piece of writing without much stress. This doesn't mean sitting down late one night and batting out a paper all at once. You should do a lot of work even before you begin to draft the assignment, and then again between the draft and the final version. In contrast to writing a microtheme, which requires you to think hard, work with the material, and put down your response briefly and in one session, with a more complex assignment you'll return again and again to the task, measuring it from different angles, rereading it multiple times, making sure the joints are glued tight, sanding it feathery soft before turning it in (and along the way, maybe even rebuilding parts of it when they don't fit the first time).

Notice the focus on *revision.* In middle school, "doing it over" may have seemed like a punishment because it wasn't "done right" the first time. This belief leads many students to think that the better people get as writers, the more easily they can pour their perfectly formulated thoughts onto the screen in elegant, compelling prose. So they try to do the same thing.

Nothing could be further from the truth. Good writers revise and revise and revise. Often an article published in an academic journal goes through twenty or thirty revisions, and even then it may come back with a comment to "revise and resubmit" (again!), or that it has been "accepted but with specified revisions." Of course, today, most revisions on paper disappear because most writers work on-screen. Take a look at the picture below of a piece of writing undergoing

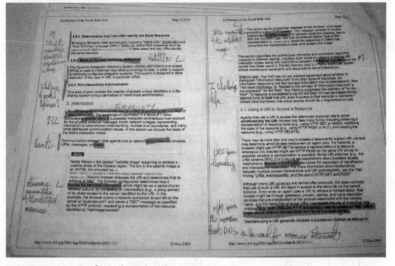

FIGURE 4.2 A Draft Undergoing Revision

KEY CONCEPT *Revision* means, literally, "re-seeing." It requires attention to major elements of a piece of writing, such as its structure, voice, and presentation of ideas. It is not *editing*, and it is not *proofreading*. See Key Concept Glossary.

revision (Figure 4.2). *That's* what makes good writing. Furthermore, the harder you work to improve your longer papers through revision, the stronger your overall writing ability will become and the more successful your final drafts will be. Nothing helps people to improve their writing abilities more effectively than the rethinking—the manipulation of language—that comes from revision.

This chapter explains the logic of techniques you can use from the moment you're handed an assignment until you're ready to produce a *full rough draft* and then *revise* it (two topics that we'll discuss separately in the next chapter). These techniques are designed to do two things: (1) keep the writing task from becoming overwhelming at any point and (2) help you to get the bulk of your ideas on-screen, before you can stand back and critically reflect on what you have produced and how to put it together. But before we dive into those strategies, we need to consider what you can bring *to* a task—that is, what you've already learned that can help you get started.

What's "Transfer," and Why Practice It?

Imagine that you've been assigned to write a microtheme in one of your courses: a summary of an assigned article. To begin successfully, you would search your knowledge and prior experience for the kind of writing known as "summary." Surely you would have written a summary before—maybe a plot summary of a novel or a summary on an essay exam of material that you had learned during a lecture. You would know that summarizing involves describing the main ideas or the "gist" of the material and avoids providing a lot of specific detail. You would know that it captures the essence of the text or ideas that you're summarizing. You would have seen ample summaries of information online, in sound bites and news reports. You would even know some stock beginnings of summaries: "The general approach used by Perkins to analyze voting trends involves ...," or "Maslow's theory can be best characterized as. ..." In drawing on this knowledge, you would be experiencing the process of *transfer*. Transfer is fundamental to virtually all mental activity that involves applying what you already know to a new situation.

> **KEY CONCEPT** In writing theory, *transfer* refers to the deployment of existing knowledge and skills (for writing) to a new situation—for example, when a student uses the knowledge she gained in a General Composition course to write a thesis statement for a paper in a Psychology course. See Key Concept Glossary.

Different degrees of transfer require different levels of mental activity. If you have a license, you know that to move forward in a car with an automatic transmission, you first put it into "drive." If you get into a rental truck, the vehicle is different. But you will *transfer* your knowledge and look for the mechanism that puts the truck into drive (maybe it's located on the steering column). This is known as *near transfer*, because the "distance" between the two different activities or contexts is not great. Now imagine that you've never learned how to shift gears, and you get into a car with a manual transmission. You know that something must engage the gears to move the car forward, but you aren't sure how to do it. In an emergency, you would "transfer" what you do know from driving cars with automatic transmissions and then problem-solve your way to figure out how to make the car move, using some trial and error (and a lot of gear-gnashing, lurching, and stalling). The situation would involve *far transfer*, because the "distance" between the two related activities is greater (see Figure 4.3).

Once you've driven a car for a year or two, your actions will reach a level of *automaticity*—that is, you don't need to think, "OK, now turn the wheel a tiny bit to the left, now a bit to the right … ." You just steer. The knowledge you use for most driving is *tacit*, or unconscious—that is, you can do it while doing something else, such as planning your day in your head.

So what does this mean for writing? First, writing is very different from driving a car. Almost all writing tasks require some conscious transfer—and many require a lot. Only a few processes reach automaticity, such as knowing that a new sentence begins with a capital letter. Writing a paper in a course requires conscious effort

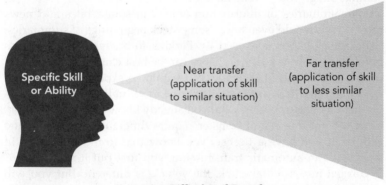

Specific Skill or Ability

Near transfer (application of skill to similar situation)

Far transfer (application of skill to less similar situation)

Increasing Difficulty of Transfer

FIGURE 4.3 Near and Far Transfer

and attention to your content, audience, purpose for writing, style, structure, word choice, and a host of other features. And when you move across contexts and must write new kinds of texts, you will almost always need to *transfer* your existing knowledge and experience, applying what you know to what you now need to do.

Second, your familiarity with the type and content of the writing task will determine the "distance" between what you know and what's required—how near or far the transfer of knowledge will be. Instead of a summary, imagine that you've been assigned to create the script for a *pitch deck* in a marketing course. What's a pitch deck? Well, it's a short business presentation, given (usually live) to potential customers, clients, investors, or other target audience to provide an overview of a product, campaign, or investment strategy, or an update. It's usually carefully scripted (in writing) but then rehearsed orally. Clearly, you would be in a *far-transfer* situation, and your need for problem solving and more information would be greater than if you were writing a summary of an article. But business professionals know the language, structure, goals, audiences, styles, and other features of pitch decks because they've practiced them for a long time. For them, creating a new pitch deck represents a *near-transfer* situation. It still may be challenging (and will require conscious thought) for them, because the context, information, and audience may be new, but they know more about how to proceed.

Many teachers complain that even in near-transfer situations, their students often act as if everything is new: "Why don't my students remember what they learned about writing (in first-year Composition or in high school or in a previous course in their major)?" They believe that students think of each course as entirely separate from all the others: discrete units of learning, independent and self-contained. In fact, research has shown this to be true in many cases. Students who have learned how to summarize in a Writing course may ask their Music History professor, "What do you want in this paper?" when they're assigned to summarize several scholars' accounts of how Beethoven composed his Ninth Symphony. Or, a teacher finds that students in a junior-level Education course seem to have forgotten how to incorporate their sources when they learned how to do this in a required sophomore-level Research course. What went wrong? Largely it's a matter of connection—of deliberately and consciously *drawing on* what you already know as you meet a new task, *linking* your prior knowledge to it. This takes some effort, and nothing changes this fact.

Here's a way to start thinking about those linkages. Make an inventory of everything you can remember learning and practicing as a writer in previous academic experiences—as far back as you can. Did you ever summarize? Describe something? Provide evidence for an assertion? Develop a thesis? Document your sources? Start a new paragraph with a topic sentence? Use a personal voice? Use (or avoid) the passive voice? Edit your sentences for clarity or brevity? Fix a sentence fragment? Comparing your inventory with those of other students can also reveal skills that you may not have learned or experienced, and then you can begin filling those gaps.

GIVE IT A TRY

Here's an assignment from a sophomore-level course in Folklore. Think about everything that this assignment is asking. Then sketch out ways you could deploy prior knowledge and writing experience to begin this task. What do you already know that could help you get started? What do you still need to learn or figure out? What action verbs are in the assignment, and what do they mean to you?

Please write an essay of five to six pages on the following writing prompt. We've discussed in class the ways Angela Carter's stories from *The Bloody Chamber* (*TBC*) reference, allude to, or even offer revisions of traditional folktales like "Bluebeard," "Little Redcape," and "Beauty and the Beast." We've also talked about how many of the folktales that we have read so far contain representations of young girls and women that are troubling. From the evil and useless "hag" or "crone" to the naïve young girl whose virginity is her most important possession, the Grimms' tales usually offer a vision of womanhood that reflects the very narrow conception of femininity common in their time.

In your essay, please choose a story from *The Bloody Chamber*. Then address how Carter's story offers a different version of femininity than the fairy tale it alludes to. In your essay, you should provide both a reading of the story from *TBC* and an explanation of the engagement with and/or critique that story offers of problematic elements from the earlier fairy tale it reimagines. **Note:** Writing this essay will necessarily require you to review/consult texts of the earlier tales from the Grimm brothers, Charles Perrault, and Jeanne-Marie Leprince de Beaumont ("Beauty and the Beast"). All of the tales, if not in your Grimms collection, are linked on our Blackboard page. Notice that for "Bluebeard" and "Beauty and the Beast" on D. L. Ashlimon's University of Pittsburgh website, there are related tales and Grimms versions below the main tale text. These may be of use to you in your thinking and writing as well.

What about Far-Transfer Situations?

It's sometimes hard to predict which college courses will involve familiar or unfamiliar higher-stakes assignments. In a general-education Sociology course, you might find assignments that you've encountered before: a research paper, an annotated bibliography, a summary, or an opinion paper. You might also find something very new—for example, a "violation of social norms analysis." How can you begin writing such a paper if you've never seen or heard of one before?

Thankfully, in most cases you'll get help. The more alien or new an assignment is to you and your peers, the more your teacher will recognize the need to *support* your work on it. As shown in Figure 4.4, which is an expanded version of the model we considered in Chapter 1 (Figure 1.3), that support can take many forms. Your teacher might have you practice certain kinds of observation or analysis before you do your own for a paper. You might be asked to draft

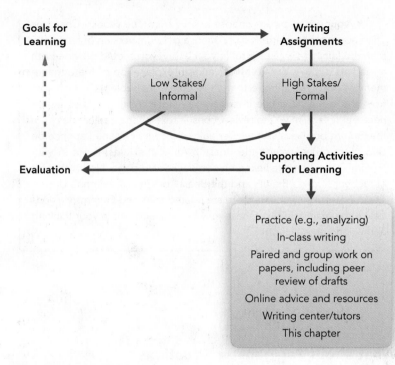

FIGURE 4.4 The Role of Support in the Design Model

parts of a paper in class and share your work in pairs. You might work in a small group to brainstorm ideas or to provide commentary on each other's full rough drafts of your papers (a process that we'll consider in more detail in Chapter 5.

Take a look at the kinds of support that a professor of Political Science provided to students for one challenging assignment on public policy. The goal of the assignment was to help students learn how to critically assess the use of statistics. Each student investigated a statistic used in a public policy debate of interest to them. The students then examined at least three different (competing) estimates for the statistic in question, and identified and discussed who created each statistic, as well as why and how it was created. After exploring each estimate, as well as its supporting evidence, they had to explain which estimate was the "best" measure to be used in the policy-making process, justifying their decision.

Here are all the activities that the professor included in the class in order to support the students' work on this assignment:

- whole-class exploration of sources (interest groups, think tanks, foundations); media coverage of a particular public policy issue; and advice on contacting staff members of elected officials

- in-class (small-group) work exploring particular sites to derive appropriate statistics; whole-class follow-up

- a topic-exploration activity online (required as homework), with a list of statistics and sources

- in-class (small-group) work focusing on the analysis of alternate statistics in a particular (prechosen) case and the process of deciding which is "best" for a policy decision

- in-class, peer-group response (in groups of three) to full rough drafts of the paper, with a strong focus on improvements through revision

- evaluation criteria provided to students before they write the paper

Wisely, this professor knew that by integrating these kinds of support into her class, she would maximize the learning potential of the assignment and get far better papers than if she let the students stumble along on their own with no sequenced work and without required revision.

Sometimes, though, your instructor may not build much, if any, support into an assignment. You're pretty much on your own, even when the territory is unfamiliar. What then? Of course, the first thing to do when you face a new higher-stakes writing task without classroom support is to focus consciously on how to deploy your existing knowledge and experience to understand what you are asked to do, *before* you start to work. The rest of this chapter offers generalized support for higher-stakes papers in the form of strategies that you can use to get to a full rough draft. But remember that these strategies are indeed *general*. In many cases you'll be assigned a very specific kind of paper with specific requirements. The best advice, then, is always to rely first on your instructor to start you on the right path—he or she will know better than anyone what strategies, knowledge, skills, and examples will be most useful.

One final bit of perspective is in order, and it returns us to the continuum in Figure 4.1. Toward the right side of the continuum, not only do we move away from purely learning-based assignments toward longer, more formal, *performance-based* assignments, but we also move toward *professionally based* assignments (ones that feel like they're located within the field that the academic work prepares you for). In your Anthropology course, if you're writing a "microethnography" of a particular subculture, such as a motorcycle gang, the project emulates and *prepares you for* the kind of work you would do as a professional cultural anthropologist, someone who often immerses herself in a culture and studies how it works, and then writes ethnographic accounts of it (*ethno* = human, *graphy* = writing). In this situation, we call the rhetorical space you're working in *conditional,* because you have one foot in the course (the immediate and real "space") and one in the profession, at least in a preliminary or apprenticed sense (the imagined space of work).

> **KEY CONCEPT** *Conditional rhetorical space* refers to the kind of writing "space" you're in when you write for a teacher, but you also try to adhere to the conventions of writing in the profession beyond your institution. It requires you to be aware of what your teacher expects *and* what is expected in the field. See Key Concept Glossary.

A good illustration of this conditional rhetorical space is an assignment given in an Art History course (for majors), which requires writing an *art label.* If you've ever gone to an art museum, you've probably seen descriptions—sometimes brief, sometimes more detailed—that give visitors information about works of art. These are located next to or below the work, and usually begin with the work's title and a caption. In many Art History courses, students (especially majors) are assigned to learn about works of art and then to write labels for them as if they were working in a museum. Notice how such assignments are located in the "space" of the classroom but are looking outward—and ahead—to the kinds of work done by curators, other professional art historians, and museum employees. (It's also a great way to learn about a specific work of art.)

GIVE IT A TRY

Spend some time searching the Internet for assignments in courses that are part of your major. Look for an assignment that demonstrates conditional rhetorical space for the students who will respond to it. How does it illustrate having one foot in an academic space and one in a professional space?

Exploring Your Subject

It goes without saying that in order to write well about something, you need to know that "something." You can't begin writing a substantial paper on the effects of high altitude on the production of 2,3 diphosphoglyceric acid in the body if you know next to nothing about 2,3 diphosphoglyceric acid or how the body accommodates to living at high altitudes. But, actually, you *can*. Some strategies that you can use are freewriting, listing, and mind mapping. These are often called processes of *invention* (borrowing from classical rhetoric).

> **KEY CONCEPT** *Invention* is a term used in rhetoric to refer to the process of generating ideas and considering them along the way to a speech or written text. It has a very long history, stretching back to the classical rhetoric of the ancient Greeks, and has become a metaterm for all strategies designed to explore a subject. See Key Concept Glossary.

Freewriting

As long as you know just *something* about the subject of your paper, doing some preliminary *freewriting* can (1) show what you *do* know, (2) reveal gaps in your understanding that will require you to read and/or do some research, and (3) set a tentative path for your paper's sections. As described in Chapter 2, freewriting is a technique that's ideally suited to getting started writing. It's especially good for avoiding procrastination—that old enemy of writers that's provoked by the anxiety associated with "writing for keeps." In freewriting, you just begin writing—wandering, really—until you get somewhere. Open a file, and just start typing, even if you end up writing the same thing over and over again. Eventually, your mind will shift into a higher gear and something will emerge. And at least you've *begun* writing, which will end up being a huge relief.

Freewriting can be *focused* or *unfocused*. In *unfocused* freewriting, you have no specific topic or area of thought when you start. Many writers use unfocused freewriting like a warm-up exercise before running or swimming. In *focused* freewriting, on the other hand, you start writing *about* a topic or idea. When starting a higher-stakes paper, this is probably the kind of freewriting that you want to practice.

Michael, a student in a seminar on utopian politics, was given the following assignment concerning the Kaweah utopian colony that started in California in the 1880s:

> The purpose of this assignment is for you to analyze and assess the kind of socialism adopted by the Kaweah colony, with special focus on the importance of land claims to the success of the colony. The paper should be approximately five pages in length and should provide a well-reasoned argument about the political viability of the colony.

To get his mental juices flowing, Michael tried some focused freewriting on the topic. He began spinning out ideas he knew about the Kaweah colony on-screen, in whatever order they occurred to him based on his reading. His writing rambled from details about the colony's history to personal opinions about its leaders' ideals to questions about the colony's downfall. After a short session, Michael felt less worried about writing his paper because he had already started it. His preliminary exploration gave him ideas, and even some usable text, for the paper. And since he hadn't read enough about the Kaweah community yet, his freewriting brought out all those murky and unspecific areas of his knowledge, showing what else he needed to learn.

Kaweah paper—
     Want to explore some of the historical and political aspects of the Kaweah colony first and then focus on why it failed as a colony. Part of it is the relationship of K. to the Federal Govt—and there's a nice analogy to other conflicts between "alternative societies" and the US—Indians before and after establishment of reservations, religious cults, and housing ordinances, article on old hippie movement and tree houses in Big Sur, etc. The K colony land claims are an important part of that whole relationship. Another issue is the internal structure of the colony. Need more on Gronlund to see where compartments came from (typical feature of some unusual systems, a kind of overstructured orderliness that ends up failing). All these bureaus and parts, and then the power structure is important.

Freewriting works especially well when you spread out the episodes over time on a single project. Start freewriting early—as soon as you get the assignment—and then do it again every few days. You'll see your focus sharpening and a plan materializing, and some of your notes may even become a good place to start or may turn into useful chunks of writing for the paper itself.

Don't get too secure, if that ends up closing down possibilities. If your freewriting leads to new ideas, go with them. Students have found themselves writing different papers from when they started, because they made useful insights and discoveries as they wrote.

Listing

Listing is a kind of abbreviated freewriting. Instead of stringing together sentences of prose (which may lead to writer's block), you just record key ideas or concepts. Soon you'll begin noticing patterns and relationships among the items in your list, and these can lead to deeper and more extensive analysis and critical awareness.

For example, Michael kept an ongoing list of information about the Kaweah colony. Among the items in his list were the following:

- influence of Gronlund
- also influenced by Edward Bellamy
- founded in 1886 as a tent colony; disbanded in 1892
- utopian socialism
- $500 to join
- problems with the government: national park in CA was established, and then the colony was illegally logging on it
- "Squatter's Cabin" only remaining structure (National Register of Historic Places)
- grew out of the International Workers Association in San Francisco
- believed in the principle of equal work and equal pay for men and women

As Michael explored the items on his list, he started creating sublists beneath each item. If he drew a blank trying to create a sublist, he realized that he needed to find out more to drill down into the specific information beneath the item. For the item "also influenced by Edward Bellamy," for example, he created the following sublist:

- Bellamy was an American author, socialist thinker
- came from family of Baptists
- wrote work of utopian fiction, *Looking Backward, 2000–1899*

As Michael dug deeper into Bellamy's work, he found that the kind of socialist thinking that inspired Bellamy also had roots in Marx and Engels and others advocating for socialist progressive labor movements. Suddenly, a theme emerged: *multiple influences on the ideologi-*

cal formation of the Kaweah Colony. Instead of a random assortment of facts and details, he had discovered a "way in," a stronger focus for his paper, through his list.

Mind Mapping

The problem with not being able to find the "right words" in order to begin writing a paper isn't a lack of "the right words"; it's that your mind isn't ready for them. Another way to avoid trying to create perfect sentences is by *mind mapping*: starting with chunks of information labeled by words or phrases. One kind of mind mapping involves creating clusters or conceptual maps, which are diagrams that reveal relationships between ideas, using minimal language.

In clustering, you center a concept at the top of a word document or a piece of paper, as Michael did with the main focus of his paper, the Kaweah colony. Then you attach related ideas to it in a cluster. Michael extended four initial pieces of information he knew about the Kaweah colony (Figure 4.5).

Like listing, each piece of the cluster can be further elaborated. For example, "Communal system" refers to the political ideology and agenda of the colony (Figure 4.6). But what sort of communal system was advocated? Here, Michael pushed further connections to further items that could elaborate on that system and its origin and influences. Extension of this cluster could be made from each of these elaborations of the communal system, and interconnections between ideas in different parts of the cluster could be shown with connecting lines.

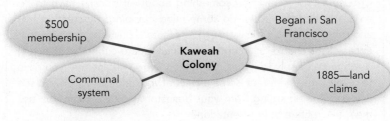

FIGURE 4.5 A Simple Cluster

FIGURE 4.6 Subcategories in a Cluster

There are many kinds of invention or conceptual brainstorming strategies in addition to these relatively simple ones. Take a moment to check out the many helpful mind-mapping programs online, such as Meister, iMindMap, Coggle, and XMind. A number of websites offer descriptions of digital mind mapping or *information-visualizing* software, some retrievable at this mind-mapping blog: http://mindmapping.typepad.com/. Professionals at the highest level of research and scholarship often use this strategy to generate creative ideas and make connections. Figure 4.7 shows one example of a mindmap created with the iMindmap software (about neurological functions of the brain). Sometimes an instructor will ask you to create a mind map as a kind of microtheme, just to get you to learn and be able to fill in information from your studies.

GIVE IT A TRY

Choose a topic you know something about—it doesn't have to be an academic topic. Then do some mind mapping: try creating lists and sublists from your knowledge, or create a cluster with nodes that encapsulate chunks of information. Then create subnodes that drill down more deeply into that information. Now imagine that you have to give a presentation on some aspect of your expertise. Can you see any patterns emerging from your brainstorming? How can you use them to structure the presentation?

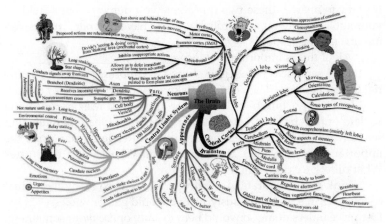

FIGURE 4.7 A Mind Map of the Brain

Finding the Heart of the Matter: The Thesis

After exploring your knowledge, you need to start considering your readers by shifting from what *you* know to what *they* want to know, a process called *decentering*. This means that you need to make sense of your material as a whole from other perspectives. What does it add up to? What does it really mean? What have you learned? Where's the heart of the matter? At this point it helps to go back to

> **KEY CONCEPT** *Decentering* refers to the process of getting out of yourself and thinking about the needs and interests of your potential readers. What do they want to know? Why? How do the purpose and context of your writing help to determine that? See Key Concept Glossary.

the details of the assignment—the guidepost for what you're really being asked to do and say.

Sorting your material may require more writing. Try to complete this sentence:

"If I've learned one thing about all this, it's _____ ."
Then go on to this one:

"The main things that make me think this are _____ ."

If you can answer these two questions, you demonstrate a hold on your subject. But you still probably won't have a paper. Try answering one more question:

"All of this is important because _____ ."

These sentences reflect issues you face in presenting your material to readers. Your readers want to know what you think or discovered (obviously), but they also want to know your reasons for saying so, laid out in order, so that they can grasp each idea separately and see how it reinforces or qualifies the others. Readers want to see the importance of what you are telling them. Why should they care? What difference does it make?

Think of the separate ideas in your notes as so many individual testimonies in a trial. Obviously, no one would gather witnesses in the first place unless doing so would help to *prove* or *document* something. In a sense, all of your brainstorming and data collection have gathered a room full of testimonies. But, unlike a court proceeding, where the problem is already established, here your job is to listen to all the testimonies and *then* decide what you want to prove or document. There's no judge (yet) and just one attorney (you), and mounds of facts, opinions, evidence, and information. You can now select those testimonies (from your readings, brainstorming, etc.) that most persuasively prove or document your point. But what *is* that point?

Across the college curriculum, by far the most popular term used for the "point" is the *thesis* of your writing. What exactly is a thesis? The term has a long history, but most teachers see it as the most important *idea or argument* you're trying to make, or the *purpose* of something you did, such as an experiment. If you could tell someone on an elevator traveling from the first to the ninth floor the main idea in the last paper you wrote, it would probably be your thesis. A paper without a thesis is like a set of directions that leads to an empty field in the middle of nowhere. In formal academic writing, a paper without a thesis looks like a jumble of ideas and facts with nothing to tie them together—no main idea, organizing point, or clear purpose that the information illustrates, supports, or extends in some way.

KEY CONCEPT A *thesis* is the central organizing idea or argument in a piece of writing. See Key Concept Glossary.

Now, it's important to realize that not all assignments need a thesis. An assignment in a Nutrition course to objectively *describe* the nutritional value of a school lunch program at a local elementary school doesn't need a thesis (although it would probably begin with a *purpose*: "This report provides a nutritional analysis of the food offered in the lunch program at. ..."). However, an assignment that asks students to *analyze* the nutritional value of the program and reach a conclusion or make a recommendation about it does need a thesis. The difference between the two assignments hinges on what each one asks you to do:

- *Objectively calculate* the nutritional value of a local school lunch program.

versus

- *Analyze* the nutritional value of a school lunch program, and *argue* for the nutritional acceptability of the lunch program.

You can see that the first assignment will require a string of statements without a thesis (nutritional value of apples, grilled cheese sandwiches, potato chips, etc.), while the second requires a *proposition*, or something you need to support with the evidence that comes from the nutritional analysis: "Although the lunch program at Mills Elementary School offers two healthy items—apples and oranges—the high saturated fat content and high levels of glucose in all of its other items, including especially its entrée choices, place it well below acceptable nutritional thresholds for schoolchildren." The difference further explains why most teachers want you to move beyond pure description when you *reflect* (see Chapter 2) and why they especially want you to engage in *critical thinking* when you write (see Chapter 3).

Notice that a thesis is usually triggered by certain operative verbs in college writing assignments:

- argue
- claim
- show or prove
- evaluate
- weigh or judge
- decide

- contend or assert
- debate

Beneath these verbs is an expectation that you'll provide a perspective or conclusion and then *document, defend,* or *support* it in some way.

Because so many college writing assignments across the curriculum take the form of an essay or argument, we'll focus here on the most common kinds of theses and their placement: assertions or claims that appear somewhere in the paper's introduction. However, be aware that theses can take different forms. The following table shows varieties of theses along with examples of the kinds of contexts in which they might be found. As we explore theses in more detail, reference will be made to some of these varieties. But, as always, look for reading models of how writing works in your particular course or discipline, and get as much guidance as possible from your teacher.

Type of Thesis	Description	Examples
Informative	Occurs in papers that provide objective explanations of phenomena; common in all disciplines but especially in scientific writing	"This paper documents the 2,000-mile voyage of newly hatched loggerhead turtles from the South Atlanta coast of the United States to the Sargasso Sea."
Argumentative or persuasive	Occurs in papers that support an argument or assertion, or that persuade readers to believe a conclusion	"More federal funding is needed to assist in the repopulation of loggerhead turtles through conservation and nest protection efforts."
Exploratory or open-ended	Occurs in papers that set out to explore a subject without an argument or conclusion; such papers often leave questions at the end	"Conclusive evidence does not yet exist for the effectiveness of loggerhead repopulation efforts. Claims for and against these efforts are equally valid."
Implied	Occurs when a thesis is not stated overtly but is implied	"Loggerhead populations continue to decline and will soon reach critically low thresholds without intervention."

| Absent; purpose defined by context and genre | No thesis is necessary when the purpose and context of the writing are obvious, such as an instruction manual or a police report | Loggerhead Nest Protection Manual for Interns: "Once a nest has been identified, it is necessary to cage the nest to protect the eggs. In the storage unit, find cages at the rear. ..." |

Developing an Argumentative or Persuasive Thesis

Because articulating a thesis around a claim is so important in academic writing, let's consider in more detail how a writer goes about developing a thesis in the context of the loose, exploratory writing that we've been describing so far.

Alec, a senior majoring in public affairs, was assigned to write a capstone senior paper in a course on Minority Issues. The paper had to involve some sort of primary research (gathering and analyzing actual data from the public, organizations, etc.). It also had to be written as a report, with recommendations for action. Being part Ojibway, Alec decided he wanted to focus on the problem of student retention among Native Americans at his university. It was well known that the number of Native Americans enrolling at his school was low to begin with, but they also had the highest noncompletion rate of any minority group. Yet no one had bothered to ask why. What circumstances led so many Native Americans to attend for a while and then leave?

After six weeks of interviewing students and faculty, examining statistics from the Department of Admissions, talking with leaders in local Indian communities, visiting reservations, reading research on student retention, and surveying various minority populations at his school, Alec had lots of fascinating and useful material. Without a careful synthesis of all the data, however, he would be unprepared to develop a claim, or thesis, in his paper. All he could say at the start would be, "This paper tries to understand why student retention among American Indians is so low at Pound Ridge University," and then dump in a lot of random material. Without a sharper analysis of the problem, what could he recommend?

After carefully examining all his material, Alec concluded that student retention was linked in a complex way to several factors, including a lack of financial support for Native Americans. The most important of these, which surfaced again and again in his interviews with students and faculty and on his trips to nearby reservations, was the idea of *academic role models*. Of over eight hundred faculty members at his university, only three were Native Americans, and one of them taught courses mainly at the graduate level. Native American students taking courses with these teachers had a higher retention rate than the rest of the Native American student population and reported feeling greater satisfaction from their academic experiences. After locating several research studies supporting the power of role models on students' feelings about learning, Alec believed he could make a strong case for the relationship between the low numbers of Native American faculty and low retention and completion rates among Native American students. From that case, he could extend a well-supported recommendation that his university should attract and hire additional Native American faculty and staff, and set up an Native American counseling center. He had, in other words, found a *thesis*.

Note that a *thesis* around a claim is much more than a simple *topic*. A topic is the "thing" you're discussing; a thesis is the "thing" *and* the central claim you're making about it.

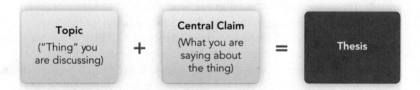

Your thesis makes up a kind of subject and predicate of your paper as a whole. A topic by itself doesn't say anything and doesn't go anywhere. It just sits there. You need a central claim about the topic to move it along and to set it in motion so that it becomes a real addition to knowledge.

Think about bees. "Bees" may be a legitimate topic, but in itself it can't be a thesis. It doesn't say anything about bees. It makes no claims for bees. A paper about bees without a real thesis will probably collapse into a mere jumble of facts about bees, and who would want to read that? If you want bees as your topic, that's fine, but claim something about them.

Think about the difference between "bees" and this claim about bees: "Recent evidence suggests that human activity is killing bees at an alarming and possibly self-destructive rate, and *unless we reverse this trend, the future of our planet's ecosystem will be in serious danger.*" Now *there's* a thesis. Bees are good for the planet, even essential, and we're killing them with pesticides. It might be true. Someone else might take on bees as a topic but defend the opposite thesis: "Recent fears about the decimation of the bee population and the end of our ecosystem as we know it are highly exaggerated, and based on scientific evidence, there is little to worry about." Both of these theses go beyond the mere "topic" of bees to assert, or predicate, something definite about them. Both of these theses are also plausible. You could imagine either one being true, although, when all the facts are in, one of them will be false.

In Alec's case, his *topic* is retention rates of Native American students at his university. His *thesis* is that the rates are critically affected by the numbers of Native American faculty at the University. As a claim, this is literally debatable (as a good thesis should be). Someone else might claim that the number of Native Americans on the faculty is irrelevant and that the real cause of the poor retention rates has to do with a lack of financial support, weaker college preparation as a result of less well funded high schools in Native American communities, or the dispersion of Native Americans across dormitories (preventing their forming a cohesive body on campus). But Alec's review of his information convinces him that, in fact, it's precisely the lack of Native American faculty that results in the low retention rate. So, that's his thesis, and in his paper he'll bring forward the necessary evidence to convince us of its validity.

Using Appeals to Support Your Thesis

Teachers in all disciplines expect you to *support* or defend a thesis with specific evidence, examples, and clear reasoning. Consider this thesis: "City ordinances that prohibit giving food to homeless

> **KEY CONCEPT** In writing, *support* refers to the evidence (facts, experience, data), logical reasoning, or other appeals you can use to convince readers that your thesis or other assertions are valid and that readers should accept them. Without support, your writing becomes mere opinion. See Key Concept Glossary.

people help to keep the streets free of the homeless by forcing them to seek help at legitimate shelters." Anyone reading this assertion will ask, "How do you know this? What evidence can you provide to support this bold statement? Why should I believe you?" If you want your assertion to be taken as something more than just an opinion (which anyone can counter by saying, "Well, that's just your opinion"), you need to offer up something more. Have studies been done on this? Do all homeless people go to shelters when they're not provided food by passers-by? Do prohibitions on feeding the homeless actually work?

The nature of "support" will vary a lot in different disciplines and in different genres of writing. In a scientific study, for example, support will come in the form of statistics or data from an experiment or investigation. In a research paper using other people's scholarship, support may come in the form of carefully selected quotations and citations to the literature. In a campaign advocating for public action, such as a pro-recycling effort, support could come from examples of communities that have profited from recycling efforts.

Type of Support	Description	Pros and/or Cons
Facts	Uncontestable truths	Difficult to refute
Statistics	Numerical data based on research or data gathering	Often believed but can sometimes be refuted with further study
Examples	Specific cases of the assertion	Enough can help to support a claim but must be seen in context
Personal experience or observation	Events that happen to the writer or to others	Can connect with readers but may be seen as idiosyncratic or "just one case"

Opinions of experts	Statements of belief from authorities	Depends on level of authority and on what basis the expert provides his/her opinion, and with what bias(es)
Anecdotes or lore	Unverifiable stories or cases	Can connect with readers' experiences or beliefs but offer poor evidence without other kinds

Often your assignment will give you plenty of information about what kind of support is expected:

> Please support your thesis with references to specific lines or passages in the story.

> You will need to support your thesis by referring to the findings of at least three research studies published in peer-reviewed journals in microbiology.

Notice that some kinds of support seem stronger than others. In our culture, empirical evidence often trumps personal experience. Quantitative data often (and problematically) gets the upper hand over qualitative or ethnographic data, even though statistics can't always capture deep meaning the way that case studies or descriptive studies can. And personal experience, when convincingly and honestly shared, often plays better than lore or anecdotes, which vary from legitimate cases to conspiracy theories and urban legends.

Rhetorical theory also gives us another set of helpful categories, referring to ways writers or speakers persuade readers of particular points of view or theses. These are referred to as *appeals*. First, the writer can appeal to the reader's sense of logic (logos), using various methods of reasoning. Second, the writer can appeal to the reader's emotions (pathos), using examples or arguments that create empathy, disgust, anger,

> **KEY CONCEPT** *Rhetorical appeals* refer to three strategies in the art of persuasion: appealing to logic (logos), emotion (pathos), or the writer's credibility (ethos). See Key Concept Glossary.

and the like. Third, the writer can appeal to his or her own status or credibility (ethos) to project the image of someone who should be believed. A dentist making a claim about the relationship between soft drinks and tooth decay is going to carry more ethos on this topic than a stockbroker, although much depends on *how* each person conveys himself or herself (the dentist could end up seeming like a charlatan, while the stockbroker may come off as earnest, honest, and well informed).

Here are some examples of each type of appeal supporting the argument that an international superfund should be established to help with the worldwide clean water crisis:

Type of Appeal	Example
Logos	"Currently, all the evidence shows that financial resources are inadequate to address the dire clean water needs of at least eight nations. Therefore, an international superfund should be established, with nations contributing in proportion to their GDP, and funding allocated on a triage basis to those most in need of clean, potable water."
Pathos	"Think of the thousands of poor children who are suffering from chronic dehydration and serious and even deadly digestive diseases from drinking polluted water and water filled with dangerous bacteria. Think of their anguished parents, themselves sick from lack of clean water, as they watch their children suffer. An international superfund should be established. ... "
Ethos	"As a clinical microbiologist, I have devoted four years of my life to studying the effects of poor quality drinking water on the populations of six nations in Africa and South America. And it is clear to me that we cannot solve the problem of safe, potable drinking water in these and other developing nations without establishing an international superfund. ... "

As these examples illustrate, arguments can take quite different forms, depending on the types of appeal employed to support them. In academia, logical appeals based on evidence and clear reasoning are highly prized. Although there are plenty of contexts for emotional appeals, they're generally not as favored. And, although it's always possible to craft a paper based on your knowledge of a topic and your expertise to write about it, you may find yourself not yet established enough in a specific field to rely strongly on the ethos that comes from extensive experience—but most certainly from how you present yourself and your ideas.

There is much more to learn about the specific ways each appeal can be exploited; for example, appeals to logic can involve syllogistic reasoning, causality, and analogy. Get advice from teachers in your specific disciplinary courses—and use the methods in Chapter 7—to begin understanding which types of appeals work most effectively in the specific kinds of writing you're asked to do.

GIVE IT A TRY

Create an assertion or a thesis that argues a specific point or perspective. Then, similar to the example above, write one statement that demonstrates an appeal to logos, pathos, or ethos. Compare your statements with those of your peers.

Deciding Where to Place Your Thesis

In much standard academic writing, your readers will be looking for a thesis in one of two places. The most common place is at the end of the introductory section: you introduce your *topic*, provide sufficient background to convince your readers of its importance, and then state your *thesis*, the claim you're making concerning your topic. This is a fairly traditional way to place a thesis, and you won't go wrong if you follow it.

A second common location is in the conclusion. In this case, you use your introduction to set up a specific problem and then review the evidence, explaining its significance as you proceed, and finally you draw all the threads together into a definitive answer—your thesis—at the end. This is the "academic-paper-as detective-story" approach. It can be a little tricky to manage, and not every paper lends itself to it, but if this structure does work, your paper will probably do a fine job of holding your reader's attention. Many scientific papers sum up, or reach their main point, at the end ("as this research study has shown ..."), but they usually signal the conclusion or thesis in an *abstract* at the beginning.

Again, be aware that across the wide territory of writing in different disciplines, emphasis on the thesis will vary and so will its nature and placement. Some very complex essays might need to lay more groundwork at the start—in two or three or four paragraphs—before they get to the main idea, and even then the thesis may be subtle (or implied). Some kinds of writing, such as project reports in scientific fields, may not really have a thesis as such because their purpose is already understood, but usually they will include some sort of statement that guides the reader and explains what the report will say or do, as in the following example:

> ... Our goal in this project was to develop a simplified production process for acetone in order to help a manufacturing company to realize greater profits.

Other kinds of texts might begin not with a statement or assertion but with a question, which implies that the paper will explore its way to an answer (or not):

> What, if anything, can be done to control the dramatic growth of kudzu and lessen its serious economic and environmental impact? Is there any solution to this rapidly spreading problem?

Whatever form of writing you find yourself needing to produce, though, the cardinal principle is to *help your readers to know where they are going and why.*

When to Develop a Thesis

When should you decide on your thesis? Answers also vary. Some experts advise you to know your thesis before you begin writing; others suggest that you write your way into one. Sometimes an idea will be so clear from the start of a project that it can safely lead you through the entire writing process, from gathering information to finding a structure to revising for style. A truly open-minded approach to your topic, on the other hand, will almost always suggest some modifications of your original thesis; in this case, sticking too rigidly to it may lead to confusion or frustration. There's no pleasure in battling the facts.

Variations will naturally occur in different courses and disciplines. If you conduct an observational experiment in psychology, you not only know what you need to say by the time you've finished the experiment and reached your conclusions but also have a good sense of how to organize it (often following a preexisting format). If you're explaining a new way to write codes for a particular digital outcome in computer science, you won't need to discover your "thesis" (which will be self-evident at the start) as much as arrange your explanation in the most logical way possible for your readers. As you think about the concept of the thesis—the main or controlling idea—be aware of how that concept works in the course or discipline you're writing in.

Imagine that after writing a full draft of this paper, Alec discovered some new statistics on returning students at his university. By matching the names of these returning students with enrollees who had dropped out (sometimes years before), Alec learned that many of the students simply took longer to complete their degrees because they left for a time to earn money for tuition. Alex would have to modify his earlier thesis somehow to accommodate this new information. He might still argue forcefully for his role-model theory, but now he would have to acknowledge that the financial exigencies of Native American students also contributed to the low retention rate. He might even argue that the problem of retention is exaggerated because it is being defined by how many students complete their degrees in four years rather than in five or six (or more) years. Simply ignoring the new information would be foolish, since an astute reader might ask why it hadn't been considered. Worse still, it would be intellectually dishonest.

It should be clear, then, that developing a thesis, or focus, for a paper doesn't always happen the same way at the same point in the writing process. But once you've managed to articulate something like a thesis, even if it is tentative, your next problem—organizing your material—will become much simpler.

GIVE IT A TRY

Choose a *topic*, such as an object, phenomenon, or person. Then look the topic up online in some reputable sources. First, to practice distinguishing between facts and claims, write down two pieces of information about your topic. Then look through the online information for any kind of controversy, disagreement, or uncertainty you can spot. Try framing a *thesis* about the topic that makes a claim or argument about it. The following is an example:

Topic: sunscreen
Fact: most sunscreens contain retinyl palmitate
Thesis: Because high doses of retinyl palmitate have been found to accelerate skin cancer in lab animals, all sunscreens containing this chemical should be avoided in favor of other kinds of protection.

Looking for Organizational Patterns

In reality, you can't ever fully separate the tasks of formulating a thesis and organizing your material. The tasks involve each other so completely that they effectively blend. In both cases, you're working with the material you've gathered to find the patterns that underlie it. You examine your material, turning it this way and that in your mind (and on-screen), to see both what it tells you about your topic—what thesis it suggests—and what patterns you can arrange it into for presentation to your readers.

As a rule, you start doing your research on a paper armed with at least a vague sort of question, as did Alec. Keeping your question in mind, you seek out, collect, and study the relevant information on it. The evidence you uncover in turn leads you to an answer to your question. Then, when you go to present your findings on paper, you reverse the pattern. You begin with the answer—that is, with the conclusion you came to, now formulated as your thesis—and you lead the reader back through the evidence that supports it.

In developing your thesis, then, you move from your question through your material to your answer:

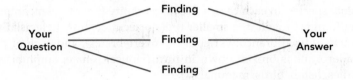

In presenting your findings, you lead your readers from your thesis through your supporting evidence:

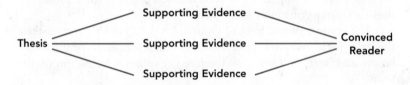

The problem is to decide how best to present your material to your readers in order to convince them of the validity of your thesis. Like a good lawyer, you have to decide how to marshal your evidence.

The problem of organization itself is twofold: (1) You have to gather your material from a sprawling, shapeless, inchoate mass into discrete, unified portions, almost servings; and (2) you have to decide what order to present them in. Two techniques have helped writers to sort out and arrange their material for presentation to their readers: organizational trees and conceptual outlines. These techniques move from a visual, schematic, spatial arrangement of information toward a more linear, prose-like form. You can use these separately or together, and in either order. You'll find them useful at various points in the development of your ideas and your paper. (As we saw earlier in this chapter, you can as easily use conceptual mapping to *explore* your subject as to sift through the information you've already explored and then *organize* it.) You should try both strategies at both stages, and discover for yourself how they suit your purposes.

Organizational Trees

You can understand the logic of an organizational tree if you think of diagrams you might have seen of the federal government or various animal species. In each case, some larger entity (government, animal kingdom) is broken into smaller units (executive branch, legislative branch, judicial branch; vertebrates, invertebrates), and each of the smaller units is broken down in turn (House, Senate; amphibians, reptiles, fishes, birds, mammals).

You can use organizational trees to organize almost any body of knowledge. They help you sort your material into its major components and see the relationships between them. They don't necessarily suggest a final arrangement of your ideas in linear English prose, but they can move you closer to the goal.

The organizational trees in Figures 4.8, 4.9, and 4.10 demonstrate the basic logic involved. Take a look at the descriptions of the topics below each tree, and see how the tree organizes information on the topic.

Obviously, these are simple examples. If you were writing more than a short paper, you would probably have several pages of brain-stormed material, which would lead to a more complex structure. The tree used to organize the anemia essay, for example, could be revised and developed in greater depth for a term paper. Carlos created such a tree for his paper about the possible uses of nanotechnology to

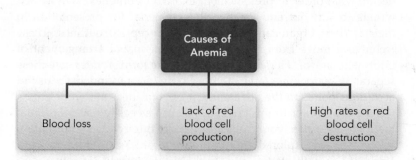

FIGURE 4.8 Chief Causes of Anemia in a Human Biology Paper

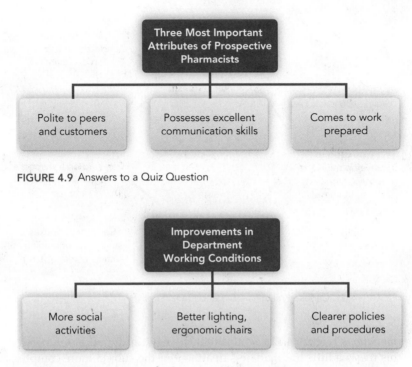

FIGURE 4.9 Answers to a Quiz Question

FIGURE 4.10 Organization of a Corporate Memo

build miniature mechanical drone insects that could fight terrorism or surreptitiously take DNA samples from someone's skin (Figure 4.11). Although nanotechnology has hundreds of applications, as a criminal justice major he began his explorations focusing on the uses of nanotechnology in fighting criminal and terrorist activity. After collecting a lot of information, he narrowed it to what he had found about the potential of miniature insect drones.

As Carlos further explored his thesis and preliminary organization, he discovered a number of serious problems with the use of such technology, in spite of its futuristic appeal. In this case, he *went backward* in his diagram and created two higher-level branches: the *potential* of the technology to fight crime and terrorism, and its

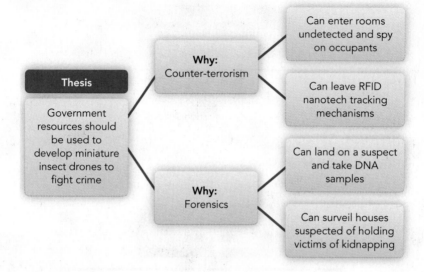

FIGURE 4.11 Carlos's Preliminary Organizational Tree

limitations (Figure 4.12). Notice that the new information tempered his thesis a little but made his treatment of the subject more complicated and sophisticated (and honest).

Notice a few things about these trees. As you move from left to right, the categories become more specific and more precise. Your large, general entities stem straight out from the main topic. Each succeeding level contains more nodes, representing more specific subtopics, arguments, or ideas. Your most fine-grained supporting facts, statistics, examples, and so forth, are arranged on the right side (or at the bottom in a vertical tree). Along any row, the abstractness of the ideas runs on par. Nodes at the same level are about equally general or specific, abstract or concrete. In drawing your organizational tree, these are the ideals to aim for. In other words, avoid creating lopsided trees or trees whose branches don't contain the same levels of specificity and detail. Also avoid trees whose smaller branches don't "fit" or follow from the branch immediately above. Think of this as an arrangement game: keep moving the nodes

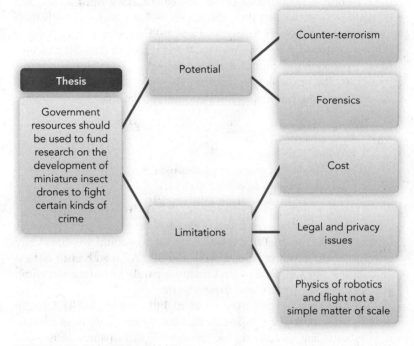

FIGURE 4.12 Carlos's Expanded Tree

around, or else do more reading and research, until the nodes in any row represent the same level of specificity. This will be a huge help when you structure the sections and paragraphs of your paper.

Outlines

Few children escape having to learn to do outlines in elementary school. Even fewer ever understand what they're all about or want use them again. None would believe it if their teachers told them that the purpose of outlines was to make our lives easier; they never did. Everyone writes the paper first, then struggles through the business of turning the paper back into the formal outline that supposedly it's based on.

The only valid purpose of outlines is to make writing easier, and if they are used wisely, they can do so. What interfered with their usefulness was the stiff, formalistic way they were taught, in "proper outline format." Every line was indented a certain amount and prefixed by a symbol: capital roman numerals, capital letters, arabic numerals, lowercase letters, and maybe—for the real obsessives—lowercase roman numerals. The structure looked like this:

Title.
I. Major arguments
   A. Minor, supporting arguments
      1. Smallish arguments or supporting facts
         a) Little, tiny supporting details
            i) Incredible minutiae

And you had to watch out if these were mixed up. The other inviolable rule was that under no circumstances could you have only one subheading at any level. If you had an "A," you had to have a "B." And if your material didn't justify a parallel heading structure, you had to make one up and force it to fit.

On the surface, this may seem of little value. But it actually reflects principles of organization that the writer really does need to understand. The underlying logic is sound. Rid of some of its stiffness, the method of outlining can help a writer to work more swiftly and easily, and to produce more coherent prose.

The most useful way to begin an outline reflects its tree-like logic. Don't start at the top and simply plow your way through the entire outline, filling it out to the fourth-level with lowercase letters as you go. That's a confusing, frustrating way to work, and gives you little room to maneuver if you change your mind about anything. Instead, write the briefest, most general outline possible—only the major headings. Get the big pieces in place before going further.

Once you've tried a number of arrangements at this level of generality, you can go back and flesh out each heading one more level down. Again, don't get ahead of yourself. Get your second-level headings in place before working down any further. Your mind should be filled at this stage with your "grand design."

After working your way through the outline to one or two levels, the rest of the development is optional. You might work it all out further yet, to the third level and on down. You might work out only sections of it and plan to keep the details of the other sections in your head as you draft. You might decide to use organizational trees for the lower levels, to show that you are not working with an either-or proposition. Or you might stop cold at two levels. The only criterion is what serves your own purpose. The longer the paper, the more levels and details you'll probably need in your outline. For shorter papers, two levels may do it. For an essay question or a memo, the main headings alone may be enough.

In Alec's case, he had already decided that the broad focus of his paper would be the causes of low retention among Native Americans at his university. His earliest outline—several main conceptual headings—reflected the nature of this data and so became a kind of investigative plan for his research:

   I. Admissions data
  II. Student interviews
 III. Faculty interviews
 IV. Site visits to reservations
  V. Site visits to community centers
 VI. Online Library research

At this point, it would have been impossible for Alec to do more with the outline because he hadn't conducted his investigations. As a plan for his research, he moved one level further down in the outline, at least for the first main headings:

  I. Admissions data
    A. % of Native Americans past 10 years
    B. Retention and completion rates compared
    C. Academic preparation compared
    D. Purpose statements?

Until he actually sat down with personnel in the admissions department, however, he couldn't be sure whether these subcategories would provide useful data (or whether, for that matter, he could even have access to information like "academic preparation"). He questioned "purpose statements" because at this point he wasn't sure whether all students had to write a purpose statement for admission to Pound Ridge. He also wasn't sure what he would do with the statements once he got them. Notice that even as he was thinking about the structure of his paper, he was also thinking about its contents.

As he moved along in his paper, Alec's outline began to reflect less the process of his research and more the organization of information in his final report. In other words, his use of outlining was initially *generative*—a way to see patterns and relationships in the subject matter and put information into categories. Then his use of outlining became *organizational*—a way to begin firming up the pieces of his project. At first, until he developed the sharp thesis described earlier, his outline mirrored some of the linked causes of low student retention:

 I. Lack of financial resources
 II. Motivational issues in native communities
 III. Cultural disenfranchisement and isolation
 IV. Lack of adequate role models on campus
 V. No counseling/advising center
 VI. Discrimination
 VII. Inadequate academic preparation

Since these categories contributed disproportionately to the problem, Alec needed to decide not just what sequence he should discuss them in, but whether they all were worth discussing in the first place or whether some of them could be consolidated into a single, higher-level category. His next outline changed as he began to focus on the role-model theory:

 I. Theories of role modeling's effects on motivation
    A. Crisp & Gruz (2009)
    B. Hess & Leal (1997)
    C. Emile (1985)
    D. Brown (1988)
 II. Retention rates at Bristol State
    A. Whole population
    B. All minorities

    C. Native Americans vs. whole populations
    D. NAs vs. other minorities, singly and summed
  III. Faculty role models
    A. Current stats. on NA faculty
    B. Past record; projected likelihood of increase
  IV. Recommendations
    A. Student counseling center for NAs
    B. Increased recruitment and hiring of NA faculty and staff

For purposes of a rough draft, this outline served Alec well. Later on, though, he recognized that his draft began too abruptly with the results of research on role models and also didn't adequately synthesize all the data from his surveys and interviews. His final outline reflected the final organization of his report, which included (in Part 3) a substantial section summarizing his interview data, and he also moved the research material from his online reading to that section:

  I. Introduction and Problem Description
    A. Retention rates at Pound Ridge
    B. Admissions data
    C. Academic preparation
  II. Disproving possible causes
    A. Financial dimensions
    B. Discrimination
    C. Preparation
  III. Role modeling as key to retention
    A. Theories/research of role modeling and motivation
    B. Interview data: students and mentors
    C. Present status of role modeling on campus
  IV. Recommendations
    A. Revising recruitment/hiring agendas for next decade
    B. Student counseling center for NAs

Of course, these topical headings would each contain substantial information, possible counterclaims or arguments, and plentiful facts and details (just imagine the synthesis of his interview data!).

Clearly, this kind of outlining process isn't like the old high school version. Instead, this kind of outlining is *alive*—a process of moving between your material and the structural dimensions of your project and back again. The outline will change. By the time you're through your fifteen-page report, you may have created half a dozen or more outlines and thrown most of them out. They will still have served their purpose.

One more proviso before we move on to drafting: as we noted before, in some cases the structure of your writing project may already be set. For example, many scientific reports follow what's called the IMRAD formula: Introduction, Methods, Results, and Discussion. (These can also be expanded—for example, there may be an Implications sections or a section on Further Research.) If you follow a specific discipline's style guide, such as that of the American Psychological Association (APA), the structure of articles is similar.

Even if the structure is not built into the kind of paper you're writing, the assignment will often contain structural clues, such as the following:

> *First*, fully describe the painting using the terms and concepts we have studied so far in the course. *Next,* provide an artistic interpretation of the painting from your own perspective, with reference to the description. *Finally*, extend your interpretation by referencing specific aspects of the artist's life and career at the point in time that s/he created the work.

Voila! You have at least the three highest levels of your structure already. Now it's just a matter of creating the subcategories, or branches of the tree: under description, you could put light/shadow, use of color, position of objects, perspective, and so on.

At the same time, resist *always* thinking that an assignment or essay question will give you a structure. Instructors sometimes (and problematically) include some subquestions after a main essay exam question or assignment, usually as a way to get your wheels spinning—to *suggest* some ideas for consideration (for an essay with its own, unique structure). It's a common mistake for students to read such an assignment and assume that the subquestions must all be answered in that order. Consider the following essay question:

> Explain what research has demonstrated about the effects of positive emotions for employees in the workplace. Consider job satisfaction, productivity, trust, loyalty, the role of culture (and cultural context), and other outcomes of positive emotions.

Here, the *main* task is to work through what the research says on this topic, in a way that makes sense to *you* structurally. The topics in the second sentence are simply possible perspectives, so it's not necessary (or particularly helpful) to write first about job satisfaction, next about productivity, and so on. Although it's logical and seems like it's "doing what the teacher wants," plodding through in this way can have just the opposite effect, suggesting that you're not thinking independently and critically about the main question but that you're just mindlessly following the cues.

GIVE IT A TRY

Look carefully at a higher-stakes writing assignment in one of your courses. Create a high-level outline based on the clues in the assignment or the assumptions embedded in the assignment's expectations (such as the use of APA reference style). If there are no clues, brainstorm two or three top-level categories that could structure the paper.

Putting It into Practice

This chapter has offered a number of *general* strategies for moving from an assignment to the point at which you can begin writing a full rough draft of a possible submission.

Here are some ways in which you can make the best use of this material:

- Keep moving between your assignment and the advice given here. It makes no sense to veer away from what is expected of you. Use the strategies as much and as often as they make sense in the context of the assignment.

- Recognize any supporting activities surrounding the assignment, and make the best use of them. Sometimes these can be implicit—a teacher might lecture in a way that demonstrates a kind of analysis expected in your paper. When in doubt, *ask*, for example: "Is the process you just went through in analyzing this aspect of heat transfer what you would like us to use when we conduct our experiment?"

- Add any of your own personal strategies—ones you are certain have been successful—to those described in this chapter so that you customize the toolbox for future writing occasions.

- Become familiar with the terminology surrounding the writing process; reread the Key Concepts, and consult the longer discussions in the Key Concepts Glossary at the end of the book. This will give you a common language for talking about writing with your teachers and your classmates.

5

Getting There: Drafting and Revising High-Stakes Papers

WHAT'S THE POINT?

After you read, think about, and put this chapter into practice, you will be able to:

- Practice strategies for getting a full draft on paper
- Understand and explain the process of *revision*
- Use one of several strategies for revising your own work in progress
- Understand the process of peer response and practice it effectively
- Know what your campus writing center offers and how to work with tutors

Don't Sweat the Small Stuff: Creating a Rough Draft

There's an interesting anecdote about the French playwright Jean Racine that tells us something about the business of drafting. Racine went to a party one night in very high spirits. A friend asked him what he was so happy about. Racine answered, "I have just written a wonderful new play! Now all I have to do is add the dialogue!"

Now *that's* a person who is ready to start drafting.

Drafting is that part of the writing process that most people think of as actually "writing" a paper. This is unfortunate, as it puts too much stress on one phase of the process, raising the stakes (and the tension) and creating procrastination (and frustration). It's better to think of the whole process as writing—everything from the first brainstorming session to the final editing—and to use the word *drafting* to mean getting the material down in paragraph form.

KEY CONCEPT *Drafting* refers to the processes— plural—of generating and organizing original ideas and information, sometimes along with others' ideas and information, into textual or multimodal form. See Key Concept Glossary.

The problems of many writers start when they rely too much on drafting. They hope they can sit down without having given the topic any careful thought and grind out one good solid draft to turn in. They're trying to develop and arrange their ideas, write their paper, polish their prose, and even check mechanics and spelling—all at the same time. They pay for this hubris in the pain of writing and in their embarrassment when their work is returned, heavily marked up with all the thinking, structuring, and stylistic polishing that they *could* have done if they had taken the time.

To draft most efficiently, you need to relax a bit and lower your expectations of what initial drafting can accomplish. You need to depend more heavily on both earlier and later stages of writing to help you produce the paper you want. We've already explored blogging, brainstorming techniques, and various ways to organize your material. The more thorough your work is in these early stages, the smoother your drafting will feel. You should come to drafting with a considered blueprint of what you want to say and the order in which you want to say it. You shouldn't have to stare out the window to get your ideas. Your ideas should exist already—as notes, trees, sketches, or whatever—beside you or in an open file on-screen, just behind your paper as you write. This doesn't mean that you toss out spontaneity or new ideas; drafting itself can be highly generative. You start with what you have and allow it to drive your writing.

Drafting also grows easier as you learn to depend more on revision, that is, the careful reworking of your paper's content, structure, and style. You can think of revision as a sort of safety net. You don't have to write a perfect draft if you're going to rework it. Revision is your chance to "shoot retakes."

Most writers agree that drafting is generally harder than revision. So feel free to spread the burden. If you see a change that you can legitimately make for the better while you're drafting, go ahead and make it. Many writers revise frequently as they draft. But if your self-criticism takes on a carping, strident, negative, defeatist tone—*defy* it. Write over the noise. You're already committed to a revision, so if your paper does have weaknesses (and it probably does), you can fix them then. Your job for now is to get words down. Sheer page count is the goal.

To accomplish this goal, writers have developed any number of useful strategies, including freewriting, which we've described earlier in this text. Let's consider several more strategies that you can easily put to work. But, first, *understand the task ahead based on your paper's genre and content.*

This section will present some general principles for drafting that will stand you in good stead and are the subject of this chapter. Be ready to adapt these principles to the specific genres, courses, and disciplines in which you're writing. Consider how the drafting process can change when a writer is working on a specific kind of text in a specific discipline:

Type of Writing	Common Drafting Processes
Complex essay (e.g., in the humanities)	Considerable recursivity. The writer discovers and clarifies some or many ideas in the process of drafting.
Research report (e.g., based on a scientific experiment)	Less recursivity. The writer may draft sections based on the structure of the report (literature review, methods, results, etc.); much of the information is already at hand from the start.
Collaborative grant proposal or group capstone project	Different members of the team may initially draft separate sections, and then those sections are spliced together and evened out; a project time line may be used to orchestrate the drafting and help meet deadlines.
Annotated bibliography	Because the bibliography consists of separate entries, each annotating a different source, the writer drafts in brief episodes, by entry; later, he or she will smooth out the style and write an introduction.
Multimedia web project (e.g., on a historical figure)	Drafting will often proceed from the outside in—starting with a main page and then linking subsidiary pages based on the organization of information, including images, video clips, or other media.

KEY CONCEPT *Recursivity* refers to a common phenomenon in drafting, in which the writer continues to discover ideas, put language on the screen or page, and revise in cycles, rather than as a linear process. See Key Concept Glossary.

As these differences suggest, some kinds of writing will involve what is called *recursivity*: the writer hasn't worked out all the thinking about a complex topic in advance, even with a lot of brainstorming, and finds that he or she continues to create new concepts and understand the topic in new ways as a result of the drafting process. In contrast, in the write-up of a human-subject experiment in, say, psychology, much of the text is already in the writer's mind as chunks of information and in working documents such as data; the methods and results, for example, don't need to be invented while the writer is drafting because they already exist, so the text will be drafted in sections. This doesn't mean that the writer will draft effortlessly. Drafting will still involve multiple decisions about the order and level of detail, the style, and so forth. But there will be a schematic, of sorts, to guide the larger organization of the text.

Some projects, especially collaborative ones, may use web-based technologies to simplify the drafting process. The most common example is Google Docs, a cloud-based word-processing system that allows people who are working on the same draft to log in and make changes to the emerging text, write comments, and interact with their collaborators. This can happen in real time so that different writers can watch their colleagues make changes or add material as they're doing it. Your instructor may ask you to use such a system in order to facilitate collaboration or even to make comments on your work as you move along.

Forget About an Audience When Necessary

Whenever you get writer's block, it's not that you feel you can't write *anything*; you just can't write anything *good*. Every sentence you write strikes you as stupid, clumsy, and empty. This problem sometimes comes from thinking too much about your audience— worrying about their impressions of your ideas and your expression of them. If you find that audience too demanding, you may want to back off and draft to the nearest approximation you're comfortable

with. If your History professor intim-
idates you, imagine yourself writing
for someone who is interested in the
subject. You might even abandon
your audience completely and fall
back again on writing just for yourself. Some writing teachers advise
doing this. They suggest that you
explain your material on paper first to
yourself and only then try to explain
it to someone else. The draft version
for your own benefit is called a *zero draft*, or *writer-based draft*. With
the draft beside you, you can then focus more confidently on your
audience and write your reader-based draft.

> **KEY CONCEPT** A *zero draft* or *writer-based draft* is a draft of a higher-stakes writing project that you write mainly to yourself as the audience in order to reduce, for the time being, some of the pressure of getting everything "right" for your intended audience. See Key Concept Glossary.

Set a Drafting Schedule

The principle of sticking to a schedule while writing a higher-stakes
paper works at all stages. It's especially important at the drafting
stage because this is the point when most writers fall prey to procrastination. Almost anything seems less onerous—changing the cat's
litter pan, doing laundry, reorganizing a closet—than getting words
on-screen or on paper. Although procrastination may help you get
some of your unappealing chores done, procrastination will also
end up leaving you too little time to revise the paper. And, as we'll
see, revision is the very lifeblood of good writing. Try, then, to set a
reasonable schedule for drafting, and stick to it. Some people prefer
a time frame (e.g., one hour between 8:30 and 9:30 a.m. every day),
while others like a production outcome (a minimum of one page per
day regardless of how long it takes). Usually, it's better to work out a
schedule in small increments than in larger ones (such as "Finish full
draft by next Monday").

Try *Semidrafting*

If drafting still causes you to freeze up, think of it as a mere transitional phase between a well-developed outline and a working,
revisable text. Your goal is no longer your paper; it's something you
can rework into a paper, like a potter's ball of clay. If the attempt to

KEY CONCEPT *Semidrafting* is the process of writing draft material that leaves gaps and/ or instructions to yourself to work on in a future drafting session when you have more time or information. See Key Concept Glossary.

write a standard draft hobbles you, you can back off and adopt a series of shortcuts and half-measures that may let you get at least something down on paper.

If it helps, you can also skip writing your material in full declarative sentences. For some paragraphs, try writing only a sentence or two and then simply draw brackets around them and set your thoughts down in short notes. Later on, you can go back and refashion your notes into real sentences. If you're writing a paper based on research, you can draw brackets and list the statements or data that you plan to include without yet quoting in full. Your paragraphs will be a mix of standard prose and assorted fragments, something like the following:

> The greenhouse effect results from the way different forms of radiation pass through the atmosphere. Light rays from the sun pass easily through the various gases in the earth's atmosphere. They then strike the ground— [explain this briefly: short waves, long waves, which move easier. Effect of CO_2 on heat transmission. Analogy with glass greenhouses. Quote Jenkins, page 37. Note increase in global CO_2 and causes thereof.] As a result, the average temperature of the globe is rising, with catastrophic results. As one scientist puts it: [Reinhardt, from GH article].

On the one hand, the writer is obviously not as close to her goal of a final, presentable paper as she would have been if she had written out her material in full. On the other hand, it has taken her perhaps one fourth of the time. In the long run, her shortcut may well pay off.

GIVE IT A TRY

Just to practice semidrafting, try composing a few lines about a topic of your choice—for example, the problem of income inequality. When you reach a point where you need more information, draw a bracket and jot down what you think you would need to find out to move ahead.

Since starting a drafting session always takes time and energy, you can help yourself by jotting down notes when you want to stop working, capturing your thoughts for the next session. Write a sketchy, fragmented semidraft of your next few paragraphs at the bottom of a page on-screen. When you sit down the next day, you can start by simply writing out these passages in full, and that often will give you the momentum you need to draft efficiently for the rest of the session. At the end of that session, jot down your thoughts again for the next writing session, and so on. Meanwhile—if you really want to keep moving ahead—*don't* minimize your file or put it away. Keep it alive and kicking on-screen so that whenever you go back to your computer, it's waiting expectantly for you to nudge it forward. (Even writing three more sentences in between other tasks or tightening and styling an existing paragraph for readability are better than nothing. Sometimes you'll be sucked right back into the text and will move it significantly forward.)

Most important (and again): whatever you do, never treat any high-stakes writing project as if it will be a "one-and-done," written and finished quickly in one sitting, often the night before it's due. Most professors have developed an uncanny ability to sniff out the one-and-dones in a pile of papers. The papers look hurried; they're not organized well; and there are revealing mistakes, such as small errors that any college student would recognize in the process of revising, editing, and proofreading. No good writers are complacent enough to think that they can churn out a really effective final text the first time through. Believing so, no matter what grades you got on your papers in high school and no matter how much you wrote for the school newspaper or your yearbook, will trick you into two misfortunes: papers that are not as strong as they could have been and, more importantly, lost opportunities to *think harder* about your writing, which leads you to become a *better writer*.

The process of reworking your prose once you have a *full rough draft* of a paper or writing project is what we'll now turn to.

It's All about Revision: What Revision *Really* Means

Many student writers tend to underestimate the need for (and power of) effective *revision*. They hope to produce a near-perfect draft the first time and limit their later work to fixing minor problems in spelling, grammar, and mechanics. Or they don't even get far because procrastination and a due date have conspired to make them bat out a paper at the last minute and hope for the best. Effective writers reverse the emphasis. They tend to write their drafts more quickly and freely and then spend a lot more time rewriting them.

> **KEY CONCEPT** *Revision* means, literally, "re-seeing." It requires paying attention to major elements of a piece of writing, such as its structure, voice, and presentation of ideas. It is not *editing* or *proofreading*. See Key Concept Glossary.

Effective writers also take the meaning of the word *revision* seriously: *re-vision*, to see something a second (or third or fourth) time. They look for more from revision than just getting the bugs out of an otherwise adequate first attempt. For them, revision means the full, systematic reworking of one paper into another richer, sharper, more readable one. They don't strive simply to make their rough draft a little less rough but, rather, to make it shine.

The "best" amount of revision will vary, depending on several factors: how much you have revised while putting a paper together; how complex the task is; how familiar you are with the genre; and what sort of academic discipline or professional community you're writing in. Some journalists, for example, can write very quickly in order to meet a deadline looming soon after an event, but they also use formulas to organize and convey their information. In scientific disciplines, research reports also fall into categories of information (such as introduction, methods, results, etc.) but inevitably will undergo some revision if the author notices gaps in the literature review or something that isn't clear in the discussion of the methods or conclusions. In most disciplines, it's just a fact of life that high-stakes documents are returned to their authors with comments, suggestions, and requirements for revision before acceptance or publication. Grant proposals often need some clarification before they are funded. Journal articles almost always require revision. Most professors who serve as anonymous reviewers for journals will say that it's extraordinarily rare for them to recommend the acceptance of an article "as is," without at least some further revision. Even in rare cases, it's almost guaranteed that a professional editor working for the journal or publishing house will mark up the manuscript with all sorts of additional corrections, adaptations to the style that the journal or publishing house uses, edits for clarity or to eliminate redundancies, and so on. Figure 5.1 shows a picture of a page of

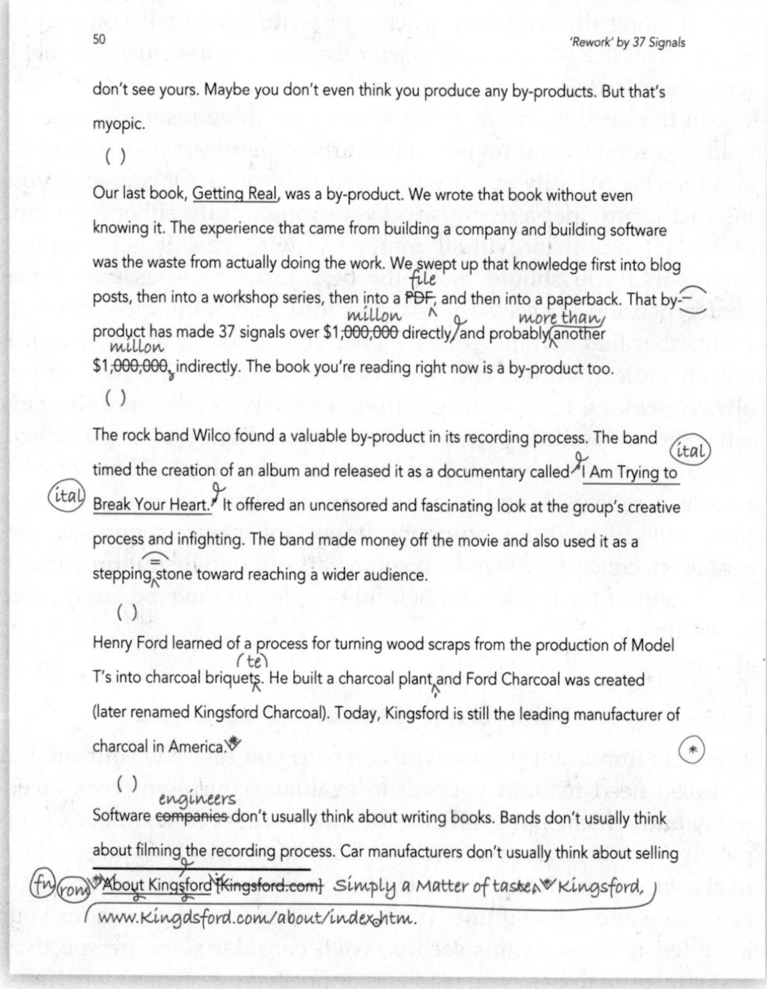

50   'Rework' by 37 Signals

don't see yours. Maybe you don't even think you produce any by-products. But that's myopic.

( )

Our last book, <u>Getting Real</u>, was a by-product. We wrote that book without even knowing it. The experience that came from building a company and building software was the waste from actually doing the work. We swept up that knowledge first into blog posts, then into a workshop series, then into a *file* PDF, and then into a paperback. That by-product has made 37 signals over $1,000,000 directly and probably another *million* $1,000,000 indirectly. The book you're reading right now is a by-product too.

( )

The rock band Wilco found a valuable by-product in its recording process. The band *(ital)* timed the creation of an album and released it as a documentary called I Am Trying to *(ital)* Break Your Heart. It offered an uncensored and fascinating look at the group's creative process and infighting. The band made money off the movie and also used it as a stepping stone toward reaching a wider audience.

( )

Henry Ford learned of a process for turning wood scraps from the production of Model *(te)* T's into charcoal briquets. He built a charcoal plant and Ford Charcoal was created (later renamed Kingsford Charcoal). Today, Kingsford is still the leading manufacturer of charcoal in America.   (*)

( )   *engineers*
Software ~~companies~~ don't usually think about writing books. Bands don't usually think about filming the recording process. Car manufacturers don't usually think about selling *(fw)(rom)* About Kingsford {Kingsford.com} *Simply a Matter of taste* Kingsford, www.Kingdsford.com/about/index.htm.

FIGURE 5.1 A Page of Copyedited Manuscript

manuscript marked up by a professional in-house editor toward the end of the process of publication (after all major and minor revisions were made).

In most of the academic settings where you're working on high-stakes, larger writing projects, it would be foolish to assume that your first draft is just fine, even if you've spent some time tinkering with it along the way. Any teacher of writing will tell you that *the biggest mistake students make in their college writing assignments is not to revise their drafts*.

In this section, we're going to consider three resources that can help you rethink and revise your drafts: *self-evaluation*, *peer response*, and *tutoring* (usually at a campus writing center). Of course, if your instructor provides a response on your rough draft, either in writing or by having an individual conference with you, it goes without saying that you should make the best, most rigorous use of that conference and, if necessary, ask questions if something is confusing. Remember that getting feedback on a draft in order to improve it is not an indication that you're somehow deficient. The best writers always seek and use feedback from a variety of readers to rethink what they've written before their text "goes live" (i.e., is published, submitted to a teacher, etc.) and can't be taken back. Think of revision as a rehearsal, and imagine how disastrous it would be for a play, musical, wedding ceremony, important speech, conference presentation, concert, or stand-up comedy routine to be put on without the benefit of feedback from helpful people (and maybe many more times after that).

Drawing on Your Own Resources to Revise

The most important person who can help you revise is yourself. But you also need to train yourself to evaluate your own work objectively and critically. It's difficult for most writers to stand back completely from their draft and read it from someone else's perspective. In the long run, though, you control your own text, and only you can shape and refine it until it pleases, informs, and persuades your intended readers. In this section, we'll consider some perspectives and strategies to help you read and critically assess your own drafts.

Step 1: Believe in Revision

We've already established that revision is partly a state of mind. If you don't believe that you can always improve your writing through revision, then revision strategies will look like so much useless busywork. But if you open your mind to the possibilities for revision, then your drafts will also open up to possibilities for improvement. The first step, then, is to orient yourself toward the process of revision. Don't come back to your draft thinking that you can just search for punctuation errors and you're done. Don't assume that you got it right the first time. And don't think that the better people get as writers, the more easily they can pour their perfectly formulated thoughts right onto the screen. Good writers revise—a lot.

GIVE IT A TRY

Take a few minutes to freewrite about your experiences revising. What messages did you get about revising in your school years? Was revising encouraged or assigned as punishment? How much do you remember revising? What effects did it have on your knowledge about writing and on the quality of your final papers?

Step 2: Become Your Audience

To draft, you may have taken the advice to forget about your intended readers if they're stopping up the free flow of your ideas. Now that you have a substantial draft, however, you want to let them back in, reviewing all that you know about them as actual, real-life people: their age, education, reason for reading your work, dominant attitudes and preferences, and so on. You then try to *become* that audience, confronting your draft as if you had never seen it before. Robed in all the mental garments of your readers, how does this piece of writing look to you? The more thorough your self-transformation is, the more accurately you can self-diagnose the strengths, weaknesses, and possibilities of your paper, and the more constructive your revision will be.

Step 3: Incubate

How soon after completing a draft should you launch into the process of revision? Maybe not too quickly. Here's why: theories of creativity—including writing of all kinds—suggest that the mind works on problems and projects in a subconscious or semiconscious way, sometimes while it's engaged in something else. The time between episodes when you focus your attention on a writing task is called *incubation*. According to research, these periods of inattention to the task can lead to new ideas that bubble up at odd moments or when you're focused again on the task.

> **KEY CONCEPT** *Incubation* refers to the time between deliberate work on a writing project when you're focusing on other things but your unconscious mind may still be working on ideas for the project. See Key Concept Glossary.

Even if you are skeptical that something actually does happen in your brain that's related to your writing project while you're jogging, walking to class, eating with friends, or watching a movie, many writing scholars claim that putting your text aside for a while allows you to come back to it with fresh insights and new perspectives. Getting "too close" to your draft can lead to frustration or boredom. Instead, always build in enough time to leave your draft alone and give yourself some rest from it. Incubation won't happen if you try to write your text from start to finish all at once, even if you revise it soon after you've finished.

Step 4: Read Your Draft through the Lens of the Evaluation Criteria

If your teacher doesn't provide feedback on your draft or build in opportunities for you to get feedback from your classmates, he or she will assume that you'll use the skills of *self-evaluation* to improve your draft. Many teachers use evaluation guides or sets of criteria (rubrics) when they reach a judgment about your final draft. If criteria aren't included with the assignment, ask your instructor whether they exist and if you

> **KEY CONCEPT** *Self-evaluation* refers to the process of standing back from your writing, often seeing it through the eyes of your intended or imagined readers, and then critically assessing its readability, structure, logic, style, clarity, coverage of information, and other features that are important to the genre and purpose of the writing. See Key Concept Glossary.

can have access to them. Then meticulously study them. After all, these are the very standards that your instructor will use to evaluate your writing. (We'll look at response or revision guides in more detail later in this chapter.)

A professor in a Literature and Critical Thinking course, titled "Whose America?," assigns students to do a "personal ethnography" by interviewing a recent immigrant to the United States. Take a look at the criteria that this professor uses to evaluate the final drafts of students' interview papers (see Figure 5.2). Notice how helpful these are for you *formatively*. For example, knowing in advance that a strong paper provides "frequent and specific details about the interviewee and the setting" will provide a useful template for revision. In fact, you can create an entire revision guide yourself, if your instructor

> **KEY CONCEPT** *Formative evaluation* refers to the use of evaluation standards or criteria as input in order to improve, rather than as the final evaluation of output. It contrasts with *summative evaluation*, which refers to the use of evaluation standards to measure some final product or performance against a set of standards. Feedback on an ungraded draft is formative, while a written assessment for a grade on a final draft is summative. See Key Concept Glossary.

doesn't provide one, by simply turning the evaluation criteria into questions: "Have I provided frequent and specific details about the interviewee and the setting?" "Where?" "How effectively?"

Step 5: Work in Stages

You don't revise your paper best by starting at the first word and grinding through, dotting the *i*'s and fixing commas as you go. *You revise most effectively by working first with the whole paper, then with the separate sections, and then with smaller and smaller details.* Such matters as using your computer's spell-checker and fixing punctuation, although important, shouldn't concern you (especially if they interfere with the flow of your thoughts) until you've attended to all of the more important matters. After all, why tinker with a paragraph that you may delete entirely?

Here's an important principle: *writing teaches the writer.* You learn about your subject while brainstorming your ideas; you understand your subject better as a result of organizing those ideas; and you find

Criteria	5	3	1	0
Establishes scene and mood	Writer uses frequent and specific details about the interviewee and the setting in order to create a clear sense of environment and mood. Readers feel like they are in the place of the interviewer.	Writer uses several details to establish a setting, but readers may have some difficulty determining the overall mood of the interviewer.	Writer occasionally uses details to establish a specific environment, but most of the writing is vague and nondescriptive.	Writing is extremely general and nondescriptive. Readers have a difficult time engaging with the paper.
Organization and Intertextuality	Writer makes clear, frequent, and compelling connections between the interviewee's experience, larger global issues, and the interviewer. The paper is organized in a logical progression of ideas and sounds more like a story than an interview.	Writer makes several intertextual and interpersonal connections. The paper may jump around between topics or may sound choppy.	Writer makes occasional connections. The paper is written more like a question-and-answer interview than an interwoven story.	The paper is almost exclusively question and answer. There is little to no attempt to weave together main ideas.

FIGURE 5.2 Evaluation Criteria for an Anthropology Interview Paper

Criteria	5	3	1	0
Author Voice	Writer "owns" his/her unique voice and perspective and develops a clear mood and style of writing.	Paper contains evidence of a distinct voice, but there may be inconsistencies.	Paper has some moments when a distinct voice is present, but there are inconsistencies and tone is mostly generic.	Writer's tone is generic and/or uninteresting.
Grammar and Editing	Paper is nearly error free. Sentences are varied and easy to read/understand.	There are some errors, but they do not detract from the meaning of the sentence(s).	There are several errors, some of which cause difficulties in understanding.	The high number of errors makes the paper difficult to read and understand.

FIGURE 5.2 (continued)

out still more about your subject as you draft. In drafting a conclusion, it's not uncommon to discover what you've really been trying to say all along. While you likely began writing with a particular thesis or idea that you would explain to the reader, some parts of your thinking might have changed. By the time your draft is done, you'll probably be more knowledgeable and have a deeper understanding of and insight into your material than when you started. As a result, you should now be able to write a more intelligent paper. As you revise, then, your first concern should be with content and purpose: what you actually said in your paper and why, and what you plan to say in the next version.

TOP-DOWN REVISION: CONTENT. To start, read your draft straight through, without so much as touching the letters on your keyboard. Scroll down, and read without stopping, as you would any article or story. Minimize the file, and try to summarize the draft, maybe writing your summary in a new Word file. Ask yourself the questions that you would ask a reader: "What does this say?" "What are the main points?" "How does the whole thing strike me?" Then imagine how you would use the material in this draft to write a new paper based on what you *currently* know about your topic and the new insights you came to as a result of actually drafting it. How can you make a smarter, more interesting, better informed paper out of what you already have? What else do you need?

Ask yourself which parts of your paper stick more clearly in your mind. What's most alive and interesting? Is your original focus in the paper—the thesis or question you had in mind when you started—still the strongest part? Or, has the center of gravity shifted? Has an apparent side issue risen up to dominate the work? If so, should you focus on that when you rewrite it? Do you even agree with what you said the first time, or have you changed your mind? (A changed mind is usually an improved mind.)

Write down your critical observations and your tentative revision plans for when you really want to start revising. Don't try to hold in your head all the changes and developments that you plan to make in your draft. Writing down and referring to your revision notes guarantees that your critical insights will actually pay off in an improved final version. Here's an excerpt from the revision notes of Eric, a student in a first-year Composition course, as he stood back from his draft on the environmental impact of plastics:

Overall my anti-plastic paper covers a lot of ground (no pun intended) about the environmental impact of plastic but I spend a lot of time on pp. 3-4 on the non-degradable issues and less on how plastic particulate matter gets distributed in the environment. I could get to the point faster about the non-degradable aspects because this is just a simple fact. The section on plastic bags in the ocean jumps around a little and there's a whole section on the myths and facts about the Pacific garbage patch that needs to be put after the general material. The quote about plastic in the ocean being equivalent to five plastic bags filled with plastic for every foot of coastline in the world needs to be repositioned and the picture of the albatross skeleton with all the plastic from its insides needs to find another place....

REVISING THE STRUCTURE. As a rule, the more carefully you shape your material before you start drafting, the more coherent the draft will turn out. The rule usually works, but it's not foolproof. There are always surprises when you draft. One line of your outline suddenly takes three pages to explain; another whole section dries up in a couple of paragraphs. Unless you're remarkably self-aware as you write, the version that winds up on-screen will not fully represent the understanding in your mind. It may be shot through with gaps, digressions, and redundancies that will be invisible as you draft but will jump out at you when you reread your draft. So, having read through your draft once to check its content, it's time to go through it again and assess how it actually hangs together.

In any kind of expository writing, you can consider organization in terms of your reader's informational needs at every point in the essay. As you revise, ask yourself repeatedly the following questions:

- Do my readers have all they need to understand this paragraph, this sentence, right now?
- Have I prepared my readers to understand and appreciate this material when they read it? Or will it feel to them as if I've towed them out to sea and cast them off without a compass?

There are two basic ways you can assess how close your draft comes to accomplishing all this: (1) You can

> **KEY CONCEPT** *Subjective flow* refers to the effect of a draft's structure or organization on you or another reader, from a purely impressionistic perspective. *Objective shape* refers to a conscious mapping of the structure or organization of your or another writer's draft. See Key Concept Glossary.

read it through, attending to its *subjective flow*. (2) You can stand back from it and consider its *objective shape*. These give you complementary kinds of information about your draft and promote more effective revision.

1. *Subjective flow*. To assess the subjective flow of your draft's structure, sit back, relax, and read through it again, from beginning to end, as you did when you were evaluating its content. This time, though, keep your fingers on the keyboard (or a pen in your hand). Read the draft quickly; don't stop to mull it over too much. As you read, keep track of your own reactions to the parts of the paper. As a newcomer to this paper, someone who has never seen it before, does it makes sense at each point? Do you have a sense of where it's going? Do the ideas develop for you in a sensible, clear, and interesting way? Does it move along at an even, pleasant pace?

Wherever you find the paper moving forward effectively, type or write a check mark in the margin. Whenever you feel that the paper is jarring or bumping, wandering off course, losing its bearings, or even contradicting something it said elsewhere, put an asterisk in the margin. It's not essential that you know what you plan to do about the asterisks at this point—only how the paper affects you. This is a diagnostic phase: record symptoms, and note your reactions in your revision notes or as marginal comments. You'll perform surgery a bit later.

2. *Objective shape*. Although reading for subjective flow often tells you all you need to know about your structure, sometimes the results are confusing or ambiguous. Especially with longer papers, you may find it difficult to form a clear picture in your mind of how your draft fits together. You need to create some sort of visual analog of your draft's structure, a diagram of its objective shape. Here's how to do this:

- Number your paragraphs, or turn on an outline function on your computer.
- Type "1" in a new blank Word document.
- Read your first paragraph; then, in just a few words, write down its main theme or idea (what it *says*) and its role in your paper (what it *does*). (You can use the "Insert Comments" function in Word to label your paragraphs.) These *does* statements will

always contain a verb relating to the function of the paragraph in your paper (such as, "*gives* an example of the idea expressed in the previous paragraph" or "*concedes* that some people do not agree with the claim just made").

- Type "2" on a new line of your document, read the second paragraph of your draft, and then write what it says and what it does.
- Continue this process until you have a full set of minisummaries of all your paper's paragraphs.

Here's an example of an annotated paragraph from the paper of a student who wrote a report of how he solved a welding problem in his class.

I couldn't alter the metallurgical structure of the plate so I brazed the washer to the plate. This didn't involve welding, which would have heated the plate way too much (around 1,200 degrees). Brazing heats the plate to around 800 degrees, way less than the maximum 1,000 degrees that the plate could be heated.

SAYS: I chose to braze instead of weld.

DOES: Explains the reason for the choice of brazing by referring to the maximum temperature I could have heated the plate to.

If you find a paragraph that's especially difficult to summarize in a few words, you've probably already found one problem. If a paragraph goes in too many directions or touches on too many topics to capture its main theme in one line, you probably have enough material in it for two paragraphs or more. Break up that lopsided paragraph into pieces that are clearer and more coherent. Look especially at the paragraph's function. If you have a hard time explaining or justifying what the paragraph is actually doing in the paper, consider merging it, rewriting it, or just tossing it out.

Once you're satisfied with the paragraphs individually, look at their overall arrangement. Have you really put all the apples with the apples and the grapes with the grapes? If the same topic shows up in several lines, you may be repeating yourself or leading your reader in circles. Ask yourself if it's clear which topics are major and which are minor or supporting topics. Can you mark off the major divisions of your material using brackets? Do these major divisions follow each other in the best order, or might you gain by moving Part

Three up between Parts One and Two? Within each bracketed major section, do the paragraph topics seem to flow in some sensible order? Or should you rearrange subtopics within one part or another?

Again, you'll be working between your structural outline—whether that's a traditional one or something like a tree or a concept map—and your draft-in-progress. Eventually, you'll see the shape of your paper as a whole, not just based on the outline, but how you have fleshed it out with details. Rearranging (and then modifying your outline) is often a necessary and crucial part of revision.

GIVE IT A TRY

Apply the *says/does* strategy to several paragraphs of a paper you're working on. If you're not currently working on a paper, try applying the strategy to a piece of text that you're assigned to read. What happened as you annotated the paragraphs? What did you notice about the way the text moved forward?

REVISING INTRODUCTIONS. The introduction in your paper tries to negotiate a type of contract with your reader: "If you, O Reader, will peruse this paper, I will reward you with such and such." First, you need to let your reader know what you have to offer. The nature of the material will obviously vary a lot by the genre and context of your writing. A marketing study might begin with an *executive summary* that states the overall purpose and nature of the text. A lab report might start with a single sentence that clearly explains the purpose of the lab: "In this lab, we explore the theory of optimal foraging and the theory of central place foraging using beavers as the model animal." In other words, state clearly the question or thesis that you intend to pursue, as we discussed at length in Chapter 4.

Your contract should also suggest the order of your information: "The three groups that were most important in settling the American West were miners, farmers, and people in trade." In revising your introduction, you will want to look for symmetry between the structure and content of the paper and what you say up front that the paper will do. Style and tone will also matter here. If you're writing something objectively scientific, you won't be using passionate language; if you're writing an editorial about a subject of great emotional importance to you, you may want to use a more persuasive tone.

Finally, revise your introduction to sell your paper effectively. This doesn't mean indulging in the pulp of TV advertising. It means showing in your introduction the real importance of your subject matter. What makes this material something worth writing about? Does it revolutionize our thinking about a topic? Does it confirm old wisdom? Are you discussing a scientific principle that's capable of making major improvements in future medical technology? If so, say so. Make it clear from the start why the material is worth knowing and why it's worth the reader's time to read about it. (A little later in this chapter, we'll look at a rough and a revised introduction that illustrate these principles.)

REVISING CONCLUSIONS. The final one hundred words of your paper can often determine whatever lasting effect it will have on your readers. In revising your conclusion, you should ask yourself what you want your readers to carry away. If you're writing a difficult, technical paper in a complex field, you might use the conclusion simply to summarize your arguments, so that your readers get your ideas straight one last time before they stop reading.

Usually, though, you can get more mileage out of your conclusion than that. In revising, consider

- suggesting new questions arising from what you've presented or researched; noting useful directions for future inquiry; or
- planting a question in your readers' minds.

Remind your readers again of the social or moral consequences of your topic, or call for vigorous action of some sort. Always think about the genre and purpose of your text in deciding how to wrap things up.

Oddly enough, if your conclusion is too conclusive, it may have a leaden, dulling effect on your readers. Instead of just wrapping things up, consider introducing some new, interesting, provocative element into your conclusion. It may keep your ideas alive for your readers that much longer.

Obviously, introductions and conclusions require careful work. Much stands or falls on how evenly and smoothly you lead your readers into your paper, and how cleanly and memorably you usher your readers out of it. Because readers are so important, thinking about them can paralyze you when you're trying to draft. Since the introduction appears at the beginning of your paper, it can stall you before you even get started. Also, what an introduction needs to say usually can't be determined without reference to the paper as a whole. Since any major change to the draft will force changes to the introduction, you don't have the information to write it well the first time anyway.

Try, then, to sketch your way through your introduction quickly in the rough draft, and get it behind you. Get it done and move on, and don't let its half-baked condition distract you. Do the same for the conclusion. Then, once you have reworked the content and organization of the paper, you can return to the opening and closing, knowing how to make them both shine.

SPIT AND POLISH. It should be clear by now that revision entails far more than just rephrasing your sentences. It means rethinking your content, rebuilding your structure, and reworking your beginning and ending—most helpfully after other people respond to what you've written. When these are more or less in place, revision still means using a healthy amount of "sandpaper and varnish." A rough, bumpy, jarring style—or a meandering bog of long, twisty, verbose rivulets of language or a diffuse, hazy cloud of bureaucratic abstractions—will offend your readers and obscure your meaning, rendering all of your previous revision futile. You owe it to your readers, your subject matter, and yourself to write as clearly and as smoothly as possible. As any professional can tell you, it requires *effort*.

Try reading your draft out loud. Your voice and ear are your best guides for revising your style. If you read your draft out loud, you'll hear most of what you need to fix. Don't trust yourself to pick this up by reading silently. The actual sounds of your words will indicate better than the marks on the page where your sentences are too choppy or where you've rambled on for too long. Don't expect to get this done in one sitting. Read through your draft several times, in between other activities. In addition to identifying the bigger problems with your draft—its style, structure, sense, use of outside material, support for your claims, and the like—you'll also find small errors that you won't notice without passing your eyes over the text again and again. Remember that the eyes of your readers (and anyone evaluating your paper) may not pass over those errors, and your errors will be found out.

GIVE IT A TRY

After completing a rough draft, try using the read-aloud strategy described in this section. Keep a list or a log of anything you notice, change, or correct as a result of using the strategy. Then compare your experience with students in your class.

Drawing on Your Peers' Responses to Revise

A staple activity in Composition courses is called *peer response* (or *peer review*). Much of the advice provided earlier in the self-evaluation section can be effectively used during peer response, except that, instead of applying that advice to your own draft, you'll apply it to the drafts of other students in your course (or to

> **KEY CONCEPT** *Peer response* or *peer review* refers to a process of getting and giving feedback on a work in progress from people in a peer group, usually other members of your class. See Key Concept Glossary.

colleagues in other contexts). Instead of repeating that advice, this section will focus on the *process* of peer response: how to conduct it effectively in order to give (and get) the best response you can to promote revision.

What's Peer Response?

If you've ever read a friend's paper and offered a reaction to it—or if the same has been done for you—you have engaged in an informal version of *peer response*. In courses across the curriculum, your teachers may set up a more formal version of this process. The following chart shows what it involves:

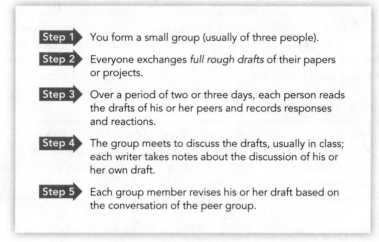

Step 1 You form a small group (usually of three people).

Step 2 Everyone exchanges *full rough drafts* of their papers or projects.

Step 3 Over a period of two or three days, each person reads the drafts of his or her peers and records responses and reactions.

Step 4 The group meets to discuss the drafts, usually in class; each writer takes notes about the discussion of his or her own draft.

Step 5 Each group member revises his or her draft based on the conversation of the peer group.

Although there are many variations of this process, at its core is the principle that getting someone else to read your draft will almost always give you insights about it that you might not discover on your own. Your peer group is a *litmus test*: how will your readers (and teacher) receive your paper? Will they struggle to make sense of it? Will they be lost in its structure or feel that you're saying the same thing over and over? Will they balk at your style or be swept up in it? Will the text flow smoothly or derail them at each turn?

Let's consider some of the features of peer response in the preceding chart.

- *Why three people?* Although groups can be of any size, a group of three people makes the workload manageable and gives you more than just one reader's experience. As a group, you also can discuss and negotiate possibilities for revision based on those reading experiences.

- *Why exchange beforehand?* In a typical class session, it takes too long to read a full rough draft, to think about it, to respond to it, and then to provide that response to the writer. Having the drafts in advance, and time to read and think about them, will yield a richer and more detailed group experience.

- *Why a full rough draft?* Although you can get peer response at any stage of the writing process—and may do so to good effect—at some point you want readers to have the experience of reading your entire paper or project from start to finish. It doesn't make sense to have readers look at a paper that stops halfway through; sure, they can comment on the introduction and part of the body, but it's all too tentative and may get revised anyway. For this reason, you'll usually be required to submit your entire rough draft to your peer group *and* to the instructor, from beginning to end, before the peer-review session.

- *Why meet in class?* Various kinds of peer response do exist, including a version in which you just give written comments to the writer (we'll consider this later; see Figure 5.4). But the live, in-class version lets you *discuss* the drafts in depth, with give-and-take.

- *Why take notes?* If you don't take notes, you may not recall all the ideas that emerge in the discussion.

Ten Tips for Effective Peer Response

Teachers often find that when students work in small groups to talk about each other's writing, several things go wrong. First, the groups stray from the task and end up socializing, or they skim through their papers, make a couple of comments, and then, after five or ten minutes, say, "We're done. Can we go?" In good peer response, *you probably need more time than what you're given to discuss all that you want to discuss.* Second, if the groups do stay on task, they focus on the wrong things (such as spelling mistakes or misplaced commas) or offer vague statements that fail to help the writer ("I liked it. It was pretty good."). Third—and as a result of these first two problems—the writer engages in very little revision, turning in a final draft that looks just like the rough draft, with a little bit of tweaking. When these problems happen, teachers often give up on peer response entirely, thinking it a waste of valuable classroom time. *In turn, a golden opportunity to improve your writing is lost.* So, how can you work in a small group to maximize the benefits of peer response? After all, it's *your* paper. Why not make it the strongest it can be? Here are ten important tips.

- Tip #1: *Do the prep work.* If you don't read—actually *read*—your peers' papers, you can't offer them a helpful response. Take the necessary time beforehand. Take notes, preferably on a printout of the draft or as inserted comments on a digital version. Read the papers more than once.

- Tip #2: *Show up.* Nothing derails peer response faster than a group member who decides not to attend the peer-response session. For this reason, teachers often count the peer-response session as the equivalent of two classes in their attendance records.

- Tip #3: *During the meeting, stay on task.* Appoint a "taskmaster" who is responsible for pulling you back to the peer response if and when you start discussing something that's unrelated. Because you're in a group and groups are social entities, it's natural to tell anecdotes or stray from your work at various points. But time is of the essence. Stay focused.

- Tip #4: *Avoid apologizing.* Everyone in a peer group is in the same boat. Don't spend a lot of time trying to minimize the effects of readers' responses by saying that you didn't have enough time to do a good job, that you're not a strong writer, or that your roommate was distracting you as you wrote. The draft is what it is. Work with it. Instead of apologizing, take a minute to tell your group members what feedback you would find especially helpful: "I wasn't sure about the middle section—how did you react to that long part about the Pacific garbage patch? Did it go on for too long or have too much detail? Were you interested all the way through? Did it add support to my thesis?"

- Tip #5: *Work from the biggest to the smallest matters.* It's very common for peer groups to zero in on tiny errors when they start working. It can come from a fear of tackling broader issues or of "criticizing" a classmate. Pointing out a misspelling may feel "safer" socially because it's objective and doesn't bring in opinion and interpretation. Also, it's easier than tackling a complex structural issue or some meaning-related matter with the content. *Don't do this.* In fact, don't even start with the small stuff. If the writer will end up tossing out an entire paragraph, why fiddle with its style or grammar? Use the questions under self-evaluation (discussed earlier) to explore larger concerns: ideas, structure, overall shape and flow, and the effectiveness of the introduction and conclusion.

- Tip #6: *Be aware of time.* If your instructor isn't giving you time cues, set a smartphone to count down the minutes until you need to transition to the next writer. In a fifty-minute class, you'll usually have about fifteen minutes to discuss each draft. If you become immersed in your discussion—that is, if you're *really* doing peer response well—the time will go by quickly. Keep on track, and remind yourselves that you have, say, five minutes left to finish responding to one member's paper. The reverse is also true: if you think you're done before (*only!*) fifteen minutes per draft, something is seriously wrong with your discussion. Instead, you should be *in the zone.* Someone should have to drag your still-working group from the room at the end of the class session. (And if that's the case—great! Continue your discussion online.)

- Tip #7: *Use the resources of your instructor.* In a typical in-class peer-response session, your instructor will roam around the room or work alone on something until beckoned. If at any point you get stuck on a particular problem that your group isn't sure how to solve, or if there's some disagreement about a solution, call your instructor over for advice. Remember that instructors will deliberately take a back seat during the peer-response process. They know that if they weigh in too heavily, you may just ignore the good comments of your peers and go with the advice of your (later) evaluator. The whole point of peer response isn't just to improve your paper but to give you experience working through writing problems—yours *and* others'. If your instructor does all the work, it subverts the learning process.

- Tip #8: *Remember that you control your paper.* What if one of your peer group members makes a suggestion that you don't think will improve your paper or that you think may even make it worse? The point of peer response is not to turn your peer-group members into teachers. That's awkward and weird, so avoid taking on the role of teacher. Your peer-group members don't have the final say. You do. Carefully consider all of their responses, but decide for yourself which responses or suggestions you want to use in your revision. That opening sentence one group member thought was too personal—does it, in fact, work based on the goals and genre of the paper? In your marginal notes, just pose the question ("Keep or toss this opening?"). Then come back to it later. On second (or third or fourth) consideration, if you particularly like that opening and know that your readers will (in spite of the group member's feelings), *leave it in.*

- Tip #9: *Leave defensiveness at the door.* If you're the writer and your peers are offering you their reading experience, don't put up a wall and a moat against their thoughts. If fact, don't think "wall" and "moat" at all; their response is just the opposite of flaming arrows and iron balls slung from a trebuchet. They come in peace, bearing the fruits of their reading. Put away the boiling oil, and open the drawbridge. Don't resist every comment, and don't meet their critiques with an ego-defending response about how you worked on your yearbook in high school or got an A in Creative Writing. Appreciate what they bring to your paper, and accept their responses openly and thoughtfully.

- Tip #10: *Try to learn about writing by tackling issues in your peers' drafts.* Think about it: how often do you see other people's work in progress? Almost everything you see is final, printed, published,

GIVE IT A TRY

Think about all your experiences working in small groups, either in school or in other activities such as clubs and organizations. Make a list of all the problems you encountered, such as a situation in which one person wanted to dominate the discussion or "have it his way." For each problem, create group guidelines, such as "individual members will not dominate the discussion but will share the floor with others." Then compare your guidelines as a class. Create a final list based on overlapping guidelines, and pledge to use them during your peer-response sessions.

slick, polished text. Peer response is an opportunity to consider writing problems and issues in something other than your own drafts. The groups aren't just about making a better paper; they're about giving you a context to enhance your writing skills.

Making the Most of Response Guides

Many teachers who build peer response into their instruction will give you a response or revision guide before you meet to discuss your drafts. These response guides are designed to help you read and respond to your own and your peers' drafts by focusing your attention on specific issues. They usually take the form of a series of questions to answer or actions that you can take to give a direct, reader-based response. Usually, the questions relate directly to the assignment's main learning goals. For example, in a Social Psychology course, the main goal of a paper could be to help you to apply the concept of crowd contagion to an experience you had that involved crowd contagion. A likely question on a response guide might be something like, "Does the writer fully explain how his or her experience demonstrates the concept of crowd contagion as we have discussed it and as it is presented in the text?" Although many instructors avoid giving questions with "yes" or "no" answers, when they do appear (like the one above), *don't just answer them with a "yes" or a "no."* Instead, offer an explanation: "The writer describes his experience in a protest crowd that had gathered outside the administration building. The details about how the crowd started to look around for things to throw help to illustrate Le Bon's idea about the reversion to primitivism and the hypnotic influence of anonymity. However, more detail could be included to show the evolution of the crowd's behavior."

> **KEY CONCEPT** A *response guide* or *revision guide* is a set of questions, usually created by an instructor, that guide your responses to the drafts of your own and/or your peers' papers. See Key Concept Glossary.

Here's an example of a peer-response guide that a professor of Geology prepared for her students to help them revise a major paper (Figure 5.3). The assignment involved creating a funding

---

PEER RESPONSE FEEDBACK FORM
First Draft of Module 6 Proposal

Name of Author: _____

Name of Peer Reviewer: _____

Instructions to Peer Reviewer: Read the draft of the proposal. Put a check mark next to sections that flow well. Put an * next to sections that are hard to understand. Then, answer the following questions.

- In your own words, describe the question that the author wants to answer:
  - Why is this question interesting and important?
  - How will they answer the question? What methods will they use?
  - How are they prepared academically to do this project?

FIGURE 5.3 Sample Peer-Response Guide for a Geology Paper

proposal to conduct research on Miocene faulting, basin development, deposition, and volcanism in the Lake Mead (Nevada and Colorado) area.

Notice that, for this professor, it's very important for students to justify the question that they want the research in their grant proposal to answer. Knowing this will focus each writer and his or her peer-group members on the nature and quality of their research question(s).

When you receive a response guide, first read the questions carefully. Think about how they're structured: What should you be reading for first? What's most important? Usually the guides are organized from broadest to least important concerns, sometimes ending in the realm of grammar, style, punctuation, and other matters of editing and proofreading (not revising). Sometimes the questions will focus entirely on larger issues of content, organization, and meaning, ignoring the least important issues for a later round of editing. Try to provide as much detail as possible in response to each question. This will give you a lot of material to share when you conduct the peer-response session.

Varieties of Peer Response

Although it's the gold standard of peer response, a face-to-face conversation about the drafts of your peers is not always possible (e.g., in online courses). Teachers and education specialists have come up with several other ways for you to convey your thoughts about your peers' drafts. Each method requires attention to the mode of delivery, but the underlying principles of thoroughness, helpfulness, and diplomacy (without coddling or ignoring the need for critique) still apply.

Figure 5.4 shows a number of different peer-response modes and their pros and cons. The scope of this chapter doesn't allow for a detailed discussion of each mode. If you're assigned to use one, be sure to become familiar with any technology it may require. For modes like podcasting or screen-capture response, try using the technology first before you provide the response "for real," in case there's a glitch with the equipment. Above all, remember that the guidelines and tips offered for face-to-face response also apply here but may need to be adapted. For example, when recording a screen-capture response on a peer's paper, you'll be scrolling through the paper and talking about your impressions, optionally answering questions provided in a peer-response guide. Your partner will be expecting you to make thoughtful comments about your reading experience based on something more than a quick skimming of the paper. Just as you would for a face-to-face meeting, prepare thoroughly. By the time you turn on the screen-capture device and the program starts recording your voice, you should be well prepared to talk about your impressions.

The following is an excerpt from one student's screen-capture response of a peer's rough draft (this is just from the audio portion, without the on-screen paper that the responder was scrolling through, highlighting various words and sentences):

> Here, like what I highlighted in purple, it says "tests that test aggression," I think you could probably change the word "test" to like maybe the word "experiment" or "observations." And here, you use "claim" twice in the

Modes	Features
Face-to-face in class	Allows deep discussion and negotiation; lines can be read aloud; highly interactive
Face-to-face out of class (teacher present)	Allows deep discussion and teacher help in structured environment with set time; lines can be read aloud
Face-to-face out of class (teacher not present)	Allows deep discussion and negotiation; takes much time; lines can be read aloud; sometimes hard to schedule
E-mail	Convenient and done on students' own time; one-way response
IM or other live chat	Allows some give-and-take and can involve several students; interactive; if in writing, less material is conveyed
Paper comments exchanged in class but not discussed	Convenient; no need for note taking; one-way response with no interaction
Anonymous comments collected and redistributed	Encourages honesty; shuffles source of response over time; one-way response with no interaction
"Hot seat" all-class comments	Each student receives response from entire class; can be intimidating and takes much time
Calibrated peer review	Is anonymous; provides multiple evaluation scores with consensus; convenient; web-based; one-way response with no interaction or discussion
Digital oral comments (podcast, e.g.)	Allows for detailed commentary and explanation; can be done at any time; one-way response without interaction
Screen-capture response (Jing, Camtasia, etc.)	Allows for audiovisual response—talk while marking up or scrolling through a paper; can be done at any time; provides detailed response; one-way response without interaction

FIGURE 5.4 Modes of Peer Response

same sentence. Here you have an apostrophe on "participant's" and you need it after the –s because it's a plural, you know, many participants. Here you have a grammar error, "continues" should be "continue." ...

Now compare a brief excerpt from another student's screen-capture response to a different peer:

> After reading your paper, I found the topic of multiverse very interesting. To start, I like in the beginning how you created a hook in your paper. To me, and probably most people as well, this message basically caught my attention and wanted me to keep on reading to figure out what you're trying to say. For this multiverse theory, is there something important that people should know about it? I mean, does it affect people in any way?

Notice how the first student really doesn't interact with the peer writer's *meaning*—the response is a catalog of small details that may get edited in a later version. The second student, in contrast, responds to what the writer is trying to do, in a broader way, and asks a question that will probably prompt the writer to include some additional material or clarify the effects of the multiverse on people.

No matter what the medium, then, remember that the most important purpose of peer response is not to play the role of a grammarian or an editor; it's to respond *as a reader* to the writer's text and its effects. Keep this principle at the front of all your peer responses (and expect the same from your peers on your own writing), and the entire experience will be far more interesting and engaging than if you just plod through with overly general statements, offer nothing but praise, or nitpick at tiny details.

An Example for Skeptics

Plenty of teachers and students will share anecdotes of their experiences with small-group revision conferences that failed. But that's less the fault of the method than the way its participants used it. Reluctant, unprepared group members, or those who focus on the wrong things, convey their thoughts in less than useful ways, or wander off topic and socialize, will make the method fail. In contrast, teachers and students all over the world will also remember their experiences when a peer-group revision conference gave them extremely helpful ideas and perspectives, generating revisions that made visible improvements to their projects. The following is just one example.

Cecily Howard was a student in a course on the History of Technology. One of her high-stakes assignments asked her to choose a recent technology (which could include a particular computer application), do some informal research on it, and then describe the technology's history, current uses and status, and possible future. The goal was to help Cecily's class to see technology and its human uses developmentally, as something shaping society and also being shaped by it.

After choosing the wiki as her technology, Cecily wrote a full rough draft. Following is the first page of that draft, in which Cecily introduces her topic.

Analysis of a Technology

Cecily Howard

Today we are living in an amazing technological age. The "communication age," as it is often called. Staggering new advances have allowed us to get information at lightning-fast speed. A recent poll showed that computer use is increasing all over the world. In developed countries as many as 65% of the population owns a personal computer. The way we communicate has been totally altered because of this technology. Many people who did not have access to information before or would have to go to a library, which can be difficult for poor or people without transportation. People without the ability to ever communicate their information or knowledge to the public can now interact in ways never before imagined. One trend in computer communication is the wiki, a popular trend that has grown on the internet. Wikipedia is an encyclopedia that popularized the wiki, which means "fast" in Hawaiian. People are now contributing to wikis and creating their own wikis. Although some people are worried that wikis will include bad information from people who don't know what they are talking about, the wiki is still expanding. With the surge in wikis, many people are now using wikis to save the time it would take for one person to add information to a web site, now any user can add information. That makes the wiki grow without "effort." Wikis are now an important part of the internet; thus it is added to the available methods of computer communication.

    At the airport in Honolulu, there is a little bus called a "wiki wiki" that runs between the terminals and the smaller terminal where the flights to the different islands. The word "wiki" means "quick" in Hawaiian, and "wiki wiki" means "very quick." The first wiki was created in 1994 by War Cunningham in Portland Oregon and it was up and running by 1995. Cunningham liked the way that Hypercard allowed information to be linked . . . [paper continues for 3 more pages].

Cecily met with her peer group for about an hour; all the group members already had read each other's drafts and were prepared to talk about their impressions. Here is a section of the transcript of their peer-group meeting in which they were focusing on Cecily's introduction.

Peter: This looks like it's, I mean, at first is about communication, I mean, communication tech—

Jessica: It starts really, like, way out there, I mean, computers, the history—

Cecily: What I'm focusing on is obviously wikis, the popularity and how, and then how they started like encyclopedias and morphed, you know, what I say later about where they are going.

Peter: Yeah, that part gets good, but you could basically draw an X through this part [indicating the first paragraph].

Jessica: —so you don't need such a way-out-there, I mean, start out faster into the wiki focus, because otherwise we don't know what it is that—

Cecily: See what I was trying to do, I need to, I was trying to focus on, like give it a background.

Jessica: But you're using all of this fluff in the beginning of this. "Many people who do not have access to information would have to go to a library. . . ." This big long sentence doesn't really add to your paper.

Cecily: I guess I was . . . I thought that if people didn't know what a wiki is—

Melissa: Right, but my point, if people know they are reading, you know, about wikis, I mean maybe a title that . . .

Peter: What about like, wikis as a, a new technology or something.

Cecily: I know, I was kinda waiting. . . .

Jessica: But you're trying to build this huge introduction to a point you can get to a little more concisely.

Cecily: So a title that would tell the reader what it's about.

Peter: Well, we don't, what if I don't know what a wiki is, I mean, you need a lead-in but not, but more on wikis. Because we go on and we think it's going to be about wikis but we're not sure, I mean, what about saying what you will do in the paper, the main point. Where are we going, sort of thing.

Melissa: And we learn a lot about the word *wiki* but not necessarily that much information about what a wiki is.

Peter: Yeah, maybe somebody has no idea what a wiki is.

Cecily: So put it up, so define or explain more and then focus on, say what the paper will say about wikis, maybe. Right.

As you can see, Cecily's group started their conversation by focusing on how her introduction began too generally—a common problem that comes from "writing your way into" your paper when you're not sure what to say, like clearing your throat before speaking. The group immediately focused on this problem, but notice how the discussion raises important issues about how *much* background to provide based on the audience's knowledge and expectations. You can almost see the learning taking place in this discussion. Even this brief snippet of the conversation—just a minute or two—yielded a lot of information for Cecily, who ended up turning in a far better paper. Take a look at the revised first page (the material that Cecily eliminated is crossed out, and the material that she added is in shaded text):

Revised Draft

The Wiki: Past, Present, and Future

Cecily Howard

New advances in computer technology are developing at an increasing pace as more and more people have access to computers. ~~Today we are living in an amazing technological age. The "communication age," as it is often called. Staggering new advances have allowed us to get information at lightning-fast speed. A recent poll showed that computer use is increasing all over the world. In developed countries as many as 65% of the population owns a personal computer. The way we communicate has been totally altered because of this technology. Many people who did not have access to information before or would have to go to a library, which can be difficult for he poor or people without transportation. People without the ability to ever communicate their information or knowledge~~

~~to the public can now interact in ways never before imagined.~~
One recent trend in computer communication is the wiki, a
~~popular trend that has grown on the internet. Wikipedia is an~~
Web 2.0-based system that allows users to also be contributors
to the information stored at the site. The first wiki, which
means "fast" in Hawaiian, was Wikipedia, a Web encyclopedia
that ~~popularized the wiki, which means "fast" in Hawaiian~~
allows people to keep adding information. Now, wikis are
flourishing and their original encyclopedia uses are expanding
with other interactive features in industry, education, and the
public sector.

   In this paper, I will first describe the development of wikis
and their original uses and intentions. Next, I will analyze what
wikis are used for based on an analysis of four wikis in three
different areas: business, education, and the public. Finally, I
will discuss the possible future of wikis and how they might be
combined with other new technologies. ~~People are now con-~~
~~tributing to wikis and creating their own wikis. Although some~~
~~people are worried that wikis will include bad information from~~
~~people who don't know what they are talking about, the wiki is~~

GIVE IT A TRY

Compare the first and revised drafts of Cecily's first page. What did
she change? What improvements do you think she made in the introduction? Point to moments in the transcript of her peer-group discussion that were likely to have precipitated those changes.

Drawing on the Resources of a Tutor or Writing Center for Learning From Your Drafts

Most college campuses have a writing center or a tutorial service that's designed to help students by offering one-to-one feedback on their writing (as well as a wide variety of other resources, such as group sessions on specific topics, visits to classes, or online advice). These centers may be large or small, may provide tutoring services in a central location or a "satellite" location, such as a dorm, and may be staffed by undergraduate or graduate students, center personnel, or faculty, or a combination of these people.

Every such center will almost always emblazon two cardinal principles somewhere about what they do or don't do:

Cardinal Principle #1: Writing centers do *not* "edit" students' writing (i.e., you can't drop your paper off at 9 a.m. and pick it up a 3 p.m. all cleaned up). They will *work with you* to help you improve your writing. Usually, they will do this in the context of a paper you're working on in a course, but they don't assume that the paper is the most important focus. Yes, you want to do well on your assignment, but your tutor(s) will also be helping you to learn how to be a better writer *through* your interactions around that assignment.

Cardinal Principle #2: Most writing centers battle constantly against a prevailing view that they serve underprepared students and that the people who use their services are deficient. Yes, writing centers do help students to develop areas in their writing that need improvement. However, many capable writers visit their campus writing center to get useful feedback, especially when they're working on assignments in unfamiliar disciplines and in genres that are new to them. Research across the United States shows that students often can increase their grades in writing-rich courses by a full category when they visit their writing center to work on all of their high-stakes assignments.

Most writing centers have both scheduled hours for appointments and drop-in hours, and some even offer online tutorial help. It's very helpful for you to visit your writing center's website and learn about the services it offers and how you can work with one of the center's tutors. Drop-in hours can help you to get someone to quickly read your draft and give you some general advice and feedback. Scheduling a visit in advance is a better option, however. Here are some suggestions for setting up and preparing for a visit:

- *Be diligent.* Follow the writing center's guidelines carefully (e.g., if you need to submit your draft in advance, be sure it's a complete draft in the correct format).

- *Respect the staff's knowledge.* Remember that tutors are hired and trained by the writing center's staff. If they are undergraduates, they were chosen because of their strong writing abilities *and* their abilities to reflect on others' writing and to provide solid advice.

- *Show up.* Like people waiting for a seat in a restaurant, there will be students who could have taken your appointment if you're a no-show. Put a reminder in your calendar.

- *Prepare.* Bring any helpful materials even if they are not required, such as a copy of the assignment or other information provided by your instructor, and a grading rubric or criteria, if available.

- *Provide some background.* At the meeting, explain what you've been asked to do and what you've done so far on your project. Tell the tutor where you think you need the most advice or what you're most worried about. Be truthful and detailed.

- *Listen carefully.* The tutorial will be more like a conversation than a lecture, but be sure to take some notes.

- *Make a plan.* Before you leave, go back over the key ideas that arose during the session; create a revision plan as soon as possible after the meeting. Remember that *you* are responsible for improving your paper, not your tutor. Unless you act on the results of your conversation, you and your paper won't improve.

GIVE IT A TRY

Visit the website of your campus writing center or tutorial service. Then jot down responses to the following questions: What services does the writing center provide? What are its hours? Who are its tutors? How can you visit? What else does it offer besides tutoring? What are its philosophy and its mission? Where is it located? Are there satellite locations?

Putting It into Practice

This chapter has focused on the processes of drafting and the importance of revision both to produce stronger writing and to become more skilled as a writer. Nothing teaches writing better than good response to work in progress and the hard work of revising. This chapter also has given you multiple strategies to work through your own drafts and revise them, and to use the responses of peers or writing tutors to propel effective revision.

Here are some ways you can put this material to work.

- Try different strategies for drafting, as outlined in this chapter, but most importantly, set a schedule for your work and stick to it.

- Learn to reread your work, preferably out loud. Too often, students finish a draft, breathe a sigh of relief, and submit it for a grade without going back over it multiple times, preferably through the lens of its intended readers.

- Start with meaning. The whole point of writing is to convey information, persuade people of a position, or explore a topic in depth. Remember that *revision* is not *editing* and it's not *proofreading*. These are three different processes that operate on different levels of a text at different times.

- Try your drafts out on as many readers as possible, not just peer groups set up in your class. Use their feedback to *rethink* what you have written.

6

In Search of Research

WHAT'S THE POINT?

After you read, think about, and put this chapter into practice, you will be able to:

- Explain the importance of research in every facet of our lives
- Understand how different disciplines conduct research differently
- Distinguish between primary and secondary research
- Formulate a research question that meets important criteria
- Locate the best sources for your project
- Understand why different disciplines use different documentation styles
- Follow the appropriate conventions for documenting your sources

Research, Research Everywhere

Think about it. Almost everything you've experienced since getting up this morning has involved *research*. If you've used a digital or electrical device of any kind—a microwave, a smartphone, a laptop, an electric toothbrush, a shaver, a toaster, a coffee maker, a TV, a refrigerator, a hair dryer, or a curling iron—scores of people's research created its technology, and scores more figured out how to harness that technology and make it work. Every conduit within a few yards of you—for electricity, natural gas, cable or satellite TV, a landline phone, a WiFi modem—leads back to decades (or centuries) of research. Do you know how those conduits work or how everything that they enable works? Their researchers do.

Look around you. Every physical thing, from chairs to books to windows to carpets to thermal coffee mugs, has involved a long history of research on its design, manufacture, and use. How do you feel? Too much salt yesterday? Or saturated fats? What's that morning coffee doing to you? Medical researchers are studying every facet of the human body and the effects of virtually everything on it. Nutritionists are analyzing the relationship of your health to hundreds of things you consume. People everywhere are engaged in the study of everything you do in your daily life, from inhaling smokeless cigarettes to skipping lunch to working out every afternoon to missing a night's sleep in order to cram for an exam (not recommended!).

Almost everything you've seen, heard, or thought about since getting up this morning is also being researched. What will the weather be like today? Meteorologists are using highly sophisticated equipment—itself the product of research—to tell you. Turn on the news or open a news page on the web: researchers have been conducting polls on political or social issues; environmental experts are talking about inquiries into signs of climate change or the loss (or rebounding) of species; historians are sharing painstaking investigations of a past president's letters; paleontologists are reporting on discoveries of ancient human remains or fossils; astronomers and physicists are using new data to speculate on the origins of the universe; child development experts and sociologists are helping parents to know whether, based on their research, children should be spanked when they behave badly; computer scientists and engineers are developing driverless cars. Look around you at the sky, earth, trees, insects, plants—they all have been the subject of extensive research. Do you hear that jet overhead? Imagine the research that went into *its* creation. Even the material in this text is based on over sixty years of technical research—large amounts of it—into how people write, learn to write, and can best be taught to write. Research is *everywhere*.

Consider this title of an article reporting on recent research conducted by a team of experts:

Evaluation of Extracellular Matrix–Chitosan Composite Films for Wound-healing Application

This article was published in the scientific journal *Materials in Medicine,* a branch of material science. It sounds complicated, right? It is, but it's one step forward in research on how materials of all kinds, such as artificial hips and pacemakers, can be improved for medical applications. In this case, the researchers studied a certain kind of synthetic film that could be used to dress wounds and maintain the right properties of moisture and consistency. In short, *research*.

Here's a title of another article:

The Sociopolitical Lives of Dead Bodies: Tibetan Self-Immolation Protest as Mass Media

Published in the journal *Cultural Anthropology*, this article reports on fieldwork that the author conducted over a six-year period in the Tibetan regions of northwestern China, where a number of Tibetans have taken their own lives, usually by setting fire to themselves, to protest the Chinese government's repression. The author's research led her to insights about the meaning and effectiveness of death and dead bodies in what she calls the "necropolitics" of current Sino-Tibetan relations. In short, *research*.

Now consider the following three titles, the products of careful, guided *research* by undergraduate college students:

Earth Sciences: "Human Impacts on Ecosystems: Comparing the Removal of the Gray Wolf (Canis *lupus*) to the Introduction of Invasive Water Hyacinths (Eichhornia *crassipes*)"

Political Science: "Oh SNAP!: The Real Cost of Cuts to the Supplemental Nutrition Assistance Program (SNAP)"

English: "Ezra Pound, Aura, and the Memory of Time-Past"

Although the students who conducted these research projects may be newer to the process of research, are just entering their fields, and aren't yet (but maybe soon will be!) recognized members of their discipline's community, *they're contributing to its base of knowledge*. In many ways, conducting research is one of the most exciting things you can do academically while you're in college, regardless of whether it's a first-year paper or a major, senior-level capstone project. If you ask a question that you have a passion to answer, in an area that interests you, your research will be meaningful, engaging, and even fun.

Disciplines are defined by the research that their members engage in. Consider the following statements of two organizations that are at the center of their respective fields of knowledge. The first statement is from the Entomological Society of America, which promotes the study of insects.

The Entomological Society of America (ESA) is the largest organization in the world serving the professional and scientific needs of entomologists and individuals in related disciplines. Founded in 1889, ESA has nearly 7,000 members affiliated with educational institutions, health agencies, private industry, and government.

Here's a similar statement from the American Political Science Association:

Founded in 1903, the American Political Science Association is the leading professional organization for the study of political science and serves more than 13,000 members in more than 80 countries.

If you were to read more about these two organizations, you would find that they serve the needs and interests of a wide range of people. The ESA, for example, includes not just insect researchers but also marketing representatives, consultants, students, teachers, and even pest management professionals and insect hobbyists. But at the core of the organization is the scientific *study* of insects: it's what drives the interests of every one of those groups.

When we think of what people in our society "do," research isn't usually the first thing that comes to mind, but research is at the core of virtually every profession, whether the profession produces or consumes it. The owner of a roofing company may spend a lot of time estimating the costs of replacing roofs, managing employees, and overseeing accounts, but large numbers of people are developing better, stronger, longer-lasting shingles and roofing products, lighter and more efficient nail guns, safer and more structurally sound ladders, and more robust computer programs for business management, and all of these significantly affect the roofer's life and business. In short, *research*.

Carrying out research isn't quite the same thing as "writing a research paper." Interviews with teachers reveal a wide range of practices and types of research, calling into question whether there even is such a thing as *the* research paper or if everyone means the same thing by it. You've also seen in previous chapters much of what writing a high-stakes paper involves, so that information won't be repeated here. Chapter 2, for example, discusses at length how to read and understand an assignment, and Chapters 4 and 5 provide strategies for developing, drafting, and revising longer papers. (You may want to review them before starting your research project.)

Even if "the research paper" is a nebulous thing, there's much less uncertainty about the practice of research itself. It's absolutely central in college education. Consider what you find in textbooks on a specific subject like social psychology, music history, or microbiology. The textbooks will only take you so far. They present the main, established, agreed-upon findings of a discipline, but they usually stop before reaching topics at the cutting edge of the discipline. Outside the topics covered in a standard textbook or e-book lies "the beyond," the living, growing field of study, the "unknown" toward which the field is striving. Sooner or later you'll be asked to explore this zone for yourself, to seek beyond the range of textbook and encyclopedia knowledge and examine the state of knowledge that is closer to the leading edge of exploration, where the conclusions are still in doubt and the most informed scholars may still disagree.

This chapter presents general strategies for conducting research and using what you find. To start, you need to develop an interesting, useful, and workable *research question*. That question, depending on your discipline, course, and assignment, may involve conducting your own study or pulling together other people's studies. Before considering what makes a good research question, then, let's take some time to understand the important distinction between *primary* and *secondary* research.

GIVE IT A TRY

Search online for one or two professional organizations in an area of interest to you—ideally your major or intended major. Look around the organization's website, especially the "About Us" link or a link to its mission statement. See what role research plays within the organization. Does it sponsor conferences or meetings at which research is shared? Does it sponsor publications or reports? What role do researchers play in the organization, and how does the organization serve their interests?

Primary and Secondary Research

An important distinction in college-level research projects is captured by the terms *primary research* and *secondary research*. In lower-division college courses, especially in general-education courses, it's common to be assigned secondary research projects. They're called *secondary* because they synthesize the results of other people's work, who did *primary* research, that is, who looked directly at their object of study rather than (only) reading what others said about it. (See Table 6.1.) Let's say you're enrolled in a course, The Psychology of Language, and you discover that over the years, some apes have been trained to communicate with people using signs or plastic symbols. Reading and synthesizing articles about the history of Koko, Washoe, Kanzi, Viki, Nim Chimpsky, and Chantek, all of which are famous primates trained to communicate, is *secondary research*. Raising a chimp, bonobo, gorilla, or orangutan yourself, spending hours a day with it in the lab teaching it to use sign language or manipulate symbols, interacting with it, and observing and analyzing how it communicates, is *primary research*.

> **KEY CONCEPT** *Primary research* refers to original research that you conduct yourself, such as a survey or a set of interviews, a controlled experiment, a search for historical documents surrounding an important event, or observations or measurements of some phenomenon, such as animal behavior or the erosion of a riverbank. *Secondary research* refers to the gathering of what scholars and researchers have done and said about the object under study—what *they* have found in their own primary research. See Key Concept Glossary.

Secondary research is usually conducted entirely with the resources of a good library, whereas the resources required for primary research will vary depending on your field. Obviously, the facilities needed for primary research on language learning in apes are difficult to come by. A few universities maintain such laboratories but not many. And it's hardly the sort of experiment you could conduct in your dorm or apartment, even with the most astonishingly patient of roommates and a college career that would span years. To take another case, imagine what's required for you to identify a new kind of Higgs particle theorized by nuclear

TABLE 6.1 Characteristics of Primary and Secondary Research

Characteristic	Primary Research	Secondary Research
Goal	Contribute a new investigation	Synthesize others' investigations
Place in paper of others' prior research	Usually before the focus on the study itself	Throughout
Role of others' prior research	Preliminary, to establish what's known	Entirely, to know (only) what's known
Your role	Conduct your own inquiry into the object of study	Collect and analyze other people's inquiry into the object of study
Example	Your own study of the effects of loud rock music versus classical music on the growth of house plants	What other people have learned about the effects of loud rock music versus classical music on the growth of house plants
Measure of success	How well have you conducted your own study?	How well have you pulled together other people's studies?

physicists but not yet identified. (Suggestion: if you want to research this, get someone else to pay for it.) Other kinds of research, though, are far more manageable. A sociological study might require that you write up a questionnaire, distribute it, collect it, and tally and interpret the results, all of which is doable within a sixteen-week semester. So is studying positive reinforcement in lab rats for a Psychology course or manipulating the breeding of fruit flies in genetics.

Don't assume, however, that all secondary research involves reading materials that are stored in a library and that all primary research means trekking through the forest, interviewing military veterans, digging up fossils, manipulating chemicals in a lab, studying lunar surfaces, or counting the calories in a school lunch program. Primary research in all fields may involve finding documents—sometimes old ones. A historian may be interested in congressional opinions about the sanctity of life in the period from 1850 to 1900. The "raw data" here will be government documents, contemporary newspapers and magazines, letters, and journals. The procedure that the researcher will use to find and analyze such information and arrive at an answer to the question that the researcher has posed will not differ significantly from the process of secondary research, except that the documents were written for reasons other than scholarship on the same or a related question. Similarly, most of the work you would do to trace the development of a discovery in biology would be archival. So would understanding the influences on the work of a particular artist or musician, or reaching a more accurate and complete picture of a particular battle or political conflict. The difference is whether you're mainly pulling together what's already been studied and then synthesizing it or conducting your own investigations (which are always *informed* by previous research).

The kind of research you do in college is also generally tied to where you are in your curriculum. For obvious reasons, many research-based papers assigned in college, especially in the early years, require secondary rather than primary research because you're finding out what's known about a topic. As you move forward in the curriculum and into your major, you'll probably end up doing more primary research; after all, you're developing the background knowledge and expertise and authority to begin contributing your own insights to the field, even if you're still in the role of learner. But even in some general-education courses, you may be asked to conduct and report on laboratory experiments and direct observations of events rather than to summarize other people's accounts. You may be asked to design, conduct, analyze, and report on an experiment that is tied somehow to the general content of the course. You may be asked to do a survey of public attitudes about a certain product in an Introductory Marketing course. You may take notes on a site visit to a developmental hospital in a course in Human Genetics, or you may find yourself writing research-based papers in a laboratory course in Chemistry, Biology, or Animal Learning. All such assignments require different kinds of research and writing tasks than does secondary research, although the same general principles apply.

GIVE IT A TRY

Using a topic or a question in an area of interest to you, locate two articles: one that represents primary research on the topic or question and one that represents secondary research. How would you describe the difference between the two articles? Try to find the *thesis* of each article and how it represents the author's goals.

Recognizing Traditions and Processes in Primary Research

Before we launch into a discussion of how you can best conduct your own research, it's important to recognize that different disciplines conduct primary research in different ways depending on the kinds of questions they ask and the kinds of phenomena or objects they study. We've seen how widely varied writing can be across different fields of study. The process of research is no different. Becoming an effective researcher requires that you learn what questions to ask and what methods to use to answer them. Consider the following examples of people engaging in research:

- The La Brea Tar Pits in California is an area that was filled with a sticky tar-like substance thousands of years ago, at the end of the Ice Age. Animals fell (or were chased) into the pits and got stuck in the tar—and preserved. In a laboratory, a researcher is meticulously cleaning and reassembling the tiny bones of an ancient field mouse recovered from a chunk of the hardened tar. Researchers at the center—and others—will then study the skeletal remains to keep adding to our knowledge of life on earth between 40,000 and 10,000 years ago.

- A political scientist has learned that middle-class citizens in the U.S. seem to rely on the economic performance of the wealthy to decide how to vote in major elections, even though such indicators may be unhelpful. She hypothesizes that the news media, which polarizes the electorate, is strongly responsible for creating these perceptions. She uses computer analysis to mine extensive corpora of data in order to test her hypothesis.

- An anthropologist is interested in what happens to cultural beliefs, rituals, and processes among Hmong refugees who have come to the United States. (The Hmong are an ethnic people who live in mountainous regions of Thailand, Vietnam, Laos, and China.) The anthropologist spends extensive time doing fieldwork—both in Laos and in Hmong-populated cities in the U.S.—to try to understand cultural adaptation and the effect of migration on existing practices and beliefs. His methods include extensive interviews, observations, and statistics such as census data.

- A relationship between obesity and the tendency to develop various cancers, especially breast cancer, has been well established. A team of cell biologists is trying to figure our what cellular processes account for this relationship. Using mice, they have been comparing various factors such as the growth of tumors, hormone levels, and mammary cell signals in different groups of mice (obese, control-fed, and formerly obese mice). As you can imagine, their methods are conducted under highly clinical conditions in laboratories.

- A writing researcher is interested in the effectiveness of teachers' responses to drafts of college students' papers. He compares responses given in the traditional way (comments written in the margins and at the end) with responses delivered orally using screencasts (brief videos that allow the teacher to scroll through a paper onscreen and talk about it to the student). He uses student and teacher surveys as well as comparisons of the revisions and improvements between students' rough and final drafts after response is given in the different modes.

In all these cases, the researchers are asking very different *questions,* using different *data-collection methods,* and applying different *analytical tools and processes* to investigate different *objects of study* for different *problem-solving purposes.*

In order to begin thinking about your own possible research projects, it helps to ask questions about the research you're already studying across the range of your coursework. Doing so can help you to begin developing appropriate frames for conducting your own primary research or becoming a more careful and informed reader of other's research. Use the following questions to get started:

- What *question(s)* is the research asking? Why is answering the question(s) important or useful? How does answering them advance knowledge?

- What *objects of study* does the research focus on? An ancient manuscript? The opinions of citizens? A living organism? A culture or subculture? A planet, moon, or galaxy? Historical documents about a person or event? A documented trend? The spread of a disease?

- What *method* or *set of methods* does the researcher use to collect information about and/or analyze the objects of study? Do those methods involve the use of statistics? Observations? Interviews? Computer analysis? Close reading? The manipulation or control of some variable(s)?

- Why are these methods most appropriate to answer the questions being asked? Could any other methods also be used? How and why?

- What broader problem(s) could the research help to solve, or how might the research extend what we know about the subject?

GIVE IT A TRY

Find a description of a research study in a particular field or discipline (including any courses you are taking). Answer the questions above to give you a general idea of how the researcher(s) are going about their work.

It All Starts with a Question

The most crucial stage in research—and the one most often botched at the start—is formulating an interesting, precise, workable, and appropriate *question* for research. After all, there are many excellent questions that you can ask but that nevertheless would not lend themselves to research.

- What's the truth about North Korea?
- How do extraterrestrials breed?
- What's two plus two?
- What are the major themes of the lost plays of Sophocles?
- Why is there air?

These are all fair questions about real (or at least possible) entities, but for obvious reasons, as questions for research they would only lead you to despair.

Although few students would tackle any of these rather ridiculous questions, they often try to research problems that are not much more workable. A high percentage of students writing research papers run into trouble by asking a question that's *too broad*, *too vague*, or otherwise *inappropriate*. Fortunately, arriving at an appropriate question for research isn't based on just luck. Mostly, it's knowing what to look for. The criteria for determining the usefulness of a research question are largely a matter of common sense, but it may help you to have them spelled out here before going any further. For a quick overview, see Figure 6.1.

If any of the answers to the questions in Figure 6.1 is "no," then go back to the drawing board. Let's explore the four questions in more detail.

Is Your Question Empirical?

Can your question be settled on the basis of some external, verifiable evidence? Can you answer your question by *looking at something?* No matter what the field of inquiry is and no matter how the empirical

Is your question *empirical*? (Can you actually research it?)	Is your question *interpretive*? (Can you go beyond "just the facts?")	Is your question *reasonable* given your circumstances (time, resources)?	Is your question *interesting* to you?

FIGURE 6.1 A Litmus Test for Research Questions

evidence is defined there, writing a research paper involves an investigation of some sort. The opposite of an empirical question is an "armchair" question—one that can be settled without getting up from your sofa and that you can simply think about in order to answer.

There's nothing inherently wrong with an armchair question. Mathematical questions often take this form, and so do some questions in philosophy. Every empirical question also has several armchair components. Before even starting to search for evidence, you have to decide, for example, what counts as evidence to begin with, where to search for it, and how it might be useful in your research. You'll probably want to work out some of the answers to these questions from the desk in your dorm room or home study.

A research question clearly requires you to *find something out.* If your question doesn't lend itself to such a process and if the whole question can be settled by chewing the intellectual cud, then no matter how excellent a question it might be in other ways, it probably doesn't lend itself to a research project.

Is Your Question Interpretive?

Although your question may be based on collecting and analyzing information, it should also have an interpretive component. It can't be "just the facts." Facts by themselves mean nothing. If someone shows you a table of numbers and says, "Isn't this incredible?," you're more likely to wonder if he's lost his marbles than to gasp in amazement. If you set out to do primary research on public opinions about genetically modified foods, then conduct a survey in various supermarkets, and then just list your raw numbers of the pros and cons, the data alone won't mean all that much; you need to make sense of it all.

Questions of the "true/false" variety or the "name that year" sort don't make especially interesting or compelling topics for research. The question, "When was John Brown born?" is obviously empirical: you can log on to your university's library portal, locate a book about John Brown, and find the answer (or even head to *Wikipedia* if you trust its entry on John Brown), but after doing so, you're still faced with the most critical question ever asked of a researcher: *so what?* On the other hand, you could ask, "How did John Brown reconcile his violent attacks on bigots, some of whom he slaughtered in cold blood, with his compassion for slaves before the Civil War?" Now you have a question that still requires evidence for its answer— in the form of letters, diaries, trial proceedings, newspaper stories, retrospective accounts by friends and acquaintances, and so on—but that also requires careful analysis and interpretation of the evidence, once you've got it. Also, these accounts may not all suggest the same answer to your question, which makes the research process all the more challenging. Your job is not only to dig up information that's relevant to your question but also to make sense of that information.

Does this mean that you're supposed to give your opinion? Well, yes, in a sense, you have to. Your information won't add up to an answer on its own. With any piece of information, you'll have to ask, "What does this tell me about my research question? What does it contribute to an answer?" It's your job to review the cases for the prosecution and defense, consider the testimony of the witnesses, study the evidence of the ballistics and fingerprint experts, and finally determine "who did it." Merely heaping up your evidence and then slipping out of the courtroom won't do the job.

Is Your Question Reasonable?

Although your question may be empirical, it may not be research-able, at least in your lifetime. Much will depend on the amount of time available to you, your background, and your resources. If you're a professional researcher and you're a short car ride from the Library of Congress in Washington, DC, or from the particle acceler-ators at the CERN laboratory in Geneva, Switzerland, you can tackle grander and more specialized questions than if you're a student working under the constraints of a tight deadline and limited library (or laboratory) resources.

This matter of feasibility shouldn't be taken lightly. If you bite off too much, you'll be panicking all the way to an "Incomplete." Here's an example: among some patients who have suffered minor strokes, there's a strange and very rare affliction called "foreign accent syndrome." Soon after their strokes or brain injuries occur, these patients speak their native language with a distinctive and authentic foreign accent. Speakers of English have been known to sound a lot like Polish, French, or German immigrants, even though they have never learned these other languages, have never visited the countries where these other languages are spoken, have no relatives or friends who speak the languages, and so on. The causes of this syndrome remain a mystery.

If you chose for your secondary research the question, "What causes foreign accent syndrome in stroke patients?," you'd be joining many professionals in neuropsychology and psycholinguistics who continue to be puzzled by this affliction. But unless you're a professional in one of these fields, it's unlikely that you could read and understand other people's research well enough to begin answering the question (much less conduct experimental research on the syndrome yourself). So, although such a question is empirical, it's not practical to set out to answer it in the context of a typical college research paper—at least, not until further evidence has accumulated. All you would be able to do is describe the syndrome and detail it with some cases, and then say, "No one really knows why this happens." The first part will be interesting, but the entire paper will be more like a book report than a research project.

The same caution applies as strongly to primary research. Let's imagine that in your Education Theory course you have a burning desire to conduct primary research comparing attitudes toward public K-12 education state by state and to correlate those attitudes with per capita state spending on education. You think an electronically administered survey with twenty-five questions will do the trick. In order to get enough data for it to be meaningful, you decide that you need a random sample of five hundred citizen responses per state. But over the course of a semester, is this reasonable? How will you administer the survey randomly? What distribution method will you use for *fifty* different states? Without money for incentives, how will you get five hundred people (or even fifty people) to take the survey in each state? Even if you get a 20 percent return, what will you do with the five thousand surveys? How will you statistically analyze 125,000 responses to the questions and correlate those responses to the spending data? Where will you get the spending data, and how will you be sure the data is accurate? Clearly, you've bitten off way more than you can chew. Your question isn't really *researchable* given your time and resources.

Is Your Question Interesting to You?

Nothing else is as important as this question. Answering a question that bores you will make uncovering every book and article like digging sewer lines in a cold rain on a Monday morning. Ask yourself, "What draws me, interests me, intrigues me?" When your research is really interesting, you won't even notice the midnight oil running low: you'll be "in the zone." Also, since research projects take a while to accomplish, you'll do yourself a favor by finding a topic you can live with, day in and day out, for a period of weeks or months, without climbing the walls.

GIVE IT A TRY

Using an area you're especially interested in, formulate a question for a *secondary research* project and another question for a *primary research* project. Then, using the questions in Figure 6.1 and the explanation of them, put your questions to the litmus test. How well did they fare? How can you modify them if they fail one or more parts of the test?

Moving from Hunch to Developed Question

When you're assigned a research project in an academic course, especially if you're not yet very familiar with the subject, your research questions won't usually just fall out of the air. They'll be the result of careful thought and reflection. Here are some steps that you can follow to develop as interesting and as appropriate a question as possible, which will meet the four tests described above.

List Major Areas of Interest

Many people's almost automatic response to having to find a research topic, even in a specific domain of knowledge like social psychology, animal behavior, or cell biology, is to go completely blank. If this happens to you, a good first step is just to list all the topics that you can think of—good or bad, dull or clever, interesting or boring, appropriate or off the wall. It doesn't matter. Put them all down. Sometimes ideas that seem silly lead to excellent ideas down the road. Suppose you're in a senior seminar on the History of Science and Technology and you're assigned to research the development of a technology. A beginning list of topics for your paper in the seminar might look like this:

television – telephone – heart monitor – GPS systems – word processing –

microwave – CAT scan – drones – flight simulator – fiber optics –

3D printing – virtual reality – cell phones – QR readers – voice recognition –

voice synthesizer – laser surgery – optical scanner – digital thermometer

There's no telling where this list is going yet. Your final question may develop from any of these general topics, or you may need to make more lists before settling on something that engages your interest. In fact, it's almost guaranteed that more than 90 percent of your list will end up in the "Delete" file. But if it gets you—finally— to a topic that you'd like to pursue, then it's all been worthwhile. (For more on brainstorming, see—or review—Chapter 4.)

Consider the Subfields That Make Up Your General Topic Area

Break up your topic into its major divisions, as if you planned to write an enormous volume on the subject and these were its main chapter titles. Then break those major divisions down further, producing a more complex tree (see pages 124–127), outline (see pages 127–132), or table of contents for the topic. Keep on dividing the topics at each new level.

Early Russian tribes

Russia during the Middle Ages

Russia under Catherine the Great

Nineteenth-Century Czarist Russia

The Revolution

Stalin, Khrushchev, Brezhnev

Gorbachev and the Liberalization

Putin and Ukraine

Each of these topics making up a volume could be subdivided even further. The last chapter of one volume, for instance, might yield:

Gorbachev's Early Struggles

Glasnost

Perestroika

The 1989 Revolutions

USSR and US Relations

Relations with the Third World

Russian Journalism
Putin as ex-KGB member

Of course, each of these potential chapters could be further subdivided. In time you would move from a global topic, such as "Russia," to a much more specialized topic, such as "Putin and Modern Russian Journalism." Or you would move from "Geology" to "Slippage Rates along the San Andreas Fault," or from "National Economics" to "(De)regulation of Banking and the 2008 Collapse," or from "I want to find out about Muslim immigration into Denmark" to "Using English-language e-pal connections between U.S. and Danish college students in four courses, I want to conduct surveys and Skype interviews to find out what prevailing attitudes exist among Danish college students toward Muslim immigration into Denmark."

In James Joyce's *Portrait of the Artist as a Young Man,* Stephen Dedalus wrote the following on the flyleaf of his geography text-book, to identify himself:

Stephen Dedalus

Class of Elements

Clongowes Wood College

Sallins

County Kildare

Ireland

Europe

The World

The Universe

You want to do something similar to this, but in reverse. You're in an Anthropology course, and you've chosen, say, to research something about African tribal communities—great, but don't stop there. So you narrow it down to tribal rituals. Terrific, but don't stop there either. Can you choose a particular tribe? A particular tribal ritual?

Someone makes you aware of an ancient tribal ritual of female circumcision—today, this is usually called female genital mutilation (FGM)—in which parts of girls' genitals are removed because of cultural tradition, with no medical benefit and with serious negative consequences to the girls for the rest of their lives. Where in Africa does this happen?

You decide that the place of greatest interest to you is Swaziland, a country being ripped apart by civil war and suffering from some of the worst health statistics in Africa. OK, good—keep going.

Maybe particular aspects of the ritual could be examined in greater and more precise detail: the history of the practice, the process, the psychological and physical effects, what's being done (if anything) to stop it, local and international attitudes, what anthropological perspective is appropriate (detached but inquisitive? horrified and invested in change?). You could end up with a question such as, "What forces are minimizing attempts to stop female genital mutilation in Swaziland, and what are the best means to eliminate those forces?"

Now you've got something like a focused topic!

Notice that, in settling on a location and question(s) for your project, you'll be shuttling between at least some preliminary investigation and a continued sharpening of what you want to investigate. For any area that's unfamiliar to you, it's impossible to know what you want to find out until you begin to find it out. So, unless you already have a lot of experience in an area, dive off the deep end, swim around, and then crawl up the shallow end with a clear sense of what you want to study.

GIVE IT A TRY

Return to the topic that you chose for the previous Give It a Try. Using the strategies described in this section, work toward a narrower, more focused question. If you're at a loss to do so, try some general searches, and then see if the information you glean would help you to choose a specific area of the topic to research.

Where should you search? Although there's much controversy about using general search engines and resources such as *Wikipedia* or Google, at the very earliest stages there's nothing wrong with checking them out for basic information. Not all of it will be 100 percent accurate, and you'll be sorting through mounds of junk to find really good information, but it's a start. Try Google Scholar, a more academic search engine that mines articles and books for reasonably well-vetted information, but realize that it will also yield some bewilderingly technical material.

Review What You Already Know about Your Topic

While you're doing very preliminary explorations, sketch a summary of your current knowledge. If this strikes you as an impossibly huge task, you're probably dealing with too broad a topic. To answer the question "What do I know about the U.S. involvement in Afghanistan?" would take you pages of scribbling and would be far too broad. The question "What do I know about the social consequences of the Afghanistan war in the United States?" is lukewarm and still shapeless. How about "What do I know about the lives of Afghanistan war veterans in the United States?"? This is better, but if you're in a course focusing on contemporary armed conflicts, you might still find yourself able to fill up several pages on your own. Would either of the following two questions be better? "What do I know about the effects of post-traumatic stress syndrome on veterans of the Afghanistan war?" or even, "What do I know about the effects of post-traumatic stress syndrome on depression, suicide, and drug use among veterans of the Afghanistan war?" Now you're getting somewhere. What *do* you know? Probably, even in a course on Middle East Conflicts, not much. You may have hit pay dirt.

Keep in mind that *too* focused a question or topic is as problematic as one that's too amorphous and vague. A good strategy is always to do a bit of searching around just to see if anyone has asked your question or if key terms in your question show up in productive ways. WARNING! Very often, students will take a minute to search around and conclude that no one, anywhere on earth, has explored the topic, because the first three Google hits didn't unearth a gold mine, so they assume that there's "nothing to find" and they want to give up on the topic. A "bit of searching" doesn't mean spending thirty seconds on Yahoo or Bing; it involves much more extensive sleuthing, using a lot of different key terms and phrases on a number of different search engines (especially ones at your library's online portal).

Here's an example. Adam wanted to find out more about a vision problem called *macular degeneration* because his grandfather was experiencing symptoms. When he typed "macular degeneration" into Google, it yielded 5,800,000 results. He realized that he'd chosen a huge topic! The first twenty-five sites were a mishmash of online medical centers, some commercial clinics, and general definitions—not very useful for a serious research project. When he tried using Google Scholar, the results seemed, well, a lot more scholarly. *Too* scholarly. Most of the links were complicated-sounding research articles published in medical journals, but their titles were all over the place:

An International Classification and Grading System for Age-related Maculopathy and Age-related Macular Degeneration

Complement Factor H Polymorphism in Age-related Macular Degeneration

Optical Coherence Tomography Findings after an Intravitreal Injection of Bevacizumab (Avastin) for Neovascular Age-related Macular Degeneration

Wary of wasting time trying to read completely baffling material, Adam decided to find some general but authoritative materials on macular degeneration. After doing a search for "medical information—vision" and scrolling through many links, he located one link sponsored by the National Institute for Health (a government agency) called Medline Plus. Trusting this site more than the commercial ones, he easily found a page titled "Eye Diseases" that listed seven common eye problems, including macular degeneration. The link to macular degeneration then offered a wealth of further general information, including diagnosis, prevention and screening, and treatment. After learning that, although vision loss from macular degeneration can be slowed, it can't be stopped, Adam decided that he wanted to research the most cutting-edge therapies. That took him to the National Eye Institute and more information.

Notice in this example that Adam had to move *around* in his searches, making judgments about the nature and quality of his preliminary sources, going up and down levels of sophistication, and not just grabbing the first pieces of information that appeared on his screen. This process of *critical source work* can save you

> **KEY CONCEPT** *Critical source work* refers to a process of analyzing the nature, quality, contents, and genres of sources during your search process, before you actually obtain the sources. See Key Concept Glossary.

large amounts of time because it allows you to judge what you're looking for *as* you're looking for it rather than trying to read the material first and then finding that it won't work for you. At this point, however, Adam's source work was geared toward refining his focus and finding a good question, not toward digging into the topic.

Transform Your Suitably Focused Topic into a Live, Interesting Question

A topic by itself is a dead, inert, stiff sort of thing, for example, "Putin and Modern Russian Journalism." There it lies. Well, what about it? What is it you want to know?

You might start by asking yourself the "so what" question. What is it about your topic that interests you? Who's affected by it? Why are you interested in Putin and modern Russian journalism? Does the topic primarily interest you as a chapter in the history of journalism, in the history of Russia, or in the career of Vladimir Putin? Or does some theoretically interesting point about communication theory or international politics hang on the answer? What makes your topic more attractive than the others that you might have chosen?

A vague enthusiasm won't help you here. You need to articulate your answer on paper. Don't trust yourself to just have a sense of why your topic is interesting. Write it out. Answering the "so what" question gains you two things. It will help focus your efforts later when you're actually doing your research, and the words you write in your project file now may very well find their way into your introduction when you create your draft. By *introducing* the topic to yourself, you'll find it easier to introduce it to someone else later.

If you really don't know how to answer the "so what" question, then the strategy Adam used may be your best option. Some preliminary searching opens up plentiful information on laws passed under Putin's presidential terms that have censored the press. That leads to some information about how reporters *self-censor* out of fear. That leads to information about stricter cyber laws that block web content that presents "extremists views" the government doesn't like.

Once you know what interests you about your topic, go on to specify your exact research question. If you think a bit, you can cook up several quite different questions about the Russian journalism topic. Following are some examples:

- How has government censorship affected Russian newspapers with the largest circulations?
- How has control of the press affected the Russian people's access to information, especially online?
- How did Russia's control of the press affect reporting of the Olympic Games in 2014?
- How does the Russian government's regulation of the press relate to the enforcement of social and political control over its citizens concerning gay rights?

These are all questions that you can derive from the topic "Putin and Modern Russian Journalism," but each requires you to find different sources of information and interpret and present your material in different ways. Your research will be much more efficient if you know which question you're actually out to answer. As you begin your research, you may find yourself refining and narrowing your focus even more.

Develop a List of Subsidiary Questions

Whatever your main research question is, the answer to it will probably not be a simple "yes" or "no" or a single name (e.g., Guy de Maupassant) or a single figure (e.g., 47 percent). If it's the sort of thing that requires a written report, it will actually be a composite answer to a number of smaller questions. Once you've formulated your main question, you should spend some time brainstorming in order to come up with as many subsidiary questions as you can.

Let's say you're involved in a group project in your Business course, and you've been assigned to assess the feasibility of implementing flexible work scheduling at a fictitious stereo components assembly plant, including the option of a four-day work week with ten hours per day. After formulating your question and writing some notes about its importance, you might continue by asking yourself, and writing in your research log, questions like the following:

- What exactly is a flexible work week? How does it compare with other scheduling options (like permanent part-time)?
- How has it been implemented at some companies?
- How has it affected productivity at places where it has been used?
- What schedules prove most popular with employees?
- What administrative problems does it cause?
- How do employees on flexible work weeks perform in comparison with employees who work a regular work week?
- How would the plant's manager have to adapt the equipment and procedures to handle differing numbers of workers at different hours?
- What is the feeling about flexible work weeks among the plant's workers?

All of this early work on a research problem is strenuous but probably one of the most interesting and useful parts of the process. It may feel easier to log into your library's website and randomly "look stuff up," but in the long run, the suggested approach not only produces a more focused, intelligent paper but also is more efficient. Any effort put in at this point will save you a lot of time later on. This again is the armchair component of your empirical research project. This is where you study the travel guides, pore over the maps, and plan and revise your itinerary. Only then will you pack your bags and head off for the mountains.

GIVE IT A TRY

Return again to the idea you explored in the previous Give It a Try. Applying the further strategies in this section, refine your question even further—to the point where you can begin researching in earnest.

Developing a Search Strategy

Around three hundred years ago, Sir Isaac Newton formulated the principles of gravitational attraction that accounted for the movements of the planets. For this he was widely celebrated. But his own account of his work is telling. "If I have seen further than other men," Newton said, "it is because I have stood on the shoulders of giants." Research means standing on other people's shoulders (whether they're giants or not). It means making the most effective use of the experiences of others to answer a question of your own, whether all you're doing is pulling together what those people have found or adding to it with your own investigations.

Research doesn't mean copying or imitating others. It means formulating a question, deciding what information would be needed to answer it, finding out if anyone has that information, and then assessing long and hard exactly what the information you find actually tells you about the question. Even if you're conducting primary research, your question needs to be informed by what others have learned. As you locate those sources, you need to read, assess, and take away from them their essential ideas and information. You have to *synthesize* what it all adds up to, what it means for your question (see Chapter 3 on synthesis). Finally, you need to present for your readers your best-considered judgment on your original question in the light of what you've learned. You argue your case, calling the most useful witnesses in the most effective way. These represent the basic steps of research, no matter what the field of study or the type of paper you're writing, and

| Know Your Resources, Search Tools, and Keywords | → | Organize, Tag, and Index | → | Create a Working Bibliography |

FIGURE 6.2 A Process for Creating a Search Strategy

they can all be done more efficiently with a little thought and a few suggestions.

As we've seen, developing an interesting, focused research question may well involve doing some preliminary exploration and searches. But when you finally have your question, you don't simply dive back into the literature and start thrashing around; it would take you too much time to gather anything, and it still wouldn't really be what you were after. Yet many students behave in exactly this way. Instead, you want to apply a very sensible *search strategy* to find the most useful sources of information for precisely the question you're trying to answer. Figure 6.2 shows you the steps in creating such a search strategy, each step of which we'll explore in detail.

> **KEY CONCEPT** A *search strategy* refers to a detailed plan for locating the best and most relevant sources for a research project, whether it involves primary or secondary research. See Key Concept Glossary.

Know Your Resources, Search Tools, and Keywords

Researchers in every discipline use specialized resources to find material that is relevant to their ongoing scholarship. People working in language and linguistics, for example, most often will use such search engines as Linguistics and Language Behavior Abstracts (LLBA) online, WebCorp, the Linguistics subsection of Open Access Journals Search Engine (OAJSE), and so forth.

This text is designed too compactly to provide you with even a few lists of resources in specific disciplinary areas. The best advice is to create your own, ongoing list of links to sites, both general and specific, that relate to your area of research. You can do this temporarily if you're in a course that's not part of your major, or you can begin a long-term list that will serve you for years of further work. Many library websites now have ways to personalize your own web page and populate it with all the resources that are most useful to you. If that's not available to you, create your own list of links on your computer. If you're not sure which reference materials are best, try looking at such resources as the Cumulative Index of Bibliographies, the International Bibliography of the Social Sciences, and the like. Your instructor and/or a reference librarian can point you in the right direction.

The same applies to the *keywords* you'll use to conduct your searches. Keywords will obviously pop up based on your research question, but it's also helpful to (1) be specific when using keywords and (2) when possible, match the terms you use to the knowledge base of the discipline. There's no point in using the word *memory* if you're researching "amnesia" or *amnesia* if you're researching "Alzheimer's Disease" or "dementia." You might stumble on the specific area when using a general term, but it will take longer to find what you need and will drown you in other material that you don't want. Furthermore, your paper will usually have a complex thesis or question (see Chapter 4), and that sentence or paragraph will almost generate the keywords for you.

> **KEY CONCEPT** A *keyword* is a common term used when searching for resources (books, articles, reports, etc.) relating to a specific topic. Such resources are often indexed with keywords, so when you use the correct keyword, those resources will become readily available to you. See Key Concept Glossary.

A good search engine will be very powerful, sifting through millions of documents and sources to find those most relevant to your key terms. If the search engine has Boolean capabilities, then you can enter two or three (or more) terms and it will delimit its search, narrowing it to those materials that relate only to all the terms, as illustrated in Figure 6.3. In that figure, the very center of the Venn diagram represents the materials that the search engine will find in which "Putin," "Russia," "press," and "censorship" appear. If you use too many terms or they're too specific, back up a bit and see what emerges. There are highly specific ways to enter your keywords in such searches, so be sure to follow the instructions at the specific tool you're using or consult a reference librarian.

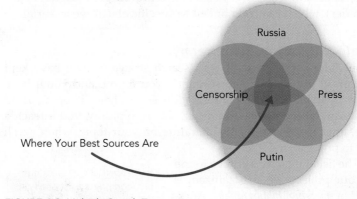

FIGURE 6.3 Multiple Search Terms

Organize, Tag, and Index

If you know you want to use a source, the most dangerous thing you can do is forget where you found it and how to retrieve it. Because you'll be creating a works cited or reference list, it pays off to write down all the bibliographic information you'll need, and it's best to use the reference style required in the paper, such as that of the American Psychological Association (APA) or the Modern Language Association (MLA). This information will include the author, title, publication, date, page numbers, edition, and so on. In the old days, researchers would keep track of their sources on index cards or in handwritten notebooks (some still do this). However, new technologies now give us a wide variety of tools to organize information and resources. One popular application, for example, is Diigo. Once you've added Diigo to your web browser, you can save specific URLs in an instant instead of cutting and pasting them or writing them down. The URLs can be categorized based on tags (such as "Russia," "the press," or "censorship"). Diigo even suggests tags for you. Later, you can search for everything saved under one of those tags, and it will retrieve it. Remember, though, that tagging a document that's inside a password-protected site may just take you to the log-in page, not the actual document. It helps also to record the DOI (digital object identifier), which is a code linked to specific electronic material.

Create a Working Bibliography

If you did a good job with your search strategy, you'll have kept track of all the sources and resources you found, and you'll have stored their bibliographic information somewhere. Keeping it all in the same place is easier said than done. Typically, you'll reach a stage, after really mining the literature on your topic, when you'll need to pull it all together.

The list of materials you've found for your project, when organized, is called a *working bibliography*. Working bibliographies aren't final; rather, they're designed to help you visualize all your sources by displaying them in the same place. They'll include printed books, articles, and electronic or online work. In primary research, they might include sources such as interviews.

> **KEY CONCEPT** A *working bibliography* is a list of all the sources to be used in a research project. It can be organized alphabetically, categorically, or by the sections of a paper. It may not represent the final bibliography because some works may be deleted or added. See Key Concept Glossary.

One excellent strategy to use when you're creating a working bibliography is to annotate each entry to indicate not only how or whether it's useful for the project as a whole, but also how it might be used and where. These are *your* annotations—reminders to yourself as you assemble your text. It's very easy to make a file copy of the bibliography later and then just delete all the annotations, leaving you with a list of references to insert into your paper.

Some instructors may require that you create an *annotated bibliography* that's separate from your research project (and often due first). If so, the next section on how to read your sources successfully will be of great help, because you need to summarize each source in a few pithy lines but still capture the gist of the source.

> **KEY CONCEPT** An *annotated bibliography* is a bibliography in which each entry includes not only the reference to a work but also a description of and/or commentary on that work, like a miniabstract. See Key Concept Glossary.

Reading, Rereading, Reflecting, and Analyzing

Every source, no matter what its medium, has the potential to be either a gold mine or quicksand. The greatest danger in conducting research is being sucked under by everything you read and being dragged down slowly, agonizingly, paragraph by paragraph, into articles that, however little they contribute to your work, you somehow can't get out of. Since it becomes such a tedious, grinding effort to read every article, you'll naturally try to get by with reading as few articles as possible. The result will be that you won't cover all the ground you need to, leaving broad aspects of your question insufficiently researched.

The other danger comes from thinking that there's too much ground to cover, so you skip over everything as quickly as possible. Studies of college students' research process show that a large number of students simply skim the first two pages of each source they find and pull out a quotation, without knowing what the entire source really says! On the other hand, maybe the articles that you *do* read fully don't yield all that they could. Sure, you read every word in them and maybe even filled a page with quotations and numbers, but still somehow your memory of the articles afterward is foggy, muddy, and clogged. This is an unpleasant way to work, and it produces feeble results.

Such problems come from an overly vague or formless plan of research. If you don't have an idea of what you're looking for, you can't ignore or reject anything. This is why narrowing your topic and formulating a precise research question is so important. The more precise your idea of what you're looking for, the more articles you can actually *avoid* reading, and the ones you do read will be more directly relevant to your topic.

Knowing what you're looking for serves a similar purpose for each source you consult or information you collect. Your task is to extract from your source the information you need quickly and efficiently. But what about the person who asks, "But isn't there something to be said for just browsing around?" Yes, there is: plenty of time, freedom in the domain of your research, and a strong sense that you'll stumble onto something really interesting—all of these do support a more exploratory approach. But let's face it: normally you're under pressure, the term is marching along, and the deadline for the project is looming ominously in your already full calendar. Surfing around online may be relaxing, but it won't get your paper started.

So what's the most effective process for reading the materials that you collect? Here are some highly useful strategies.

Search for the Gist

First, try to come to an overall understanding of what you're reading. You might start by reading just the beginning and ending of the article and noticing whatever subtitles it may have in between. That should give you a good idea of where the article is going, its main point, and how it goes about defending or illuminating that point. You should formulate some hypothesis about the article's major directions before trying to plough through it. At least try to see the forest before wandering around among the trees.

Read the article quickly, from beginning to end, and try not to take any notes. The minute you start writing down interesting statements or paraphrasing ideas, you stand in danger of bogging down in irrelevant detail. Move through the article easily and quickly in order to grasp its main outlines in its entirety.

Write a Summary

Once you've read the article through, try to write an abstract or summary of it in your notes. Holding the entire article poised in your mind, how would you state in a few pithy sentences what the writer was saying? If you're not sure you can do this yet, glance back over the article. Reread the opening and closing sections. The author may have stated her thesis quite directly and simply somewhere. Which one sentence best captures the gist of the piece? (See pages 214–215 for more detailed directions on how you might set about doing this.)

Bullet the Main Ideas

When you've defined what the author is saying, sketch in the major supporting points and arguments. Try to get down how she attempted to prove her point or how she illustrated it. Did the author rely on experimental procedures, anecdotal evidence, chains of logical deduction, or some combination of these? At this point, you're still examining the article from the author's perspective rather than from the perspective of your own question. What did the author claim, and how did she support it?

Come Back to Your Project

Now that you've sketched in the thesis and method of the work, you can start thinking again of what in it might be relevant to your own topic. Without looking back, what do you remember that struck you as useful in trying to settle the question you've framed? Is the author's main point itself relevant to your concerns, or is one of the chains of reasoning relevant? Were there anecdotes or statistics that the author used for her purpose but for which you would prefer to turn to another source for anecdotes or statistics?

Focus on Your Question Again

Now think again of what it is you're trying to answer: your own question, not the author's. What material in the article is useful to you? Find it, reread it, and then get the pertinent parts down in your notes. Your notes may consist of straight summaries and paraphrases of ideas from the article. Or you may want to get down the precise words that the author used. If you do decide to quote directly, you need to transcribe the passage exactly and flawlessly, down to the placement of commas and periods; or, better still, find the relevant pages and cut and paste the material into your text—*being sure to differentiate it from your own* (a subject we'll come back to shortly).

If you're conducting primary research, take some time every so often to reflect on the significance of what you've observed. What's happening? What do your early findings suggest? What other questions do they raise? What other experiments or field observations would you want to carry out if you could? In retrospect, what flaws might exist in the design of the research? What are the implications of your findings for other questions—maybe even for other fields of study?

After you've finished collecting your data and before you sit down to draft your report, try to state for yourself what the findings mean, what answer they give to your original question, and maybe what they suggest for future research. That is, take a little time to think about what you've done and the meaning of what has happened as a result. Don't immediately dive into technical descriptions of your method and results. Think about the question you defined (so very carefully) earlier in your work, and consider exactly what your results tell you about it. Was your experiment or observational study, after all, the best way to address the problem? Did it give you a definitive answer? Did it leave parts of your original question unanswered or only ambiguously answered? Where might you go from here, or where might another researcher go from here, given the results of your current research?

By now you should have the following material saved on your computer:

1. The precise bibliographical reference of the material.

2. An abstract or summary of the material.

3. An outline of the major arguments or pieces of evidence that the author presents to prove or illustrate her point.

4. Paraphrases, summaries, transcriptions, or highlighted photocopies of the passages in the article that are most useful in answering your specific research question.

Now Stand Back

You have what you came for. You've found the most relevant articles, and you've preserved in your notes the most useful material in them for answering your own research question. Now you want to spend some time thinking aloud about what the information actually means. Try to answer in your notes some of the following questions:

- Why is this material important? How does it affect my understanding of the issue I'm examining? Does it support a hypothesis of mine concerning my question? Does it challenge my understanding and force me to rethink my position?

- What's surprising about this material? Is the article itself internally consistent, or does the author contradict herself in different parts of it?

- How does this material fit with other things that I've read? Does it reinforce earlier sources? Does it correct earlier sources in some detail or point of reasoning? Does it refute outright points made in other readings?

- If the material I've read does conflict with other sources, is the conflict apparent or real? Can both positions possibly be true, or is one of my sources necessarily wrong? If only one source can be correct, which one is correct? What makes me say that?

The art of research is emphatically *not* to march ahead with a preconceived opinion about something, find some sources that support your position and cite those as experts, and find others that refute your position and debunk those. All that does is to entrench you in your original position, perhaps making you more articulate in your prejudice but making you no less prejudiced. Research should be the active attempt to build on the work of other thinkers, observers, and writers in order to understand something *better*—and that means *differently*—than you did before. That's why this reflective phase of the research process is so vitally important. You get nowhere just collecting facts. You need to think long and hard about what the facts mean. This is where you make your most distinctive contribution, in reassessing what others have learned and thought. This is where you go beyond bagging intellectual groceries to making genuine culinary art.

Though this may slow down the research part of your job, you'll get the practical payoff when it's time to draft. You won't find yourself sitting with a stack of photocopied articles and notes or dozens of saved PDF files on your computer, wondering where to begin to make sense of it all. You'll arrive at the drafting stage of your work with a well-developed sense of what you now know. In fact, you'll probably find many passages already written in your notes that you can clean up a little and incorporate into your draft. For the rest, even the sections that you have to draft fresh will come to you more easily because you gave your material such long and careful consideration. There won't be the slightest danger of turning in a "string-of-sources" paper. The paper will be yours, not theirs. It will belong to and represent you, not your sources.

GIVE IT A TRY

For a source that you've found as part of a research project—or that you can find easily on a topic of your interest—follow the strategies described in this section in order to read the source carefully and insightfully. Try to write an annotation of the source that will help you to recognize its content when you're working on a large research project.

Writing the Research-Based Paper

The process of drafting, revising, and editing a paper based on outside sources is not in itself much different from that of any other kind of writing. All that's contained in Chapters 4 and 5 applies here as well. (If you haven't read Chapters 4 and 5 yet, you should. They're very wise.)

One other piece of general advice: before starting on your draft, put all of your files away for at least a day, and then, without looking at them, write a sketch of your paper. After spending days or weeks doing your research, you have filled your mind with so many specific pieces of information you've found that you may have lost the overall sense of what your paper is about. You need to step away from your sources, clear your mind, review your original question, and then try to summarize for yourself, in no more than a page, what you now believe is the answer to your question. Once you've written such a "pre-abstract" of your paper, you can develop your blueprint—maybe a tree or an outline—from that and then return to your sources to see where and how you'll incorporate them into your paper.

Let's turn now to putting the paper together.

Audience ... Again

How you present what you know will depend heavily on who you're writing for (see Chapter 4). In professional settings, this issue is usually settled from the start by the actual situation you're working in. You know who your primary audience is, who else might see your report, and so on. In popular and scholarly writing, the audience is determined by your choice of the publication to which

you will submit your paper. You'll write up your research on genetics and unipolar depression differently for professional readers of
the *Journal of Consulting and Clinical Psychology* than you will for the
drugstore magazine rack browsers of *Psychology Today*.

In the classroom, an instructor will sometimes designate a reading audience for you, as demonstrated in Chapters 3 and 4: "Write
up your findings on automobile emissions testing as a report, with
recommendations to the state legislature." But more often, the audience isn't specified in advance. In that case, you should fall back on
what we call the "default audience." If you don't know who else to
write to, write for yourself as you were before starting the research.
What did you already know about the topic? What preconceived
ideas did you have? Attribute such knowledge and preconceptions
to your readers as you write.

Using Sources in Your Paper
Many writers have trouble knowing when to include an outside
source, whether to summarize or quote it directly, how to format it
on the page, and when and how to credit it with a footnote, endnote, or parenthetical reference. Some writers are so overawed by
the problem that they dodge it completely; you'd never know from
their papers that they'd even done any outside reading if they hadn't
included a bibliography.

Other writers defer to their sources continually. Such a writer
may be reading and thinking about a particular issue for the first
time. The writer feels like a rank amateur, a total novice, the new kid
on the block. Then he starts reading the words of people who have
been working on the problem for years and are highly qualified to
discuss it. Faced with all of this, the writer panics, doesn't dare offer
his own opinion, and simply transcribes quotations of everything
that he has collected, glued together with a thin tissue of connecting
prose. (Teachers sometimes call this *patchwriting*.) Instead of standing on other people's shoulders, he's hiding between their legs. The
anxiety is understandable, but all it produces is a "string-of-sources"
paper. Long reflection, a careful comparison of different sources, and
a certain boldness will produce better work—and it will at least give
evidence of more active thought.

Remember this from our earlier discussion: *your paper should represent your own best considered judgment on your research question in the light of what you've learned.* The paper has your name on it, represents your opinion, and should headline your vision of the problem from start to finish. *You* lead in the paper and draw the outside sources in with you whenever you need them.

How and When to Include Outside Sources

If you've done your homework, you're going to know far more than you can explain and substantiate in the space available to you—in either primary or secondary research. So you need to be efficient. Your first duty is to get across to your readers, as clearly as possible, your final, informed understanding of the issue. Your second duty is to present the most compelling evidence for your position that you can. This second duty will require you to include passages from your source material and, in primary research, your data and its analysis, to prove or illustrate your point.

Your own writing must play the leading role in your paper. Your readers aren't primarily interested in your sources. If they were, they'd be reading your sources' work instead of yours. Readers want to hear from *you.* You raised the question in your introduction and persuaded them of its importance. Now your readers want to hear *you* tell them the answer. Whenever you can present something as well by yourself as you can by referring to an outsider, go ahead and do it yourself.

Have a positive reason for including every source in your paper. Don't add sources simply because you feel a need to "put in some quotes." There's obviously nothing wrong with including sources, but since they require space for their presentation, you should make sure they're carrying their weight. This will help you avoid the pastiche: a patchwork quilt of nothing but the words of other people.

Purposes of Outside Sources

Every source you refer to should have a legitimate reason for being cited. One of the most common mistakes in writing research papers is dropping in references just to show off to a teacher, to prove that you've been "researching." Unless it has a distinct purpose that is recognizable in the flow of your text, a reference is only so much baggage (and announces itself as such). Table 6.2 shows some of the various purposes that sources can serve in your writing.

TABLE 6.2 Some Uses of Outside Sources

Purpose of Source	Description
Authority	An outside source can speak with an authority that is greater than your own on some aspects of your paper. Such an "expert witness" might simply supply a piece of the puzzle; for example, it's up to you to decide how we should reduce the national debt, but a Washington economist might at least be able to provide authoritative numbers on what the debt is. At other times, the witness might be directly defending the same point you're making but from a position of greater expertise. If your readers won't believe you on the advisability of arms reductions, perhaps they will believe a senator, a general, or a secretary of state. Just be careful in this case that you don't let an outside source do all your talking for you.
Illustrating the problem	Some sources do nicely as examples of the very problem you're discussing. Popular magazines can provide a single anecdote to capture the human interest of a broad class of problems. Hearing about the trials of one farm family can convince readers of the importance of otherwise seemingly abstract questions concerning agricultural policies.
Reflecting public or scholarly consensus	You might present an assortment of outside sources to reflect the range of views on some issue. You might cite a statement by one senator arguing that the family farm is economically outmoded and should be allowed to die out. Back to back with that, you might cite a second senator who strongly defends government intervention to keep family farms alive. This helps define the problem that you're addressing and suggests the variety of viewpoints that are available. If you choose to hold off providing your own opinion until the end of your paper, such an opening creates a sort of narrative tension that should keep your readers' attention to the end.

(continued)

(continued)

Purpose of Source	Description
Sparring partners	You might also cite an outside source as a "sparring partner," that is, someone to argue with. The full significance of your opinion might not be clear to your readers until they see a vigorous, articulate statement of an opposing view. Such opposition clarifies and sharpens your own opinion. You want to be careful, though, not just to set opposing arguments against one another, as if your paper was a boxing match and you were sitting outside the ring, calmly watching (with no opinion whatever) as your sources bloodied each other's noses. The early stages of drafting often lead to such a structure, but making up your own mind about the validity of the various points is essential for the conclusion of your research. Saying "there are a lot of opinions about this matter" doesn't help your readers a bit. There are a lot of opinions about most matters.

Summary, Paraphrase, and Quotation

Your options for how to include the testimony of your various witnesses are summary, paraphrase, or quotation. Again, the economy principle applies. Present whatever you need to from your source, but do so in the least possible space. Because *how* to use these three methods of incorporating others' voices into a research project gives so many students trouble, it's worth taking some time to explain just how they work.

SUMMARY. The most condensed form of incorporating outside material is *summary*. Before you can write a summary, you obviously need to know the source itself thoroughly, or you risk misrepresenting it. If all you need is the gist of some idea, boil it down into your own words—as few as will do the job—and present that. Your main concern is accuracy. You want to present the idea, argument,

> **KEY CONCEPT** In the context of source work, a *summary* is a piece of text that condenses key information from a source—or sometimes the entire source—in the writer's own words, without replicating parts of the original text. See Key Concept Glossary.

or story in its most condensed, crystalline form without distorting or misrepresenting it, which is harder than it sounds. Since summarizing is the most space-efficient means of presenting outside material, you should consider it first. If you need more than just the essence of the idea, argument, or story, you'll need to move on to paraphrase or quotation.

PARAPHRASE. A *paraphrase* is a thorough, detailed restatement of someone else's text or ideas. It's one way you can maintain a consistent style within your own text, clarify something that may be confusing or difficult to understand in the original, or slightly condense a longer passage. In comparison to summary, there's a closer relationship between the amount of text in the original and in the paraphrase. For example, for a paper in political science, you may need to paraphrase the main contents of a recent senate resolution, in order to bring it from legalese into plain, accessible English.

> **KEY CONCEPT** In the context of source work, a *paraphrase* is a restatement of an idea from a piece of text in new words (not those of the original). It is sometimes used to "translate" a difficult text into an easier one or to clarify some aspects of the original. See Key Concept Glossary.

You might also be using something written in one context to illuminate your ideas in another. You might paraphrase the accounts of certain geological studies for a feasibility report on the location of a new office building. Here again, in effect, you would be translating the writings of geologists for business executives who are interested in a purely practical question. In both cases, you're presenting the structure and content of other people's ideas without breaking the texture or continuity of your own prose. You're using their ideas, but the words are yours.

The greatest danger in paraphrase lies in that last sentence—in keeping the language of the original source from seeping into your text. If you want to use the language of the original source, that's fine, but be sure to mark it as a quotation and to not pass it off as a paraphrase. To do so can sometimes lead to a charge of plagiarism. In fact, when you're actually writing a paraphrase, it's best to keep the original out of sight until you're done. The language of a paraphrase has to be entirely your own, consistent with the language of the rest of your paper, and not colored by the words of the source itself.

QUOTATION. If you find that the language of the original does tempt you, you probably should consider the third way of incorporating outside material—by direct *quotation*. You rely on direct quotation when the language of the original offers something that you can't replace in a summary or a paraphrase, and the words have a special value above and beyond simply the information they carry.

> **KEY CONCEPT** In the context of source work, a *quotation* is the exact copying of a piece of text from a source into your own paper, with an acknowledgement of where the piece of text came from. Quotation is often used because the language of the original is important for readers to see in its exact form. See Key Concept Glossary.

The expression in a piece of text may be so unusually *colorful, pithy, or precise* that no paraphrase could improve on it. Or the words may give your readers a feel for the personality and mind of your source that you couldn't capture any other way. Consider the following statement from *Plain Speaking* by President Harry Truman:

> I fired General MacArthur because he wouldn't respect the authority of the President. I didn't fire him because he was a dumb son of a bitch, although he was, but that's not against the law for generals....

It's hard to imagine how anyone could paraphrase a volley of words like that and not kill it: "Truman stated that it was not General MacArthur's lack of intelligence that provoked the dismissal, such a lack not traditionally constituting grounds for dismissive action, but ... ." As President Truman's statement stands, it's terse, provocative, funny, and has the fingerprints of that tough, no-nonsense Missourian all over it.

You'll probably also want to rely more on direct quotation when your source is someone already of interest to your readers rather than someone they've never heard of. You paraphrase anonymous experts; you quote celebrities, of whatever stripe. You paraphrase articles in physics journals; you quote Stephen Hawking. You paraphrase articles from *Foreign Affairs*; you quote ex-presidents. You paraphrase a commentary on Milton's famous poem, "On his blindness"; you quote the poem itself. The direct quotation puts your reader in more immediate contact with your source so that the warmth and color of the original personality comes through. If readers enjoy the closer contact, they won't thank you for standing in the way with a paraphrase when you can throw the door wide open and invite the person into your text with a quotation.

You should also quote when you need to establish with unusual care a point made by your source. For example, if you plan to argue against something that one of your sources said, you should quote the statement exactly. If you paraphrase the idea, your readers will suspect you of distorting the opponent's words to make an easier target. To play fair in such a situation, reproduce the source's words, letting the source speak for himself or herself, and then go on with your critique.

The same thing applies if you're relying heavily on the support for your position given by somebody else. If your case depends on the statement of a particular witness, you'd better give the witness's words verbatim. Here again, your readers may not entirely trust the accuracy of a paraphrase.

How much should you quote? The minimum that will do the job. Pull out the words you need and use them as precisely as possible and no more. In presenting the statement from President Truman, you might blend paraphrase and quotation in this way:

> Truman claims to have dismissed General MacArthur not for being "a dumb son of a bitch" but because "he wouldn't respect the authority of the President."

This preserves the fabric of your prose, saves a little space, and still captures the saltiness of the original.

Disciplines vary a little in the ways they use these three options to bring in outside source material. In the humanities, expression is often as important as the ideas being expressed. In the sciences and social sciences, ideas and concepts are not usually rendered in especially unique, stylized, or complex ways, so direct quotation takes a back seat to paraphrase and summary. Take a look at this excerpt from an article in the social science section of the *Journal of Gerontology*:

> Support for frail older persons living in the community is generally provided by family and friends, with supplementary support from formal helpers (Horowitz, 1985; Stone, Cafferata, and Sangl, 1987).

This pattern is typical for all ethnic groups, although the composition of the support network may vary by race and ethnicity (Cantor, 1979; Mindel, Wright, and Starret, 1986; Taylor, 1985, 1986; White-Means and Thornton, 1990).

In this excerpt, which is typical of work in the social sciences, the authors summarize broad statements with references to entire works; the works—their overall conclusions—and not the specific words, are what's important.

In contrast, here's an excerpt from an article about a Victorian novel, *Moonstone,* from the journal *Victorian Literature and Culture*:

Disability, then, is located and defined by scholars as something "constructed on top of impairment" (Corker 3); disability is "not so much the lack of a sense or the presence of a physical or mental impairment as it is the reception and construction of that difference" (David, *Bending* 50); disability is "a linchpin in a complex web of social ideals, institutional structures, and government policies" (Linton 10). In turn, the current or "New Disability Studies" is a system for interpreting and disciplining bodily variations" and the "relationship between bodies and their environments," an analysis of the "set of practices that produce both the able-bodies and the disabled," and, ultimately, "a radical critique" of the "set of practices that produce both the able-bodied and the disabled" (Garland-Thompson, "Making Freaks" 132).

Here, the author wants to be sure that the ways that other scholars have analyzed contemporary definitions of disability are rendered in their exact words, not as paraphrases or summaries.

GIVE IT A TRY

Find two articles in different fields of study, such as the history and biology or sociology and literature. Study the way that the articles use outside material. Do they mainly summarize, paraphrase, or quote directly? What can you say about their practices relative to the content they're working with and the disciplines they come out of?

A Few Matters of Form

In the world of research, words are often viewed as property. This is because they bring credit and credibility to those who wrote them (and the ideas they represent). In some cultures, borrowing someone else's words, whether the source is cited or not, is a way of honoring that person. In cultures where cooperation and the equal sharing of commodities is the norm, it may seem acceptable to take someone's ideas and words and just repurpose them as one's own. In the United States and most Western cultures, where individual competition and personal gain are emphasized, it's important—and required—to give credit for original ideas, words, and other creations (artwork, still and moving images, computer code, and the like). The words associated with original thinking and research "belong" to whoever wrote or spoke them. To present someone else's words as your own is plagiarism, a kind of misconduct that can get you into very hot water. You can present other people's words as much as you like, but you need to indicate clearly which words in your text are your own and which words originated with someone else.

However, the idea that text is property varies across kinds of texts and their purposes. For example, even in higher education certain documents are not as strongly associated with specific authors or career trajectories as, say, books and articles. These include committee reports, syllabi, lesson plans, outcomes statements, and the like. Ask professors what would upset them more: if someone plagiarized one of their research articles or if someone "borrowed" a description of an assignment that they had developed for a course without attributing it to them. You can guess the answer. But this doesn't lessen the need to provide sources when possible. The reason to cite a committee or some entity that has no "author" is less a matter of giving credit to specific people (for their own gain) than to provide the *source* of the words or for someone who may need to know (perhaps for their own research). For example, the archives of an English department held a very old policy requiring teachers to fail any student paper that had three or more grammatical errors. This policy might be of special interest to someone studying changes in teaching practices and underlying theories of writing. Citing the source ("Archives, Department of English, Average State University") doesn't give any of the policy's authors credit. But it gives readers crucial information about where the document was found and how they might obtain it themselves for their own purposes.

Citing sources, then, is important for more than one reason:

1. To give credit to someone for their original creation, so that their work can be acknowledged and so that their careers can be supported;

2. To help readers to find the original source if they want to locate it for their own purposes;

3. To keep researchers honest in their representation of other people's work;

4. For students, to show instructors the difference between your own ideas and words and those of others, so they can make an accurate assessment of your work.

Over the years, different codes have been developed to mark the parts of a text that are borrowed; these vary from discipline to discipline, and for this reason, they can lead some well-meaning students to err without intending to. If you compare the two excerpts above, you can see how a student trained to write in the reference style of the first excerpt might inadvertently put exact words into her paper, include the author of those words in parentheses, but forget to mark the exact words *as* the author's (using quotation marks). It seems like a minor issue, but it's very important.

In this section, you'll find some options available to you and the codes required for incorporating the words of others in your own text. Apologies in advance if this is about as fascinating to read as a set of instructions for running a washing machine. But if you want clean clothes, you'll study it.

Short Quotations

If you're incorporating only three or fewer lines of someone else's words, you should simply mark the passage with quotation marks and leave them incorporated into your own prose, as the following example illustrates:

In his essay on biography as a literary form, Johnson writes, "I have often thought that there has rarely passed a life of which a judicious and faithful narrative would not be useful." Johnson thus rejects the idea that only the famous should have biographies written about them.

Longer Quotations

If the quotation runs longer than three lines, it should be separated out from the body of the text, indented five spaces, and single-spaced, as follows:

> Though aware of the difficulties faced by one doing scholarly work, Johnson holds out the promise that long, hard effort will be rewarded.
>
> Every man, who proposes to grow eminent by learning, should carry in his mind, at once, the difficulty of excellence, and the force of industry; and remember that fame is not conferred but as the recompense of labour, and that labour, vigorously continued, has not often failed of its reward.

Partial Quotations

You're also free, as suggested above, to borrow only those phrases that you need. You're never obliged to quote passages in full, as long as you indicate any changes you make. You can, for instance, incorporate short excerpts of the original words into your paraphrase, provided they're marked, as the following example illustrates:

> Johnson insists that scholars should keep in mind both "the difficulty of excellence, and the force of industry" when at work.

Fragments of Quotations

You can delete words from either end of a sentence that you're quoting, or from the middle of it; you would indicate the deletion by an ellipsis (three spaced periods). If you cut off the end of a sentence, insert the final punctuation mark (period, question mark, or exclamation point), followed by the ellipsis, as shown in the following example:

> According to Johnson, "Every man, who proposes to grow eminent by learning, should . . . remember that fame is not conferred but as the recompense of labour. . . ."

Altering Quotations

Sometimes you might find it convenient to change a quotation from the first person to the third person or from one verb tense to another. You can make such changes by altering pronouns and verbs and by placing your changes in brackets [like these]. For example, you might find it more graceful to present a quotation used earlier in this chapter with the following:

> In his essay on biography as a literary form, Johnson wrote that "[he had] often thought that there [had] rarely passed a life of which a judicious and faithful narrative would not be useful."

Smoothing Quotations

The previous example suggests one final principle in the formatting of quoted material, and that's to run your own words and the quoted material together as gracefully as possible. If you splice words from your source into your sentence, keep the syntax consistent and smooth, and make the sentence sound as unified as possible.

However you choose to incorporate the words of your source, the same basic principles apply:

1. Use what you need, but don't pad.
2. Mark clearly whose words are whose.
3. Mark clearly any changes you make in the quotation.
4. Make sure that your changes do not fundamentally alter the meaning of the original material.
5. Splice your own prose and the quoted material together as gracefully as possible.

Documentation (Another Few Exciting Pages)

When you incorporate the ideas or words of another person into your text, it's not enough to mark them as such, as demonstrated in the previous section. You need to *state somewhere in your paper precisely where you got them.* You need to provide enough information so that your readers, if they choose, can look up the source for themselves. That is, you need to give the author's name, full title of the book or article, the name of the magazine or the publishing house that published it, when it was written, and so on. Since this information usually consists of two or three lines, you almost never present it in your text. Instead, you place some sort of a notation in your text next to the borrowed material and present the source location somewhere else— either in a section at the end of your paper or in a footnote at the bottom of the page. This is what's meant by *documenting your sources,* or just *documentation.*

> **KEY CONCEPT** *Documentation* is the process of showing the exact source of each reference (however included) to information that you bring into your paper from elsewhere. Documentation can include information about books and articles, speeches, interviews, films, ideas, and other material. See Key Concept Glossary.

Why all the fuss? Many if not most of the readers of any scholarly article are themselves researchers in the field, working on and writing about problems similar to those discussed in the article they're reading. If a source has proved to be important to you in your research, the odds are high that it will be valuable to your readers in their research as well. For this reason, your readers will want to know exactly where you found your material. They'll want to be able to go to their own libraries, find the journal or volume you used, and read the source in its entirety for themselves. Part of your job is to make this possible by giving full bibliographic information for every source that you use.

Much of this strikes everybody as being incredibly picky. But the fact is, you can cause your readers a lot of trouble if you don't pay attention to your documentation. Try looking for an article sometime when the information you've been given has the wrong page number or year. (And bring your Advil with you.)

Over the years various systems for presenting documentation have been developed. The system of footnotes and alphabetized bibliography that you learned in high school represents only one among many systems. Different fields, different publications, and different companies all have their own particular forms and strategies. There's no point here in giving you the details of any one system. Instead, find an example of something published in your field, and learn how documentation is handled in that field. Let's now consider some general tendencies across disciplines.

Placing the Information

Since the information that a reader needs in order to locate the book, chapter, or article cited in another work is often extensive, a reader won't find this information in the body of the text itself. You won't see anything like the following:

> The history of research on this question shows disagreement. As Todd and Palmer noted (Todd, G., and Palmer, B., "Social Reinforcement of Infant Babbling," *Child Development*, Vol. 39 (1968), pp. 591–596), social and vocal reinforcements seemed to increase the amount of an infant's babbling. Dodd and Nakazima, however (Dodd, B., "Effects of Social and Vocal Stimulation of Infant Babbling," *Developmental Psychology*, Vol. 7 (1972), pp. 80–83; Nakazima, S., "A Comparative Study of the Speech Developments of Japanese and American English in Children," *Studies in Phonology*, Vol. 2 (1962), pp. 27–39) disagree.

Citing sources in this way would obviously strangle anyone's reading to death. In addition, if a reader wanted to look up Todd and Palmer's article, and the piece the reader originally found it in was a long one, the reader would have to spend a lot of time just relocating the bibliographic reference in the mass of prose surrounding it.

Instead, virtually every discipline relies on a system of notations in the text referring the reader to full bibliographic information somewhere else. The notations can be asterisks (*) and daggers (‡), but more often they are numerals. They point the reader either to the bottom of the page or to a list of notes at the end of the article, chapter, or book.

Another increasingly common method is to use parenthetical documentation. In this method the notation consists of a pair of parentheses (called an *in-text reference*) containing very little information—just enough to allow the reader to find the source in an alphabetically arranged list at the end of the article, called variously *References* or *Works Cited*. There you can find the rest of the information that you need to locate the source. This does away with the need for a separate list of footnotes or endnotes *and* a bibliography. The alphabetic bibliography alone does the work of both.

For instance, you might see an in-text reference such as the following:

> Identical twins proved concordant for schizophrenia at a rate four times that of fraternal twins (Kendall, 1979, p. 246).

It becomes a simple matter to find the appropriate article in the bibliography (under "Kendall"), jot down the full reference, locate the work at your online library portal or at the library itself, turn to page 246, and check out this piece of information for yourself.

What do you need to document? To be on the safe side, *document anything that you didn't bring to your paper yourself.* Anytime there's something in your paper that you got from an outside source, mark it as such and indicate where you found it. You have to document everything you borrow, whether it's a direct quotation or only a paraphrase. You do not document your own ideas, items of common knowledge, or famous sayings.

Later on, if you're addressing an audience of experts, the rule changes slightly: the most precise principle then is to *document anything that is not common knowledge among your audience.* Thus, you may need to document a fact about Benjamin Franklin for a history class that you could skip footnoting if you were writing for historians of the American Revolution. If it's a fact that any qualified expert would immediately recognize as coming from Franklin's *Autobiography*, you could leave it undocumented in your paper. On the whole, however, you'll never go wrong by documenting anything that you had to go and get.

You'll often find as you write that you have an interesting insight, piece of information, or opinion on something that you'd like to share with your readers but that doesn't really fit anywhere in your paper. It's a sort of colorful leftover scrap of material that you can't quite bear to throw away but that you can't incorporate into your paper either. Or it's an *aside*—an interesting idea that would otherwise interrupt the main flow of your information or argument. This is what a *content footnote* is for.

> **KEY CONCEPT** A *content footnote* is a remark or aside that clarifies or elaborates on ideas in the main part of the text but that would otherwise interrupt the flow of its ideas; it usually appears at the bottom of the page but sometimes appears in a series of notes at the end of the text. See Key Concept Glossary.

Content footnotes are more common in some disciplines, especially in the humanities. You mark in your text where the scrap of material should go, choose the footnote option in Word, and write in the space it takes you to at the bottom of the page. Now you've put the scrap of material where the reader (if he or she chooses) can attend to it, but you haven't disrupted the main argument. Since your readers understand that such footnotes are asides, you can afford to be less formal in them than in the body of the work.[1]

> ### GIVE IT A TRY
>
> Look through some articles until you find a content footnote. Then describe what the purpose of the footnote is and why it was better to place it outside the main body of the article.

Form of the Full Citations

Once you've figured out where the full bibliographic information should go in your paper and the system of textual notations that you want to use to point readers to the information, you have one task left: to work out the exact pattern of bibliographic references themselves. For your particular discipline or journal, you have to know what information is required in a footnote, endnote, or bibliographic listing; you have to know what order the information goes in; and you have to know how it's to be punctuated. This calls for precise, almost microscopic observation. It's not fun, and it can be extremely tedious, but it's necessary.

As we'll see in Chapter 7, each discipline uses its own documentation or reference style to show readers the source of any outside information included in the text. These styles have developed somewhat organically, to best match the way the discipline works with and conveys its knowledge. Let's consider a couple of very common examples, the differences between the Modern Language Association reference style and the American Psychological Association

---

[1]A content footnote is often, by the way, a great place for wry commentary. The footnotes of Gibbon's *Decline and Fall of the Roman Empire* are sprinkled generously with such dry, sardonic one-liners. And, yes, you are now reading a content footnote.

reference style. (A number of other systems exist for different disciplines, such as the Chicago Manual of Style, the style preferred by the Council of Biology Editors (CBE), or the Vancouver, Harvard, ALWD, or Bluebook for law. Sometimes a specific journal will have its own unique reference style, and you need to follow its guidelines when submitting a manuscript.)

When you cite a source in a paper that uses the MLA documentation style, the references you include inside the text will appear inside parentheses, following an "author-page" style. The author's last name is included, followed by the page number where the cited material is found. That points the reader to the end of your paper, which will include a Works Cited page and the full reference of the material you just cited. A typical MLA in-text reference to a peer-reviewed journal article looks like this:

> Daniels argues that the story's character reflects the Cinderella archetype but does so "with a strange contemporary twist" (116).

Here, the full reference for Daniels' work will be found in the Works Cited, and the pages of the entire article are indicated there. (Many rules for dozens of variations will be found in the *MLA Style Guide*, such as what happens to the in-text citation when there are two articles by Daniels.)

In contrast, consider the APA in-text citation style. The reference you include in the text will also appear inside parentheses, but in this case you will put the author's last name followed by the year of publication, as shown here:

> Hobart's research shows that when three-year-olds are given a box full of toys reflecting different gender stereotypes (gender-neutral dolls with feminine clothes vs. masculine clothes), the children's selections match their own gender, suggesting "very early gender imprinting" (Hobart, 2010, p. 19).

Here, the in-text citation also points to the References list at the end of the essay, where Hobart's article can be found alphabetically, followed by year of publication.

As discussed in Chapter 7, even minor differences in disciplinary reference styles can reflect differences in the ways that knowledge is conveyed in those disciplines. For example, some styles favor the reference of entire works ("this research study showed that ..."), while others point to specific language within texts that may be important for interpretation ("this scholar says these things in this way ... ").

These differences are also seen in the list of works consulted. In any reference system, you need to give the name of the author(s) exactly as given in the original source (sometimes with full first and middle names, sometimes with just initials); the exact title and subtitle (if any); the publisher or name of the journal that published the piece; the date of publication (and if it's a book, the place); and, if it's an article, the numbers of the pages on which it appears. If the source is a speech, a pamphlet, a broadcast, a film, or some other less usual form, you'll need to provide different information. In the absence of citation requirements given by your instructor, you can learn how all of this is to be arranged and punctuated by studying examples from most of the work you're citing. If a particular reference system is mentioned (and one usually is), then obtain the manual and follow it. Always ask your instructor if he or she has a preferred reference style if one isn't indicated. You can also find websites that show the basic information for most reference systems.

The pairs of examples below show differences in the reference style for four basic kinds of references that you might use for a paper that follows either the MLA or APA guidelines. The purpose of these examples is not to serve as a guide for including sources in your paper. Rather, they're designed to call your attention to the very specific features of each system, such as how authors' names are included, how journals' volume and issue numbers appear, and what happens when there is more than one author. As you compare the two styles, notice their differences, including what's capitalized, what order the information appears in, and how numbers and dates are handled. At first, these differences may seem picky or trivial; but reference styles are like URLs on a computer: enter just one wrong keystroke, and the computer (or, in the case of references, your teacher or editor) will notice. Have patience for exactitude and it will serve you well.

Although you can rely on the samples below to guide you in creating a simple reference list, they don't go very far. There are many less common kinds of sources whose citation styles are not included here, such as films, interviews, or unpublished reports. Again, it's good advice for you to get hold of the preferred style guide (in print or online) and have it available as you write your research-based papers.

Each sample entry is annotated to call attention to specific information. It's best to read the entries in two ways: first, look at and compare the references themselves to see how different media (book, article, etc.) are cited. Second, read the annotations, which call attention to the differences between the styles.

The Basic Format of a Book with One Author

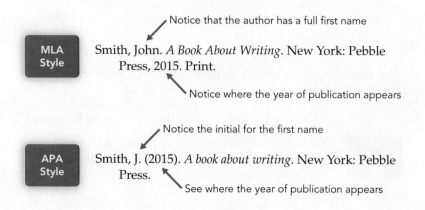

Notice that the author has a full first name

MLA Style

Smith, John. *A Book About Writing*. New York: Pebble Press, 2015. Print.

Notice where the year of publication appears

Notice the initial for the first name

APA Style

Smith, J. (2015). *A book about writing*. New York: Pebble Press.

See where the year of publication appears

The Basic Format for an Article with One Author in an Academic Journal

Notice that the article title is in quotation marks.

MLA Style

Smith, John. "A Study of How Writing is Taught in the United States." *Journal of Writing Instruction* 13.1 (2012): 16-28. Print.

Notice how and where the volume and issue number appear, with the year in parentheses

(continued)

Notice that in APA, only the first initial of a
work's title (plus proper nouns) is capitalized

APA
Style

Smith, J. (2012). A study of how writing is taught in the
United States. *Journal of Writing Instruction,* 13(1),
pp. 16-28.

See the way the pages
are indicated? Compare
with the MLA format.

Compare the APA's method of
indicating the volume and issue
numbers with the MLA's method

The Basic Format for an Article with Two Authors in an Academic Journal

Notice that the second author is
in reverse order of the first author

MLA
Style

Smith, John, and Sally Jones. "A Study of Two College
Student Writers Overcoming Writer's Block."
Writer's Psychology Studies 42.3 (2014): 111-136. Print.

Notice that in MLA, the form of the reference
(print or web) is indicated at the end. Not so in APA.
(Look back at the previous MLA references.)

Notice that the second author's first initial and
last name follow the same order as the first author.
Notice that APA uses ampersands (&) for "and"

APA
Style

Smith, J., & Jones, S. (2014). A study of two college
student writers overcoming writer's block.
Writer's Psychology Studies, 42(3), 111-136.

The Basic Format for a Chapter in a Collection of Academic Essays

the chapter title, followed by the editors' names.

Smith, John, Juan Rodriguez, and Polly Sanders. "A Case Study of Students' Online Writing." *Writing, Youth, and the Internet.* Ed. Frank Pruett and Mellissa Edwards. Sandstone, MO: Landlock Press, 2014, pp. 66-78. Print.

Notice the difference between the APA and MLA information about the edited collection in which the chapter appears.

Smith, J., Rodriguez, J., & Sanders, P. (2014). A case study of students' online writing. In F. Pruett & M. Edwards (Eds.), *Writing, youth, and the internet* (pp. 66-78). Sandstone, MO: Landlock Press.

See where the page numbers appear in each style of citation. In APA style, they come after the book title and not at the end.

Putting It into Practice

This chapter has focused on the process of putting together a document based on either primary or secondary research. That process, as should be clear, is complicated and requires sustained effort and plenty of time. This is why, if you're assigned to write a research paper of any kind, you begin early and return to the task often until it's due. Chapters 4 and 5 offer plentiful material on how to come up with ideas, structure them, and then draft, revise, and edit your high-stakes paper. This chapter focuses more specifically on arriving at a manageable, interesting research question and finding plentiful information on that question, whether for the purpose of providing background for a primary research investigation or pulling together what's known in a secondary research project.

The following are some ways in which you can put this material to work.

- Create a timeline for your project from beginning to end. Use the sections of this chapter to create deadlines or due dates for each part of the project ("general question: Sept. 10; refined question: Sept. 18; preliminary exploration of sources: Sept. 29; five good sources: Oct. 8"), and so forth.

- Share your ideas often with other people. Run your research question by someone who can give you good advice about how clear, interesting, and manageable it is.

- Find out which documentation style you need to use in the paper, and then get hold of the manual. Study it *as* you collect information.

- Create an indexing, archiving, and tagging system for yourself that works best for you. Whatever you do, record the source of everything you find that can be useful. (Countless hours down the line can be wasted trying to remember where you found that terrific article whose source has disappeared into the ether.)

7

The Comparative Anatomy of Texts

Species of Writing

To take part in any cooperative social activity, you need to learn the language. There's no use shouting "Touchdown!" at a bowling tournament or discussing a new death metal rock album in the vocabulary of classical music FM radio: "Notice the sensual tone of the breakdowns and scorching tech death, the pig squeals playing in delicate contrapuntal harmony to the breaking of glass and screaming in the melody." You have to talk the talk.

The same thing is true in writing. Every shared activity, whether it's work or play, develops its own forms and styles of writing. To be part of that world, you need to learn to write its prose. A recent MBA graduate needs to be able to read, understand, and write each of the kinds of letters, memos, and reports that will most likely show up on her desk. A new PhD psychologist, if he enters clinical practice, will need to write testing reports, interview summaries, chart notes, discharge summaries, and treatment recommendations. If he enters into academia, he'll probably be writing conference talks, journal articles, and research reports, whose form and style will depend heavily on what psychological field of study he belongs to. A research article on communication anxiety written in American Psychological (APA) style is different from a psychoanalytic case study, a geological field analysis, or a civil engineer's report recommending the use of specific equipment to clear land for a building. The approach the writer follows will dictate the form and style of the documents she writes.

As we saw in Chapter 6, published guidelines, such as style sheets and handbooks, can help you master the text forms and rhetoric of these different worlds. If there's a style sheet or manual for your subject area, get hold of a hard copy or an online version—for keeps, not just to finish an assignment. You should sit down with it and scroll or skim through it at random, just to see what sorts of information it contains and what problems and topics it covers. Then you should keep it within easy reach of your keyboard or a click away on your computer at all times. You don't have to memorize much from such a guide; you simply have to know when to use it and how to find what you need.

No matter how up-to-date and thorough your style guide is, don't rely on it entirely. Not all businesses do their progress reports and year-end summaries alike. Not all scholarly journals, even in the same field, accept articles with the same format, language, and documentation. Worse yet, all of these conventions change over time. New approaches to a subject generate new ways of writing about it. Sometimes, in fact, entirely new subjects appear on the intellectual horizon, bringing in their wake new terms, new ways of organizing information, and new structures for theorizing and observing—and hence for writing. Think of computer science, for example.

Trying to learn all of the various conventions, forms, and styles you might ever need to use would be an endless, frustrating, and horrible job. Fortunately, it's not necessary. You don't have to learn every possible text in every context. Instead, you need to develop the ability to *anatomize a text*, to examine it, take it apart piece by piece, figure out how it was constructed in the first place, and then use that knowledge when building a text of your own. You need to know what parts to look for, how to analyze their organization, and then how to draw a sort of blueprint or schematic of the text that will guide you in your own writing. You don't need a hundred separate rules for a dozen different texts; just go out and observe the characteristics of the creature itself so that you can paint one of your own. You need, in other words, a kind of guide of techniques for reproducing what you find in the field, along with a sharp eye and a little patience.

This chapter will provide you with the guide. You'll need to contribute the sharp eye and the patience.

Basic Anatomy: A Guide

The one theme this book has pushed hardest is that *writing varies a lot across different communities of practice*. Learning how to write effectively in a new context—a new course, a new major, a new job—will require you to try consciously transferring your existing knowledge and experience into this new community. This will be necessary, but it won't be sufficient. You need to *read* the context and *read* the kind of communication in it in order to figure out how to think and write like a member of the community. Let's explore how.

Surveying Your Rhetorical Environments

To understand any particular kind of text, you need to understand the role it plays and the function it performs in its environment. What does this kind of text *do?* The various academic disciplines and professions have each developed a wide range of documents for different tasks and purposes. Just think about all the different types of writing produced by both parties in the process of hiring somebody for a job. There's a job listing (in both a print and an electronic version), a cover letter, a resume, maybe a formal job application (print or online), maybe a digital portfolio, an invitation for an interview, the acceptance of that invitation, the interviewer's report, maybe one or more follow-up letters, a hiring letter, an acceptance letter, a formal contract, an official job description and catalog of employee benefits, and maybe legal documents reminding the human resources department about equal-opportunity requirements. Each is a different kind of document with its own structure and language, and with its own particular bit of work to get done. These documents also may even vary in different kinds of businesses and professional settings.

To write any one of them, you need to understand how it fits into the entire involved process of matching a candidate to a job in a specific place.

In scholarly fields, the paper trail leads through the development, application, and dissemination of knowledge. As we saw in Chapter 6, the development of knowledge usually entails some combination of looking and reflecting or analyzing, so you'll find some works of research, some works of theory, and some of both. In most fields, people will try put the knowledge they gain to some practical use. You should be able to find works in almost any field on the application of what's known, from clinical or technological studies to how-to writing. Finally, new knowledge is *interesting*. Readers at all levels want to know what's going on in the various disciplines, and there are always experts and journalists ready to explain it to them. One biochemist's work on liver enzymes might spawn three articles in the professional journals, five reports in medical magazines on the development of new techniques for the treatment of cirrhosis, several brief items in the popular science monthlies, and ultimately take its place in the "Enzymes" chapter in a biology or chemistry textbook.

As a first step, then, in learning to read, understand, and (ultimately) write any specific kind of text in your field, you need to survey the types of writing that your field generates. Since you know some of them already—your field can hardly *be* your field if you haven't already read something in it—you should start by reviewing the kinds of texts you're already aware of.

Such an inventory will get you started, but it won't be comprehensive. To complete your survey of the types of writing in your field, you'll need to do some browsing, some of it certainly in the library, either physically or online. That's where you'll find the research and theoretical works, the attempts at application, the explanations for other experts or for lay readers—all the books and articles written by the people who find the subject most interesting. The library is also where you'll find the bibliographies, indexes, and reference works in your field, which help to coordinate the original sources and make them more accessible. (You should make a point of asking the reference librarians to explain these to you, beyond the general advice in Chapter 6.)

Luisa, who aspires to be a lawyer, wrote the following list of the kinds of writing lawyers do, but she also discovered that people playing different roles in the legal profession will be responsible for writing different kinds of documents.

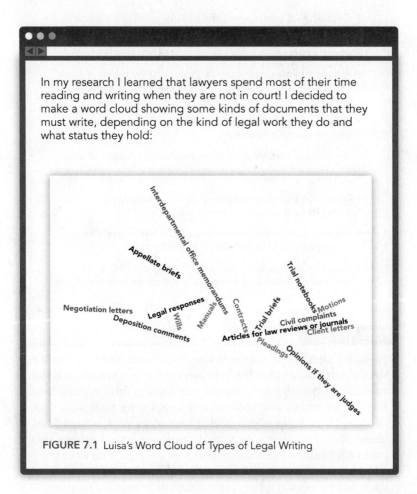

In my research I learned that lawyers spend most of their time reading and writing when they are not in court! I decided to make a word cloud showing some kinds of documents that they must write, depending on the kind of legal work they do and what status they hold:

Interdepartmental office memorandums

Appellate briefs

Trial notebooks

Negotiation letters   Legal responses   Contracts   Motions

Deposition comments   Wills   Manuals   Trial briefs   Civil complaints

Articles for law reviews or journals   Client letters

Pleadings

Opinions if they are judges

FIGURE 7.1 Luisa's Word Cloud of Types of Legal Writing

For most fields of study, you should be able to find examples of each of the following kinds of texts:

- Volumes of theory or research by one author (or a team of authors), written as an expert to other experts

- Collections of essays by several authors, all on one topic, and sometimes drawn from a conference at which the authors spoke

- Books addressed to a popular audience (including textbooks)

- Articles in professional journals, presenting the results of one expert's (or team's) thinking and research to other experts in the field

- Articles in popular magazines explaining recent ideas and discoveries to nonspecialists

- Reviews and criticism of all the sorts of books described above

- Summaries or reviews of the recent research in a particular area

- Books and articles seeking to apply the knowledge in a particular field to practical problems

- Encyclopedias or handbooks, sometimes highly specialized, summarizing aspects of the field in short articles

- Indexes, catalogs, and bibliographic works organizing the publications in the field and guiding the reader in finding them

GIVE IT A TRY

List all the kinds of texts related to your field that you're already familiar with, and decide what function they serve in the field as a whole. If you have trouble getting started, list the books you're using in class. They count. Then access your library online (or go there physically), track down some examples in your field of each of the kinds of texts listed above, and write down their titles. Note where in your library's web portal the books and journals for your field are kept, what kinds there are, what they look like, and how to find them again when you need them (use the tagging system in most popular browsers). Take notes.

Learning to Dissect a Text

Now that you have some sense of the rhetorical environment of your subject, you need to capture and dissect one type of text that inhabits it. For the rest of this chapter, you'll be analyzing, step-by-step, one particular piece of writing. You'll sketch the skeleton, find and label the major organs, note how the connecting tissues hold it together, and subject parts of it to microscopic analysis. You'll also note its overall color and texture. You can do this easily on a Word version of the article you choose, or you can use a markup program for other forms, such as PDFs. You can also work the old-fashioned way: print out a copy, and write in the margins. When you're done, you'll be in a position to take a further step: begin making a creature of your own. Once you know how a chemistry lab report, a historical essay, or an article in biblical exegesis works, you can carry on an in-depth study in the area, presenting what you learn in such a way as to contribute to the ongoing conversation that is the discipline itself.

GIVE IT A TRY

To follow along in this process, find an example of one kind of writing in your field. It should be fairly recent: an article from a nineteenth-century journal won't help you to see how people in the field communicate *now*, as interesting as it can be to see how they worked *then*. Work from an on-screen manuscript or a photocopy that you can access as you read the rest of this chapter. Think of yourself as writing a sort of lab report in rhetorical anatomy.

Start with an Overall Assessment of the Genre

We've considered *genres* from various perspectives throughout this book, so you know what the term means. You also tacitly recognize certain genres: you know what the half-size newspaper-like publications at the checkout counter of the grocery store contain, with headlines like "Two-headed boy found in mysterious mountain cave" and "President had seven children out of wedlock." You also know what the paperback novels on the wire racks close to that same checkout area contain, with titles like *Endless Love* and pictures on their covers of a sensuous woman standing in the moonlight by the beach, her diaphanous negligee brushed gently by the sea breeze. You know the purposes, language, contents, and styles of these texts. Your job now is to become as familiar with the genres of specific academic and professional disciplines. The content may not be quite as racy, but it's essential for the progress of knowledge, and it can be very interesting as you gain expertise in your field.

A great deal of academic publishing will be in the genre of the scholarly or research article published in a *peer-reviewed journal*. Such journals can have extremely high standards and are therefore prized places to publish one's work. They may have very large readerships, mostly other scholars and professionals, but sometimes journalists who look for groundbreaking discoveries that they can report in the news.

> **KEY CONCEPT** A *peer-reviewed journal* is a professional or academic journal whose articles have been reviewed, usually anonymously, by "peer" experts who serve on the journal's editorial board or are on a panel of designated reviewers. This process ensures that articles published in the journal are of high quality and have scholarly integrity. See Key Concept Glossary.

At the same time, a journal isn't a genre. It *contains* genres. Some journals publish only one kind of text—say, research articles. But most also publish other genres, such as book reviews, notes and comments, or marginalia. The *Journal of Agromedicine*, for example, includes editorials, book reviews, brief reports, occasional symposiums, and even in one issue, a "Cowboy Poetry Roundup" section, the result of a poetry contest that took place at an international symposium in Saskatoon (who says academic journals are always dull and dry?). But the most important contributions to the field of knowledge will usually be scholarly articles. In many fields, these are from twenty to thirty published pages, but in some fields, such as chemical engineering, they can be much shorter. As you choose your sample text, then, try to get a sense of its genre. This will be further particularized as we go along, but for now you need an overall impression. A book is a book—but what kind of book is it? Popular? Scholarly? An article is an article, but how long is it? In which section of the journal does it appear? Is it a review? A research report? What can you figure out about its overall purpose? What does the journal look like? What does it say about itself? How is it organized? Who is on its editorial board? Where is it indexed? Who publishes it? How often is it issued? (Here's where you're mostly observing the creature to get a general idea of how it behaves and what it looks like.)

The Author(s)

A logical next step in analyzing the piece of writing that you have chosen in your field is to notice who wrote it. In the early stages of study in your field, the author's name may not mean much to you, so go beyond it to the author's credentials. Is the author a professor, some other sort of expert, maybe a journalist specializing in the area? Has the author published in the field before? Don't guess at this. Find whatever evidence you can. Is there a college listed under the author's name? If so, you have strong reason to believe that the author is a teacher or a researcher there. Does the bibliography list other works by the author? Does the journal or book contain a brief biographic sketch of the author anywhere? If so, where? What does it tell you? In many cases there will be two or more authors. What else does that tell you? Are they all from the same place? Look at the order of authorship: are their names alphabetized? If not, it's likely that the first author is the "lead" or "most important" author. Sometimes people who play a subsidiary role, such as technical assistants, are included because they contributed but they are not the lead author. Sometimes a person who obtained a grant is the lead author and those hired to work on the project are secondary authors. In scientific fields, it's not uncommon to find articles with many authors— even dozens or thousands of authors, as in the record-breaking, thirty-three-page physics paper published in the journal *Physical Review Letters*, whose 5,154 authors are all part of two huge research teams that have experimented in the Large Hadron Collider laboratory located in Switzerland. (Of course, you wouldn't be expected to know all about those authors, but it would be helpful to find out something about the teams they work on and maybe look at the first two or three authors if they are the "lead" authors and not first by alphabetic organization). Write down the author's or authors' name(s) and whatever you know about his, her, or their credentials. Also note down where you found this information.

The Audience

Although you're usually given the name(s) of the authors and their credentials, you'll probably need to infer the audience of an article indirectly. Whenever authors are writing, they are picturing their readership, the people they believe will most likely read their work and appreciate it. How they conceive of their audience will affect their work at every point. Who reads this sort of work? What is their general educational level? What is their level of specialized training in this field? Is the audience generally educated readers or PhDs doing research in the area?

What kind and degree of interest will readers bring to this work? Does the author have to catch the reader's attention, or can the author assume that no one reads about seasonal changes in the territorial behavior of the African fat-tailed gecko unless they're already doing research in the field and have a lifelong passion for reptiles? Does the author hope to find readers both among specialists and the broader reading public?

Some of this can be inferred from the nature of the journal carrying the article or from the publisher of the book. Most professional journals describe their readership and intellectual mission in a short paragraph at the front of the issue. *Pharmaceutical Nanotechnology*, for example, tells you that its readership is especially interested in manuscripts "detailing the synthesis, exhaustive characterisation, biological evaluation, clinical testing and/or toxicological assessment of nanomaterials." (Notice the spelling of *characterisation*, a giveaway that the journal is not published in the United States—in fact, it's an international journal published by Bentham, which has offices in several countries and uses British spelling). A rather different journal, *Ultimate Reality and Meaning*, describes its mission and authorship this way:

> This interdisciplinary academic journal is published quarterly by an international association of thinkers who have an interest in research on human efforts to find meaning in our world. It publishes studies dealing

with those facts, things, ideas, axioms, persons and values which people throughout history have considered ultimate (i.e., that to which human mind reduces and relates everything and that which one does not reduce or relate to anything else) or as horizons (i.e., world views in the light of which humans understand whatever they understand) or as supreme value (i.e., for which someone would sacrifice everything and which one would not lose for anything).

Given such information, what can you reasonably infer about the readerships of these two journals? How does that information affect the way you would write for each of them? Will either one of them be anxious to publish your research on "The Effects of Sounds and Music on the Stress and Physical Responses of Laying Hens?" (Yes, there are effects.)

> ### GIVE IT A TRY
>
> Describe the expected readers for your chosen work. Note their educational level, probable specialized training, and why they would be interested in reading it. What are the clues leading to your conclusion?

The Author's Purpose

In a general sort of way, you could describe the author's purpose for a work even before reading it. Authors write to advance the knowledge in their fields, to disseminate what they know to others, to win fame and glory, to earn an honest living or raise their chances of promotion—or because, like a few among us, they're never entirely comfortable when they're not writing. But here we're looking at something much more specific. What is the explicit, stated purpose of the particular work you're examining? What does the author come right out and say that she's trying to do? (In many cases, the purpose will be a *thesis*, as discussed at length in Chapter 4, but consider the other varieties of main points described there as well.)

If you're examining a book, you should find the purpose stated in the Preface or Introduction—or even in the title. If you're examining an article, the purpose ought to surface somewhere in the opening paragraphs, possibly in the very first sentence. The purpose will sometimes be stated in an unconcealed form:

"The purpose of this experiment is to. . . ."

"This article examines the. . . ."

"To date, no research exists exploring the relationship between. . . . This study was designed examine this relationship empirically. . . ."

Sometimes the purpose will be presented as a problem:

"What happens when. . . ."

"Though many scholars believe . . . , this leaves unexplained why. . . ."

The purpose may only be implicit. The author presents a thesis statement, and the purpose of the article is to convince the reader of its validity. If there is no explicitly stated purpose, trying to distill the main point into one pithy sentence may be the closest you can come:

The importance of Sherman's march to the sea lay more in the effect it had on the presidential election of 1864 than on its intrinsic military utility.

Research examining the effects of social media on the academic writing of students has been particularly unrevealing; few studies have considered the *intellectual* rather than the *textual* consequences.

A business letter, of course, usually states its purpose in the very first sentence:

I am writing to complain about the poor service I received when I brought my Tibetan spaniel to your clinic for its annual checkup.

The author's statement of purpose is the one sentence that is most likely to help you grasp the significance of the piece overall. Pinpointing the statement of purpose is also your first major observation. Notice *where* the statement appears in the work and what form it actually takes so that you'll have at least some knowledge of the conventions when you write your own version of this kind of text.

GIVE IT A TRY

Find the author's statement of purpose, and copy it *verbatim* into your notes. Then write down where it was located—in what part or what section of the piece. If it was labeled or marked, make a note of that, too. If there's no explicit statement, write down in your own words what you think the author is trying to achieve. This may be simply convincing the reader of the validity of the author's central thesis, whatever (and wherever) that is.

The Title

The title of the book or article is a sort of calling card or invitation. Its purpose is to seek out an appropriate audience and to introduce that audience to the written work. As a result, the style of the title depends on the nature of the readership the author is seeking. For an article trying to catch the eyes of busy or frustrated shoppers waiting in line at the supermarket, the title has to be sufficiently catchy, intriguing, or even puzzling to lure the readers to the first paragraph (or make them toss the magazine into the cart): *Guacamole in the Boudoir? Jaylo Tells All!*

In academics and business, on the other hand, most of the reading we do is work related. We already bring to it an interest in a very specific kind of content—for example, the behavior of electrons in a magnetic field, the application of Rawls's theory of justice to medical ethics problems, the causes of the 2008 financial crisis, or a statistical comparison of gun violence in the United States compared with the same in Northern Europe over the past three years. If an article covers the area we're interested in, we read it almost automatically; we don't really need a sexy title to arouse our interest.

The titles of academic articles and business reports, therefore, tend to be long, detailed, and sort of colorless when compared to popular writing. This doesn't reflect a failure of creativity; it's simply a convenience. What the reader wants is as thorough, explicit, and precise a label on the article as possible—not "Beautiful Crested Birds with White Plumage Show Their Passion Even When Watched," but

"A Study of the Mating Behaviors of Australasian *Calyptorhynchus* in Zoo Environments." Of the columns of articles listed in a bibliography, readers want to pick out and read only those articles that are most relevant to their own research. The reader of an article on photosynthesis in saguaro cacti will probably first make contact with the title in a bibliography of some sort. That reader wants a statement of the article's ingredients, for example, "The Effect of Differing Levels of Soil Silicon Content on Photosynthesis in *Sereus giganteus.*"

Titles in scientific disciplines tend to be as explicit as possible without (m)any embellishments, such as this title from the *Journal of Advanced Research in Mechanical Engineering*: "Thermoelastohydrodynamic Analysis of Elliptical Journal Bearing (Two-Lobe)." Some titles, especially those in the humanities and social sciences, try to combine color and thoroughness. The main title will tend toward the snappy or engaging. This is followed by a colon and a subtitle, with the subtitle doing the actual business of labeling the contents. So you may get something like this: "A Kiss Is Just a Kiss: Heterosexuality and Its Consolations in Sir Gawain and the Green Knight," published in the journal *Diacritics*; or "The Rapture of the Ride: Hearing (Dis)abled Masculinities in Motorcycling," which appeared in the *Journal of Sociology*.

GIVE IT A TRY

Copy into your notes the title of the article you're examining. What kind of work is the title doing? How thoroughly does the title present the major topic of the article? Does it make any attempt to sell the piece, above and beyond simply listing the contents?

The Skeleton

The "skeleton" of an article refers to the structural framework on which it's built. You can see the skeleton most clearly in the subheadings that divide the text. In some articles in the humanities, you may find no subtitles at all—at most, maybe sections marked with Arabic or Roman numerals, or merely divided by an extra blank line. In other articles, especially in some fields, the articles will be carefully sorted into different labeled sections: for example, Introduction, Method,

Results, Discussion. These sections, as noted earlier, are often standardized. Journals published by the APA (or journals that follow its style guide) expect to see their contributors' articles sorted into the sections and labeled with precisely the subtitles above. If you label your sections "What the Problem Is," "What I Did," "What Actually Happened," and "What I Make of It All," you'll be working against the field's conventions. Other works, such as this textbook, make use of subtitles, but they don't follow any standardized rhetorical format, although their physical layout is dictated by the publisher's own in-house conventions, which are usually based on industry standards.

Besides the name and arrangement of the sections, you also need to take note of the placement and capitalization of the subtitles. How does the article distinguish major sections from minor sections? How are the various subtitles positioned: are they centered, flush left, or indented? What words in the subtitles, if any, are capitalized? Are any of the subheadings in bold font or in italics, and if so, which ones?

The Major Organs

Whether the text you're studying has an obvious, explicit skeleton—subheadings, numbered divisions, and so on—it always has an *organization*. That is, it has *organs*, interworking parts, and interrelated components. It's not a mass of pure, undifferentiated prose. It's constructed of different sections, each with its own purpose and meaning, and each depending on the others to give the article its full significance. The results of a study mean nothing without a statement of the problem. A book review without at least a brief synopsis of the book's content is incomplete; it simply doesn't *work*.

If there are subheadings, they obviously will delineate and maybe even describe for you the major organs. But even without such labels, you need to locate and identify them. Before reading the article in detail, glance over it quickly. Read just the opening paragraphs of each section. Then read the opening sentence of each paragraph. Try to find the logical breaks in the work. Where does it finish one task and pick up another? Where, for instance, do you find transitional sentences moving you from one topic to the next one?

> With this understanding of Bultmann's notion of "demythologizing" to build on, let us turn briefly to his notion of "kerygma."

Once you've located the major parts, read each one over quickly and try to decide what it's doing. Is it defining a problem? Reviewing past research? Summarizing another writer's position? Refuting an argument? Outlining a method of research? Reflecting on the broader significance of the author's conclusions? Surely it's doing *something*.

Minor Organs (or, Even an Article Can Have an Appendix)

Locating and noting the function of the major organs of a book or an article may give you a complete schematic of it. Then again, it may not. It may, in fact, miss a number of minor organs that are not included in the body of the work. Books, for instance, almost always have title pages, publication information, sometimes a dedication, a Preface, a Table of Contents, maybe a List of Illustrations, and then, after the final chapter, an Appendix, Bibliography, and Index. Many articles have an Abstract wedged between the title and the Introduction, while others have key word lists, the author's credentials, and a list of Works Cited (or References) at the end. As with the major organs, you need to find these minor organs, notice where they are located, how they're formatted, and what useful work each one does. What do you think an abstract at the beginning *does* for readers? Again, the point of all of this is not just to understand the article better—although for sure, you'll be a much better reader as a result—but to see how writing works in the field and to be able to cast your own observations and thoughts into this kind of format.

GIVE IT A TRY

Figure out the skeleton and major organs of your chosen text. Locate the major organs, and analyze what each one is for. Mark on your article where each section starts and stops. Draw a diagram or schematic of this organization, or create one. Then try to state as clearly as possible the different functions of each organ. What is each section of the work *doing*? Now find and describe the minor organs, the minor parts of the article or book that are not included in the main body of it. Note their placement, format, and function. From your notes, be able to create these when you try to write a similar document.

How Outside Sources Are Used

Chapter 6 explained why you might sometimes paraphrase or quote someone else's text in your own work. The knowledge in any discipline is built up slowly, brick by brick, with every researcher studying the work of his or her predecessors and then going beyond it, adding to it in some significant way. It's this kind of continual mutual borrowing that allows a discipline to grow, to explore new areas, and to test and verify its claims. Because it's so essential, each discipline has found standardized, systematic ways for writers to incorporate and comment on each other's work as they present their own work.

To take part in the ongoing conversation of your field and to write the kind of text you want to write, you need to understand *why* outside sources are cited and *how* they're worked into the fabric of the text itself.

Find the places in your text where the author has summarized, paraphrased, quoted, or even merely mentioned the work of a previous writer. Note first how many such references there are. Does the author do a fairly thorough review of previous research up front, only occasionally mention other scholars, or not bother with them at all? (Any of these may be appropriate.)

Note also *where* these summaries, paraphrases, or quotations occur. A brief review of research in a scientific article will probably appear early on, in the introduction, and then the authors will launch into their own experiment or inquiry, maybe citing a couple of scholars to support their methods. On the other hand, if you're reading a review of a recently published collection of Winston Churchill's correspondence, you'll probably find quotations from the letters scattered throughout.

How much of each previous work was used? Are the references to the work of the earlier writers actual quotations or only paraphrases and summaries? If they're quotations, how long are they? A phrase here or there? A few sentences? Or does the author sometimes quote passages at length? Sometimes, you'll find strings of authorities cited to make a point, as if the writer were conducting a poll on the issue:

> Other researchers, however, have found just the opposite (Baker, 1996; McCarthy, 2004; Urbaine, 2001; Winslow, 1987).

Once you've noted all this, you should be in a position to answer the really vital question: *why* is the author pulling in these previous works? If we assume that the author is trying to make a case, to convince us of something, we need to ask what purpose each citation serves. To ask the question another way, how would the author's case be weakened if the material were missing? What does it add, above and beyond what the writer can tell us, in the writer's own words?

Here are a few purposes such cited material can serve:

- It can offer direct testimonial support for the main point that the author is making: "Jones, in her 2012 monograph, reaches similar conclusions."

- It can prove or illustrate some point: "An example of this comes from the work of Farnsworth. . . ."

- It can act as a "straw man," a representative statement of a position that the author is attacking: "The logical flaw in such a stance appears clearly in the following passage from Schaeffer. . . ."

- It can help define the precise nature of the problem that the author is trying to solve. "Though Jones (2001) believes that . . . , research by Hendrix (2006) suggests. . . . My own study is designed to test Jones's hypothesis under more tightly controlled conditions than Hendrix was able to achieve."

- It can establish the writer's authority to say something new about the topic by implying, "I really know my stuff. I'm thoroughly acquainted with the previous work on this question." This could take the form of a string of citations: "An exhaustive review of the literature on the reduction of ocean species since 1970 shows that . . . (Abrams, 1997; Chanovic, 1993; Farnsworth, 2005; Lalicker, 2015; Pruett, Samuels, & Ross, 2001; Ross, 2002; Stainton & Miles, 2012; . . .)."

Giving Credit Where Credit Is Due

Writers are obliged to give credit to other people whose ideas and words they cite in their work. Assigning credit and providing such bibliographic information in your text is what *documentation* is all about, as we saw in Chapter 6. The underlying principle is the same across all disciplines, but over the years (centuries even!), different disciplines have developed different methods and styles for doing this. These differences will be noticeable if you read articles in the social sciences, sciences, and humanities—each reference system will behave differently. Part of your anatomy of a text, then, involves figuring out what system is being used within the community of practice in which and for which the text is written. And—you guessed it—you need to master these conventions to join the written conversation in your field.

To figure out the citation and references practices in the field of your chosen article, find all the places where the author makes use of the work of previous writers and scholars. Describe in your notes where you find them, how many you find, how extensive they are, what form they take, and what purpose each one serves. Find where in the article the author gives the full bibliographic information for the sources cited. Note if these are footnotes, numbered endnotes, or an alphabetical bibliography, or some combination of them. Then notice and describe the system of flags or markers used in the text to point you toward the fuller citations. Refer to the material in Chapter 6 to record the precise form that the references take.

It's important to note that some disciplines have agreed on these conventions across their various journals and books. All of the journals put out by the American Psychological Association, for example, use what's called "APA format." Most journals of literary studies use the "MLA format," developed by the Modern Language Association. These systems also have evolved over time for purposes of efficiency and clarity, and because new online media have created a need for new types of references. Both of these organizations also publish style guides or publication manuals that explain their documentation systems (along with many other matters of form) in exhaustive detail. Other fields publish style guides as well, such as the Council of Biology Editors. You should check to see if a style guide exists for your discipline, and, if it does, keep a copy of it on your computer or by your desk. Some disciplines may not have a uniform (published) style guide, but scholars working in them simply use the reference style preferred by each journal to which they submit articles. Many style guides have abbreviated versions (for the most basic references) online. (If you need a good general guide and are allowed to use it, check out the *Chicago Manual of Style*.)

GIVE IT A TRY

Study the footnotes, endnotes, and/or bibliographic listings in your article. For each *type* of listing (government document, speech, etc.), work out in your notes the schematic, showing what it contains, how the information is arranged, and how it's punctuated.

Use of Graphics

Graphics and visuals may not appear in the article you're analyzing, but at some point, they'll come up and will need close attention. You'll need to look at where they are used, how they are constructed and labeled, what purpose they serve, and how they are coordinated with the author's text. The following chart provides some features to look for:

Location	Where are the graphics used? Largely in one section (Results) or throughout the article? How heavily does the author depend on them?
Construction	How are the graphics constructed? Are they tables, graphs, schematics, flowcharts, maps, or exploded diagrams? What's on the x-axis, and what's on the y-axis? What special symbols do they use? Are these symbols standard or idiosyncratic?
Labeling	How and where are the graphics labeled? Are they figures, or are some of them labeled "Table" or "Diagram"? Does the label appear above or below the figure on the page? Is there anything else on or around the figure, such as a parenthetical reference if it's borrowed or a caption if it requires some explanation?

Purpose	What purpose do the graphics serve? How is this picture worth a thousand words? Could the same information be given in prose? If not, why not? (A major skill in learning how to write is knowing when not to write—when you'd actually do better to draw or insert a photo or a graph.)
Integration with text	What does the author say about the graphic in the text? Sometimes the writer will simply mention the graphic in passing and assume it's self-explanatory. Others require a careful introduction, some explanation of how to read them, and a careful discussion of what they illustrate for the purposes of the author's argument. This will, of course, depend on the complexity of the graphic itself and at least somewhat on the audience for which the author is writing.

Figure 7.2 provides an example of a graph that appears early in an article titled, "What Happens When Extremists Win Primaries," published in the *American Political Science Review*. Notice that the graph is labeled "Figure 1" and titled at the top, and that there is a further note at the bottom, but much more is said about it in the body of the text. As you can guess, figures such as this are essential in work that reports statistics or other data, conveying a lot of information in a small space.

Figure 7.3 shows a page from an article in *The Journal of Infectious Diseases* titled "A Human Domain Antibody and Lewis^b Glycoconjugate That Inhibit Binding of *Helicobacter pylori* to Lewis^b Receptor and Adhesion to Human Gastric Epithelium." (The little "b" superscript after Lewis refers to the "b" type of this antigen, which is sometimes abbreviated Le^b.) This article focuses on the identification of an antibody that inhibits adhesion of *Helicobacter pylori*, a bacterium associated with gastric problems such as acid reflux, to the epithelium. The page shown in Figure 7.3 includes two kinds of visuals. Figure 4 of the article has two images; image A is a picture of the bacterium adhering to the gastric mucosa in a section of human stomach in the absence of the inhibitor, and image B shows it in the presence of the inhibitor. Figure 5 in the article shows differences in bacterium levels in human stomach sections when the bacteria were cultivated under

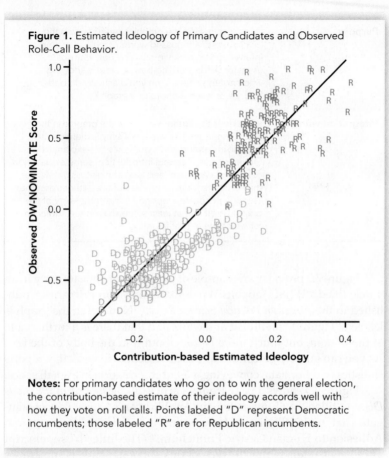

Figure 1. Estimated Ideology of Primary Candidates and Observed Role-Call Behavior.

Notes: For primary candidates who go on to win the general election, the contribution-based estimate of their ideology accords well with how they vote on roll calls. Points labeled "D" represent Democratic incumbents; those labeled "R" are for Republican incumbents.

FIGURE 7.2 Example of a Visual in a Political Science Article

different conditions using the inhibitor. No direct mention is made of these figures in the article; rather, they provide visual support for what is being presented in the text.

In printed articles, visuals are often difficult to include; they may lose some resolution in the printing process, and are expensive to print in color. One advantage of online journals is that they allow for high-resolution, color images as well as graphs and charts that can be made interactive (allowing the viewer to chose different ways of presenting the data or to "drill down" into specific data). In fact,

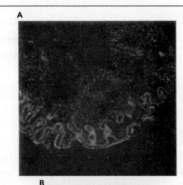

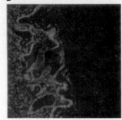

Figure 4. Adherence of fluorescein isothiocyanate isomer I-labeled *Helicobacter pylori* to gastric mucosta. Sections of human stomach were incubated with fluorescein isothiocyanate isomer I-labeled *H. pylori in* the absence of an inhibitor (a) and in the presence of domain antibody 25 at 10 ug/mL (b), illustrating the reduction in binding.

specificity may be a major factor that determines inhibitory activity. The epitope to which domain antibody 25 is directed has not been mapped, although it may overlap with the binding site kof BabA for Le^b. Binding studies with chimaeric BabA constructs indicate that the BabA binding site is within residues 212-614 [24].

Domain antibodies have potential for topical applicaion to prevent infection with *H. pylori*. In previous studies, domain antibodies that blocked adhesion mediated by the MP65 man-

noprotein adhesin and that secreted aspartyl proteases of C. albicans cleared infection when applied vaginally in a rat model of vaginal candidiasis [20]. Furthermore, orally administered lactobacilli engineered to express single-domain (llama-derived) antibody fragments directed against surface components of rotavirus conferred protection against diarrhea ina mouse model of rotavirus infection [25]. These studies indicate that single domain antibody fragments are sufficiently stable to retain activity at mucosal surfaces and the Fc-mediocated function is not essential for protection against infection. In addition to stability, domain antibodies can be produced on a large scale by fermentation in microbial systems cna can also be modified by in vitro affinity maturation to increase affinity using phage display technology [13, 14]. Affinity maturation could potentially increase the efficacy of domain antibody 25. Because gastric mucosal Le^b and microbial BabA molecules are exposed on the membrane surfaces as multiple copies, it could be advantageous to present the domain antibodies themselves as multivalent structurers (eg. by incorporation into micelles).

We also investigated glycoconjugates as inhibitors of *H. pylori* adhesion. In agreement with previous findings [6], both Le^b HSA and, to a lesser extent, sLe^b inhibited attachment of *H. pylori* to human stomach epithlium. Poly-o-lysine glycoconjugates represent a synthetic alternative to neoglycoprotein con-

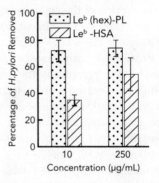

Figure 5. Removal of bound *Helicobacter pylori* from Lewis^b (Le^b) stomach sections by Le^b glycoconjugates. Sections with bound H. pylori were incubated for 1 h with the inhibitors at the concentrations shown, and after washing, residual microorganisms were measured in the standard assay. HSA, human serum albumin; Le^b(hex)PL, poly-o-lysine conjugates of Le^b hexasaccharide.

FIGURE 7.3 Example of Visuals in a Medical Research Article
(SOURCE: Younson, Justine et al. A Human Domain Antibody and Lewis b Glycoconjugate That Inhibit Binding of Helicobacter pylori to Lewis b Receptor and Adhesion to Human Gastric Epithelium, *Journal of Infectious Diseases*, November 15, 2009, p. 1581. Reprinted with permission.)

visuals no longer have to remain still; brief video clips can show processes taking place in labs under microscopes, bits of interviews with subjects, animal interactions, and so on. The "article of the future" is likely to include more visual imagery, both moving and still, as a consequence of digital technology.

> **GIVE IT A TRY**
>
> Examine the figures in your article, if any, and answer the above questions about them. Write the answers in your notes, and save them for future reference.

Coloration

To return to our biological metaphor, by now you should have a thorough account of all the rhetorical inner workings of the article that you're studying. You've examined its environment, its skeleton, and its major and minor organs, and you've put its documentation under the microscope. Your notes should contain a comprehensive anatomical description of the creature. You now have one more observational task, and then you're almost done. You need to examine the overall prose style of the work—what we might call its *coloration.*

Prose style can best be considered in terms of the writer's *persona*. Your persona is the image of yourself that you project to another person (the word originally meant "mask" in Latin). Whenever you speak to somebody, you communicate a message, some piece of information, *and* you try to make the other person see you in a particular way. This isn't a form of fraud; it's simply inevitable. You do the same thing in writing. The persona that you adopt as a writer shows itself in the style of your prose. Compare the personas of two writers who have created different tent signs placed on tables in a busy coffee shop:

> **KEY CONCEPT** *Persona* refers to the sense of self that you project through your choice of language (words, sentence structure, etc.) or, more generally, your writing *style*. It is related to the concept of *ethos* described in Chapter 4. See Key Concept Glossary.

> Sign #1: "Please be considerate of the next patron(s) who may be waiting for your table and bus your cups and dishes to the plastic bins by the door. Many thanks for helping!—Jimbo, owner"

> Sign #2: "**DO NOT** leave your dishes and utensils on the table! **Everything** must be bused or disposed of at the door! **No exceptions!**—The Management"

Clearly, the image that the first writer conveys is of an approachable, courteous person who cares about the needs of all his patrons. The image conveyed by the second person is of a martinet who lays down the law and treats customers like soldiers in boot camp.

As a rule, someone who is writing in his or her discipline is writing either as an expert to other experts or as an expert to a lay (general) audience. If a biologist, say, is describing her research on octopus intelligence to other biologists, she won't preface her report with a humorous account of her childhood collecting sea creatures in the Florida Keys. Her professional colleagues, reading her article with an eye toward advancing their own research on the higher mollusks, won't be interested—not right then, at any rate. But if she's writing for a popular magazine—*Smithsonian*, say, or *National Wildlife*—her readers may be happy to have the weightier scientific material broken up with her personal reactions and anecdotes.

The same audience considerations will control the biologist's prose style. To her colleagues she will write formal scientific prose; she will present herself in the *role of* a fellow scientist. To the readers of *National Wildlife*, she'll write more casually; her prose will sound like intelligent, succinct, lively speech. She'll *sound like* a bright, fun person with a consuming interest in animals—a sort of energetic, likable next-door neighbor who just happens to have a doctorate in marine biology. Note that neither persona is "false"; she's a scientist, and a smart, fun collector of animals. Her choice is simply which side of herself to present in which context.

The first thing to notice about the prose of the article you're analyzing, then, is how professional versus how casual it is. You'll probably see this first in the level of formality of the writing. Is it business-suit prose? Lab-coat prose? Or does it suggest a sweater and jeans? (As we saw in Chapter 2, your learning blog or notebook is one of the few places where cut-offs and a tee-shirt are welcome.)

Consider snippets from two different articles. The first is from the journal *Criminology* and comes from a research article titled "Testing for Temporally Differentiated Relationships among

Potentially Criminogenetic Places and Census Block Street Robbery Counts."

> We follow the lead of Bernasco and Block (2011) and enter spatially lagged versions of our potentially criminogenic facilities variables to model the observed spatial dependence in census block street robbery counts (Anselin et al., 2000; Elffers, 2003).

The second comes from an article titled "America's Real Criminal Element: Lead," published in *Mother Jones*, a popular magazine that covers a wide range of issues in politics, the environment, culture, and science:

> The biggest source of lead in the postwar era, it turns out, wasn't paint. It was leaded gasoline. And if you chart the rise and fall of atmospheric lead caused by the rise and fall of leaded gasoline consumption, you get a pretty simple upside-down U: Lead emissions from tailpipes rose steadily from the early '40s through the early '70s, nearly quadrupling over that period. Then, as unleaded gasoline began to replace leaded gasoline, emissions plummeted. Gasoline lead may explain as much as 90 percent of the rise and fall of violent crime over the past half century. . . . Intriguingly, violent crime rates followed the same upside-down U pattern.

Notice the dramatic differences in the coloration of these two pieces. The first is ultraformal and scientific, pushing the authors (and readers) to the background and sharpening the focus on their study. The second is much lighter, employing a more common vocabulary, drawing the reader in through the use of the pronoun "you" and using casual expressions like "it turns out" and "pretty." The respective authors made these decisions based on a good understanding of their audiences, publication contexts, and purposes for reading (scholars who don't mind spending a lot of time understanding highly complex inquiries versus the general reading public interested in learning and thinking about what might cause crime rates to have changed over time).

What constitutes professional prose also differs from one field to the next. The prose of an art critic, for instance, is often colorful and impressionistic, and full of metaphor and imagery. Anthropological studies of various cultures' religious ceremonies may be richly descriptive but in a scrupulously objective way. A mathematician uses prose only to glue together the strings of abstract symbolic notation that do the real work. As a result, the prose is austere, precise, often wonderfully clear, but suggestive of nothing beyond the exact denotative meaning of the terms used. In a field like psychology, where the scientific or humanistic status of the subject is itself at issue, the austerity or richness of a writer's style may reflect how the writer construes the discipline in the first place. Styles can also change across *types* of research within a field. In educational research, for example, a controlled experimental study of two teaching methods may be rendered in a very clinical style, backgrounding the author(s), while a piece of qualitative research involving lots of observation might be rendered in a more descriptive way, revealing the researcher's own role within the environment.

Most writers, even if they work mostly within their fields, also change their prose continuously, just as people do when they dress for an important formal social event in the morning and then for a family barbecue in the afternoon. Below is an excerpt from the well-known popular book of (Dr.) Lewis Thomas, titled *Lives of a Cell*. Can you imagine Dr. Thomas using that same prose style when writing a medical report in his role as president of the Memorial Sloan Kettering Cancer Institute in New York?

> Viewed from the distance of the moon, the astonishing thing about the earth, catching the breath, is that it is alive. The photographs show the dry, pounded surface of the moon in the foreground, dead as an old bone. Aloft, floating free beneath the moist, gleaming membrane of bright blue sky, is the rising earth, the only exuberant thing in this part of the cosmos. If you could look long enough, you would see the swirling of the great drifts of white cloud, covering and uncovering the half-hidden masses of land.

For that matter, can you imagine something like the following paragraph appearing in the book you are now reading?

> Rather, [the case study subject's] transfer difficulty may have been exacerbated by the existence of several production sponsors loosely tied together, each inhabiting a different professional or public discourse context with only temporal, situational goals to unite them rather than continually reinforced sets of practices as might be seen in a busy nanotechnology lab.

(Yours truly was wearing a jacket and tie that day.)

The Question of Jargon

Every discipline over time creates its own vocabulary, its shop terms, and its jargon. Often these serve a vital function. They provide names and labels for ideas that otherwise would take too long to describe whenever they were mentioned. On the other hand, if you use them too freely (or incorrectly), they can sound pretentious and ugly. They can also distort the meaning of what you're trying to get across. Two safe principles for the use of jargon are to be *sparing* and to be *precise*.

Don't use jargon when ordinary English words will do. Don't show off. Use it only when it's genuinely necessary in the context of your writing and study within your discipline. Try to use plain, standard English as often as possible. English is still the first language of the most rarefied of specialists. Anything you can write in plain English has a higher chance of actually being understood than its jargonistic translation.

On the other hand, when you're working within your discipline and it's necessary and appropriate, feel free to use the specialized terminology, but *get it right.* Don't call *mass* "weight"—it's not. Don't call *punishment* "negative reinforcement." They're not the same. Don't use "phenomenology" when you mean "epistemology," or "ideology" when you mean "phenomenology." And if you don't know what the term means, look it up or don't use it at all.

One final note about specialized terminology. Sometimes disciplines can go overboard in the development of fancy terms for simple concepts. One critique of this practice suggests that the discipline is trying to make itself seem highly important by denying access or understanding to common people. The overuse of jargon makes nonmembers "outsiders" who don't really understand what goes on in the field, which might itself be insecure about its own contributions or worth to humanity. To some extent, disciplines try to self-regulate their prose, calling into question its excessive impermeability. On the other hand, there may be very good reasons for specific terms to develop. Take the word *dyad*, which is used in some of the social sciences, such as communication studies, psychology, and sociology. In communication studies, a dyad refers to a pair of individuals who are usually talking to each other. So why not use "face-to-face" for "dyadic"? Face-to-face implies that the individuals are physically present, but some dyads may be communicating on the phone or online. *Dyad* is more precise. In sociology, a dyad often refers to two people who are maintaining some sort of relationship, often socially significant. "Face-to-face" won't capture that. Nor will "couple" or "significant others" or "pair of friends." A good practice, then, is to study specific jargon-like terms to see if they are, in fact, needless jargon or are used to encapsulate shared understandings about the object of study.

GIVE IT A TRY

Turning once more to the article you are studying, what do you notice about its prose style? How professional or casual is it? What does *professional* seem to mean in this case? How would you describe the persona of the author? Does the prose change at all from section to section, or is it uniform throughout? Finally, write down any special terms you find, and define them as precisely as you can. Then try to figure out whether they are legitimate specialized terms or could be replaced with something simpler and more direct. In this critique you should also consider the context and nature of the publication—for example, whether it's a specialized journal or one designed to reach a broad, public readership.

Three Rhetorical Dissections

Throughout this chapter, you've been analyzing a chosen text, following along through each procedure, pulling away tissue, exposing the working parts, noting the major and minor organs. You should have a good sense of how doing this can give you plenty of insights about the way that writing works in a specific disciplinary (or professional or public) setting.

Now let's further strengthen your skills at textual anatomy by looking at some more examples of published texts. We'll conduct detailed analyses of a mathematical proof, a social-psychological research study, and an interpretive article in literature and film: one each in the sciences, the social sciences, and the humanities. (The originals are printed in full at the end of each section.) The first example, the mathematical proof, shows you how much you can figure out about the construction of a text without even understanding the subject matter (if you do, so much the better). Even the question of the proof's validity isn't particularly relevant here. We're simply describing as fully as possible how the proof actually works on paper so that, if we did have a contribution to make in this area, we'd know how to present it for publication in this journal.

A Mathematical Proof

TITLE. The article is titled "A One-Formula Proof of the Nonvanishing of L-functions of Real Characters as 1." The title is obviously more functional than decorative; it labels the content without making any attempt to sell it. It is what it is.

AUTHOR AND AUDIENCE. The article appears in a journal called *The Mathematical Association of America*, which is clearly the organization that publishes it. The author, Bogdan Veklych, works at the Massachusetts Institute of Technology, one of the most prestigious universities in the world, so we know that he is highly expert in his field. That's all we can glean about him, based on his affiliation, which appears at the end of the second page. His audience consists of other professional and academic mathematicians, including students. Few will read this piece without having significant mathematical knowledge; many will be math professors. But note that the proof is suitable for an undergraduate college course.

PURPOSE. The author states his purpose first in a one-sentence abstract at the top of the first page and then explicitly in the first two lines (after providing a "universal agreement" about the difficulty of a step in a calculation): "In this note, we present a proof of this fact. . . . " Notice the plural "we" even though there is only one author.

SKELETON AND MAJOR ORGANS. The article doesn't present any overt structure; there are no subheadings. Instead, the structure takes the form of an extended argument, with premises and conclusions (indicated by "hence" and "thus"). Because the article is so brief, it really doesn't need subheadings; however, some proofs include labels, such as "Theorem 1," "Theorem 2," and so forth, and "Conclusion."

MINOR ORGANS. The only extras contained in the article are the abstract and a brief acknowledgment of a person who provided editorial assistance, as well as the brief section marked "References."

USE OF OUTSIDE SOURCES. The writer uses only four outside sources for this work. All of the references to these sources in the article appear in the introductory material, and all of them refer to other mathematicians' proofs.

DOCUMENTATION. The flags for the sources within the text are bracketed numbers following each reference to an author; the numbers correspond to the numbered references at the end of the article. The schematic for the reference style looks like this:

> 1. First initial, Last Name, *Name of Book*, Name of Book Series, Name of Publisher, City of Publication, year of publication.

In the case of a journal article (the third reference), the schematic differs:

> 3. First initial, Last name, Title of article, *Title of Journal* [abbreviated] Volume of journal (year) page numbers.

If you intended to write for this journal, you would need to study a few more articles first (and look at the form of the other two references). There might be other aspects of the citation style that you'd need to know, depending on what you were citing.

GRAPHICS. There are no figures, drawings, diagrams, graphs, or other visual aids; however, formulas play a prominent role, especially the enlarged formula at the center of the article.

COLORATION. Stylistically, this is mathematician's prose *par excellence*. Since the nature of the material is inherently complex, the writer has made his prose as clean, simple, and direct as possible. Here are the opening lines:

> It is universally agreed that the most difficult step in proving Dirichlet's theorem on primes in arithmetic progression lies in showing that the L-function, $L(s, x)$, attached to a real nonprincipal Dirichlet character x, does not vanish at 1. In this note, we present proof of this fact, suitable for the undergraduate classroom.

Here you have two declarative sentences, the first laying out a claim based on a long history of "universal agreement" and the second promising to support that claim with a proof. Professor Veklych is writing as a mathematician to mathematicians, many of whom teach undergraduate college students. The prose, if simple, is ruthlessly formal and austere. There's really no hint of color—no humor, irony, or clever turns of phrase. The use of "we," common in proofs even with one author, is a way of further removing the author ("I") from the equation, so to speak.

JARGON. Finally, the article is necessarily full of special terminology. In the world of mathematics, even common English words take on special meaning. Words like "infinite," "nonprincipal," and "function" don't mean nearly the same thing as they would in an article in, say, educational research ("The teacher's function in this setting involves. . . ." or "Students have almost infinite choices of activities based on this lesson. . . ."). Other terms, such as "holomorphic," may have few or no equivalents in other fields. Obviously, any misuse of the special terminology and symbolism would reduce an article like this to gibberish.

To render the ideas here into common English prose, including all the mathematical notation in the proof, would require dozens of pages and serve no purpose for this audience.

A One-Formula Proof of the Nonvanishing of *L*-Functions of Real Characters at 1

Bogdan Veklych

ABSTRACT. We present a simple analytic proof that L-functions of real nonprincipal Dirichlet characters are nonzero at 1.

IT IS UNIVERSALLY agreed that the most difficult step in proving Dirichlet's theorem on primes in arithmetic progressions lies in showing that the *L*-function, $L(s, \chi)$, attached to a

The author is very grateful to an anonymous referee and to Susan Ruff for extensive editing help.

real nonprincipal Dirichlet character χ does not vanish at 1. In this note, we present a proof of this fact, suitable for the undergraduate classroom. It is similar to those given by Davenport [2] and Serre [4], but it avoids the use of infinite products and the explicit use of Landau's theorem on Dirichlet series. It does use basic complex analysis and the idea behind Landau's theorem. There are proofs that bypass complex analysis, which are, however, more complicated than the proof below. Of these, a proof by Monsky [3] is perhaps the simplest. Another example is a proof by Apostol [1].

We shall use two standard facts, that the Riemann zeta function $\zeta(s)$ is holomorphic in the half-plane Re $s > 0$ away from $s = 1$ where it has a simple pole and that the L-function $L(s, \chi)$ of a nonprincipal character χ is holomorphic in all of Re $s > 0$. These facts are easily proved by summation by parts (see, for instance, [2]). We shall assume that there is a real nonprincipal character χ for which $L(1, \chi) = 0$ and derive a contradiction by considering $F(s) = \zeta(s)L(s, \chi)$. By the cited facts, $F(s)$ is holomorphic in Re $s > 0$ except possibly at $s = 1$, but since the zero of $L(s, \chi)$ at 1 cancels the pole of $\zeta(s)$, $F(s)$ is holomorphic everywhere in Re $s > 0$. All we shall need, however, is that $F(s)$ is holomorphic in a disk centered at 2 (or any number greater than 1) that contains $\frac{1}{2}$, or equivalently that $F(2 - s)$ is holomorphic in a disk centered at 0 that contains $\frac{3}{2}$.

Multiplying for Re $s > 1$ the absolutely convergent Dirichlet series of $\zeta(s) = \Sigma k^{-s}$ and $L(s, \chi) = \Sigma \chi(l)l^{-s}$, we obtain a Dirichlet series $\Sigma c_n n^{-s}$ representing $F(s)$ in (at least) Re $s > 1$. Its coefficients c_n are the Dirichlet convolution of 1 and χ, so c_n is the sum of $\chi(l)$ over all l dividing n. Thus, by the multiplicativity of χ, c_n is the product of the contributions of the form $1 + \chi(p) + \cdots + \chi(p)^a$ of the primes p dividing n, where a is the exponent of p in the factorization of n. We use the fact that $\chi(p)$ can take only the values 1, -1, and 0 to conclude the following.

1. If a is odd, the contribution of p is $1 + a$, 0, or 1.
2. If a is even, the contribution of p is $1 + a$ or 1.

Hence, $c_n \geq 0$, and if n is a square, $c_n \geq 1$. It follows that the sum $\Sigma\, c_n n^{-1/2}$ diverges; by $c_n \geq 0$, it is not less than the similar sum over $n = m^2$, which, by $c_{m^2} \geq 1$, is not less than $1 + \frac{1}{2} + \frac{1}{3} + \cdots$. We'll combine the divergence of this sum with our previous observation about the holomorphicity of $F(2-s)$ and several basic facts of complex analysis to get a contradiction.

For $s \in [0,1)$, we observe that $F(2-s)$ is equal to the following:

$$\sum_{n=1}^{\infty} \frac{c_n}{n^{2-s}} = \sum_{n=1}^{\infty} \frac{c_n}{n^2}(e^{s \log n} - 1) + \sum_{n=1}^{\infty} \frac{c_n}{n^2}$$

$$= \sum_{n=1}^{\infty} \sum_{k=1}^{\infty} \frac{c_n}{n^2} \frac{s^k (\log n)^k}{k!} + F(2)$$

$$= \sum_{k=1}^{\infty} s^k \sum_{n=1}^{\infty} \frac{c_n}{n^2} \frac{(\log n)^k}{k!} + F(2)$$

(the change in the order of summation is permitted since in the double sum all terms are nonnegative). The very last expression is a power series in s, and we've just shown that it converges to $F(2-s)$ for all $s \in [0,1)$. Hence, the radius of convergence of this power series is at least 1, so it defines a function holomorphic in $|s| < 1$. It coincides there with $F(2-s)$ by the uniqueness of the analytic continuation. Therefore, this power series is the power series expansion of $F(2-s)$ around 0, as the latter is unique. By our previous observation that $F(2-s)$ is holomorphic in a disk centered at 0 and containing $\frac{3}{2}$, its power series expansion around 0 must converge to it for all s in this disk, in particular, for $s = \frac{3}{2}$. Thus, we can set $s = \frac{3}{2}$ in the power series and then read the displayed formula backwards, as the change of the order of summation is again permitted. We see that $\Sigma c_n n^{-1/2} = F(\frac{1}{2})$, but $\Sigma c_n n^{-1/2}$ diverges, as we showed above, which is the contradiction.

REFERENCES

1. T. M. Apostol, *Introduction to Analytic Number Theory*. Undergraduate Texts in Mathematics, Springer-Verlag, New York, 1976.
2. H. Davenport, *Multiplicative Number Theory*. Second edition. Revised by H. L. Montgomery. Graduate Texts in Mathematics, Vol. 74, Springer-Verlag, New York, 1980, http://dx.doi .org/10.1007/978-1-4757-5927-3.
3. P. Monsky, Simplifying the proof of Dirichlet's theorem, *Amer. Math. Monthly* 100 (1993) 861-862, http://dx.doi .org/10.2307/2324663.
4. J.-P. Serre, *A Course in Arithmetic*. Graduate Texts in Mathematics, Vol. 7, Springer-Verlag, New York, 1973, http://dx.doi .org/10.1007/978-1-4684-9884-4.

A Social-Psychological Study

TITLE. Now let's turn to a second example for dissection: an article that reports on a study that associates writing about traumatic events with improved physical health (yes, there's a fairly substantial body of research supporting that relationship). Notice that there's a subtitle after the colon: "The Necessity for Narrative Structuring." In its directness, the title grabs the reader's attention and implies a relationship, but then immediately it's qualified by the subtitle. Readers in this field may already be familiar with research showing that when people write about traumatic events in their lives, they often become healthier; but this article is *adding to* that relationship by suggesting there's more to it than just any kind of "writing."

This article appears in the *Journal of Social and Clinical Psychology*, which is published by Guilford Press. The article's title is well designed to show up on many computer searches because it has important keywords: "writing" and "trauma," for example. A quick glance at the journal's masthead suggests that it's a legitimate scholarly outlet for professionals working in the fields of psychology and social psychology, both academic researchers and those in clinical practice. Its editors and editorial board include respected experts, and it has a strong "impact factor," a statistic reflecting how often material in the journal is consulted and cited—that is, its influence. Other psychologists (and students doing research papers) will have no trouble guessing whether it's relevant to their own professional interests, once they find it.

AUTHORS AND AUDIENCE. Just below the title we find the authors' names, first Joshua Smyth, followed by his affiliation at the time of publication—Syracuse University, a major, respected research institution—and then Nicole True and Joy Souto, both at the State University of New York at Stony Brook, another research-extensive, state-supported university. Nothing else in the article tells us more about the authors, but notice that the contact information for the first author (Smyth) appears in a footnote at the bottom of the first page. (A quick search outside the article easily leads to Dr. Smyth's impressive credentials and current position at Pennsylvania State University.) Information about the other co-authors is more difficult to find; many search results lead back to the article itself. Because the authors are not listed alphabetically, it's safe to assume that Smyth was the primary author and researcher and True and Souto may have played a lesser, supporting role (even serving as assistants or statisticians). There are four additional articles by Smyth cited in the reference list but none by the other authors. Overall, we have a strong reason to believe that the information in the article is trustworthy, objective, and credible, and not the ranting of armchair pseudopsychologists in some politically slanted publication. Based on the journal, the audience for this piece is obviously researchers in psychology and social psychology but also people in related fields, such as sociologists, social workers, health professionals, and perhaps personnel in high schools, colleges, and universities who are interested in ways that the effects of traumatic experiences can be lessened. The audience may even include journalists who are investigating the question for more publicly-oriented pieces. The audience includes both graduate and undergraduate students who are researching (social)-psychological issues.

PURPOSE. The purpose of this article is, again, captured pithily in its title: it will show that writing about traumatic experiences does something, but that the something requires a certain kind of writing. The *abstract*, a common feature in social-scientific and scientific journals, tells us concisely what the article is about through its genre: it's a *research report*. Here we learn that the authors will answer the question in the title by showing that when they ask some subjects to write about various assigned topics and other subjects to write about their own traumatic experiences, and when they ask the trauma groups to write either in a fragmented way or as a coherent narrative, those who write about their own traumatic experiences using narrative structures are the most likely to report positive health benefits than the other groups. The abstract doesn't explain *why*—but as readers, we can expect the authors to explore the implications of their study at the end.

Why is the abstract here? First, to give a quick overview of the article, which helps readers learn what to expect—it's literally an aid to reading. Second, to offer a synthesis that can be useful if someone is trying to pull together a lot of literature quickly in order to read it later. Some researchers might even cite this piece based on the abstract alone, but this can be risky, since the abstract misses much of the detail in the article.

SKELETON AND MAJOR ORGANS. Unlike the mathematical proof, this article gives us clues to its organization. The subheadings, in list form, look like this:

Writing About Traumatic Experiences

Methods

    Participants

    Materials

    Essay Evaluation

    Procedure

Results

Discussion

References

Even without specialized knowledge in psychological research, these headings give us a pretty good idea of what's covered in the article. We also get an overall sense of what the authors are doing: *organizing* the study into its parts. Notice, however, that before the skeletal structure is indicated with subheadings, there's a general, unlabeled introduction that provides background (in many articles, such overviews are preceded by a heading such as "background," "introduction," or "overview").

The first couple of sentences offer a simple, general assertion (writing about traumatic events improves physical health), followed by references to previous studies that support that assertion. The third sentence then claims that although the prior research has shown the relationship, it hasn't really shown *how* writing about traumatic experiences enhances physical health. An exploration of the theoretical assumptions behind the relationship follows for a couple of paragraphs, until we reach some questions that the researchers explored in their study. Keep in mind that all this is prefatory. The real meat of the article starts with the subheading "Methods," which will explain exactly what the researchers did to answer their questions.

MINOR ORGANS. Within the major sections of the article, only one (Methods) contains any subsections—four of them. In turn, only one of these Methods sections (Materials) contains further subsections: "Impact of Events Scale," "Symptom Report and Activity Restriction," and "Mood Report." Unlike subsections such as "Methods," these are more specific to the study and will therefore not be generally recognizable by readers not familiar with similar kinds of instruments.

Notice also that there are two footnotes. These contain specific information that the authors may have felt would intrude on the flow of the main text and was therefore not needed there. You'll probably find fewer footnotes (or endnotes, which are footnotes all stacked up at the end of the article) in social science journals than journals in the humanities.

USE OF OUTSIDE SOURCES. Of the eighteen references that appear at the end of the article, four are authored or coauthored by Professor Smyth, suggesting that he is drawing on some of his own investigations and extending them. This only adds to his credibility, since it suggests that he's creating a trajectory of knowledge about writing and health. Another multiply-cited researcher is Pennebaker, who has three references (and, if you care to search for his work, turns out to be one of the foremost authorities on writing and health). If you read carefully, you'll also see that Pennebaker teamed up with Smyth on one of Smyth's articles, lending additional credibility to the article. As is typical in social-science research, many of the references appear early in the text (fifteen), and thereafter the number of references continues to decline as the study is reported, picking up somewhat at the end in the Discussion section. For an article of this length and a study of this size, the number of references is typical and represents an effective balance between the requirement to build on prior research and the need not to overwhelm the reader with everything ever written on the subject.

DOCUMENTATION. Because the article uses the APA reference style, each source is marked with parentheses containing the author's last name and the year of publication. All coauthors are listed; if several studies are listed inside the parentheses, they are separated by semicolons.

> . . . (Pennebaker, 1993; Smyth, 1998).

If the author's name appears in the text, though, it's not repeated in the parenthetical reference:

> This may reflect the need for increases or improvements in narrative formation, as suggested by Pennebaker, Mayne, and Francis (1997).

The full bibliographic information for each outside source is presented in a section called "References." The list is arranged alphabetically and contains articles published in journals, conference papers, chapters in edited collections, one book, and a manuscript (Smyth) submitted for publication. (If you were to scan the reference lists in other articles in this issue, you could draw a reasonable conclusion that this particular field builds knowledge more readily through articles published in peer-reviewed journals than through books or other kinds of documents.) You would draw the reference schematic as follows:

Lastname, FirstInitial, & Lastname, FirstInitial. (year). Title of article. *Title of Journal*, Volume #, xxx–xxx.

GRAPHICS. The article contains one brief table and two figures that depict the effects of writing on "activity restriction," a measure of health, and "avoidant thoughts," a measure of how much the traumatic experience is intruding on one's usual thinking. The first is labeled "The effect of writing group on activity restriction" and the second is labeled "The effect of writing group on avoidant thoughts." In the text, both graphs are explained as followed:

Individuals asked to form a narrative reported less restriction of activity because of illness $F(2,107) = 8.17$, $p < .01$ (see Figure 1) and showed higher avoidant thinking than the other groups $F(2,107) = 3.70$, $p < .05$; see Figure 2).

COLORATION AND JARGON. The prose style of the article is somewhat mixed. It begins with a paragraph that is easily accessible to the average educated reader:

Writing about traumatic events produces a variety of health benefits, including improvements in physical health, psychological well-being, and measures of physiological function (Pennebaker, 1993; Smyth, 1998). Writing has recently been shown to lead to symptom reduction in patients with chronic illness (Smyth, Stone, Hurewitz, & Kaell, 1999). Less is known, however, about how writing produces these benefits. Early theories suggested that the cumulative strain of inhibiting disclosure about traumatic experiences was deleterious, and could be reduced via writing, although this explanation is not well supported (for discussion see Smyth & Pennebaker, 1999). One broad explanation for the effects of writing is that the act of converting emotions and images into words changes the way the person organizes and thinks about the trauma. By integrating thoughts and feelings, the person can more easily construct a coherent narrative of the experience. Once in narrative formation, the event can be summarized, stored, and assimilated more efficiently, thereby reducing the distress associated with the traumatic experience. This cognitive processing is thought to be reflected in alterations in intrusive and avoidant thoughts associated with the trauma (Greenberg, 1995).

As the article moves along, the author then transitions into somewhat more complex language, as demonstrated in the following paragraph:

> Multilevel random effects models (PROC MIXED in SAS) were used to test effects of group, time, and the interaction of group and time (group*time) on symptoms, activity restriction, intrusive thoughts, and avoidant thoughts. Time was coded as number of weeks postwriting (1 to 5), and baseline scores of each dependent variable were used as covariates. Composite symptom and activity restriction measures were computed by summing all reports of symptoms or restriction at each time point. Group (control, fragmented, and narrative) was unrelated to symptom report, all $F(2,107) < 1.0$).

The challenge for some readers of this prose will come from its description of the statistical analysis. However, for the most part the article is not impervious to many readers in spite of these sections in the results. Few specialized terms are used, and those that may seem unfamiliar, such as "intrusions" and "avoidance thinking," are understandable in the context of the article. But the formality of the prose still evokes the persona of a psychological *scientist*, with the emphasis on science.

Every writer sooner or later runs into the problem of balancing discipline-based terminology and plainness or ease of comprehension. The advice here can itself be put plainly: use the jargon when it helps. Otherwise, write the clearest English you can.

Effects of Writing about Traumatic Experiences: The Necessity for Narrative Structuring

Joshua Smyth
Syracuse University

Nicole True and Joy Souto
State University of New York at Stony Brook

Although writing about traumatic events has been shown to produce a variety of health benefits, little is known about how writing produces benefits. The degree to which individuals form narrative structure when writing may predict health improvements. This study manipulated narrative formation during writing to test if narrative structure is necessary for writing to be beneficial. A total of 116 healthy students were randomly assigned to write about control topics or about their thoughts and feelings regarding the most traumatic event of their life in one of two ways: list in a fragmented format or construct a narrative. Individuals asked to form a narrative reported less restriction of activity because of illness and showed higher avoidant thinking than the other groups. The fragmented writing group did not differ from controls on any measure. These data (a) demonstrate that instructions to form a narrative produce a different response to writing than instructions to form fragmented and control writing and (b) suggest narrative formation may be required to achieve health benefits.

WRITING ABOUT TRAUMATIC events produces a variety of health benefits, including improvements in physical health, psychological well-being, and measures of physiological function (Pennebaker, 1993; Smyth, 1998). Writing has recently been shown to lead to symptom reduction in patients with chronic illness (Smyth, Stone, Hurewitz, & Kaell, 1999). Less is known, however, about how writing produces these benefits. Early theories suggested that the cumulative strain of inhibiting disclosure about traumatic experiences was deleterious, and could be reduced via writing, although this explanation is not well supported (for discussion see Smyth & Pennebaker, 1999). One broad explanation for the effects of writing is that the act of converting emotions and images into words changes the way the person organizes and thinks about the trauma. By integrating thoughts and feelings, the person can more easily construct a coherent narrative of the experience. Once in narrative formation, the event can be summarized, stored, and assimilated more efficiently, thereby reducing the distress associated with the traumatic experience. This cognitive processing is thought to be reflected in alterations in intrusive and avoidant thoughts associated with the trauma (Greenberg, 1995).

It is believed that if an individual is upset about a traumatic event, memories are not integrated into a personal narrative, possibly resulting in the memory being stored as sensory perceptions, obsessional ruminations, or behavioral reenactments (Janet, 1909; van der Kolk & van der Hart, 1991). In severe cases, such as posttraumatic stress disorder, treatment of individuals often focuses on the processing of the memory (Foa, Roghbaum, & Molnar, 1995). Traumatic memories are more disorganized than other memories and it is argued that treatments aimed at organizing memory should be particularly effective (since more organized memories are easier to integrate into existing memory (Foa & Riggs, 1993)). Narrative formation may be a particularly important strategy for imposing organization. Decreasing disorganization over time has been associated with improvement in narratives from victims of personal trauma during exposure treatment (DeSavino et al., 1993). This suggests that the organization of stressful memories, particularly with narrative structure, may be a critical factor in the beneficial effects of writing about stressful events.

One problem with processing, organizing, and integrating traumatic memories seems to be that they lack linguistic components and therefore cannot be effectively communicated or organized (Smyth & Pennebaker, 1999). Emotional writing about traumatic or stressful events may be beneficial because it is effective at forcing the re-coding of the traumatic memory into narrative language. Although this theoretical explanation that writing produces a restructuring of memories through narrative formation seems plausible, it needs to be explored in the context of writing about traumatic experiences. Pennebaker and colleagues developed a computer program (the Linguistic Inquiry and Word Count) to measure emotional and cognitive categories of word usage in the essays. Using this approach, a re-analysis of essays produced in six writing studies found that improvement was predicted by changes in insight and causal words over the course of writing (Pennebaker, Mayne, & Francis, 1997). Specifically, people whose health improved, who got higher grades, and who found jobs after writing went from using relatively few causal and insight words to using a high rate of them by the last day of writing. The authors note that the essays of people who showed this pattern of language use appeared to be constructing a story over time (Pennebaker, Mayne, & Francis, 1996). This suggests that building a narrative is a critical factor in the beneficial effects of writing, although the research support is correlational.

This study investigated in an experimental fashion whether narrative formation during writing about traumatic experiences is necessary for improvement. Previous research has demonstrated that the expression of both thoughts and feelings about a traumatic event are necessary for improvement (Pennebaker & Beall, 1986), although it is not clear to what degree this overlaps with narrative formation. Is the expression of thoughts and feelings in conjunction sufficient for improvement or is it the explicit construction of a narrative that leads to improvement? To examine this issue, we created three writing conditions. The control condition asked individuals to write about neutral topics. The narrative condition asked individuals to write about their thoughts and feelings regarding a traumatic experience and to do so in a narrative way (i.e., to tell a story). The fragmented condition asked individuals to write about their thoughts and feelings regarding a traumatic experience, and to do so in a fragmented way (i.e., listing them in a telegraphic, unintegrated fashion). Although numerous definitions of narrative exist, we chose to focus on the organization and story-telling aspects because these are presumed to be the salutary aspects (Pennebaker, Mayne, & Francis, 1996; Smyth & Pennebaker, 1999).

Our primary hypothesis was that expressing thoughts and feelings in a nonnarrative format would not result in health improvements, whereas writing in a narrative structure about traumatic topics would produce improvements in health reports. A secondary hypothesis was that if narrative formation alters the memory representation of a traumatic experience; intrusions should decrease as narrative structure increases. Writing in a narrative format should produce decreases over time in trauma-relevant intrusions and writing in a nonnarrative format should not produce such reductions.

METHODS

Participants
Participants were 116 undergraduate student volunteers (69% female) ranging in age from 18 to 35 years (mean = 18.8 years). The sample was 59% Caucasian, 17% Asian, 8% Hispanic, 8% African American, and 8% reporting other races. Participation fulfilled a research requirement for the students' psychology course.

Materials
Impact of Events Scale. The Impact of Event Scale (IES) is a scale of commonly reported experiences of intrusion and avoidance to measure subjective distress caused by a traumatic event (Horowitz, Wilner, & Alvarez, 1979) and has been used as a process measure in other trauma disclosure studies (Lutgendorg & Antoni, 1999). Participants identify the most traumatic

experience of their life and respond to 15 items assessing the frequency of intrusive thoughts about the event or attempts to avoid thinking about the event over the past 7 days. All items use a four-point response key, "not at all," "rarely," "sometimes," or "often" and the IES has demonstrated adequate psychometric characteristics (Horowitz, Wilner, & Alvarez, 1979).

Symptom Report and Activity Restriction. Symptom report consisted of a self-report measure of common symptoms over the last week taken from previous research on the health effects of writing in a student sample (Greenberg, Wortman, & Stone, 1996). The specific symptoms were fever, dry cough, productive cough, congested nose, sinus pain, sneezing, hoarseness, muscle aches, aching joints or bones, muscle pain or cramps, fainting, diarrhea, rash, constipation, ear ache, vomiting, indigestion, headache, abdominal or stomach pain, water retention or bloating, endometriosis (cramps), and premenstrual symptoms. Participants indicated whether they had experienced any of the symptoms over the past 7 days (yes/no format). For each symptom participants reported, they also indicated if the symptom had caused them to stay in bed, miss school, or reduce other activities they had planned to do during the previous week. Activity restriction was included to measure the behavioral response to symptoms and was coded as the total number of items checked.

Mood Report. Affect was assessed immediately before and after writing by four adjectives describing positive affect (happy, joyful, enjoyment/fun, pleased) and five adjectives describing negative affect (depressed/blue, unhappy, angry/hostile, frustrated, worried/anxious). The adjectives were rated on a 7-point scale, with scores ranging from 0 *(not at all)* to 6 *(extremely)*, and are those used in previous research (Smyth, Hockemeyer, Andersen, & Stone, 1999). The psychometric characteristics of this approach are satisfactory and are reported in detail elsewhere (Diener & Emmons, 1985).

Essay Evaluation

Essays were evaluated on a 7-point scale, with scores ranging from 0 (not at all) to 3 (moderately) to 6 (extremely) for how emotional, how personal, and the degree to which they showed narrative structure (this was defined as showing the organization characteristics of a story, most notably a clear beginning, middle, and end). The length of the essays was coded as the number of words used. Essays were coded by three graduate student raters who were first trained by coding 200 essays from a previous writing experiment. Essay coding was conducted blind to experimental condition. There was considerable agreement between raters overall (interrater reliability = .83) and for each of the three primary rating categories (how emotional = .84, how personal = .79, narrative structure = .87). When differences between raters existed, consensus between raters on the appropriate evaluation was reached and that score was used.

Procedure

After informed consent was obtained, participants completed the IES and the symptom and activity restriction report. Participants were then randomly assigned to one of three experimental groups—control, fragmented, or narrative. Participants were provided with a writing tablet containing an insert with writing instructions for their group assignment and mood assessments. Participants completed the first mood form and wrote on their assigned topic for 20 minutes at which point they were signaled by the experimenter to finish writing and complete the second mood report. Essays were returned into a sealed box. Although most research uses multiple (typically three) writing sessions, it was reasoned that increasing the number of sessions would increase the likelihood that the fragmented experimental group would form a narrative, despite instructions to the contrary. Additionally, investigators have previously produced strong health effects of writing using a single session (Greenberg, et al., 1996).

The control group was given the following instructions:

We would like you to write about the following assigned topic. You should write about the specific topic in detail without discussing any of your thoughts and feelings surrounding the topic, but rather focus on a factual description. Today we want you to write about your plans for the *previous week*. Again, describe them in detail without referring to your thoughts or feelings associated with them.

The instructions for the fragmented experimental group were as follows:

You were recently asked to answer some questions about the most traumatic or stressful event of your life. We would now like you to write briefly about that event. The important thing is that you list the deepest thoughts, feelings, emotions, and sensations you experienced as a result of this event. You may choose to write about whichever aspects of the event you want, but whichever you choose, they should be aspects that have affected you very deeply. It is critical that you let yourself go and touch those deepest emotions, thoughts, and sensations that you had.

Some people find listing thoughts, feelings, and sensations about a stressful event upsetting, and may cry, feel sad or depressed afterwards. This is quite normal, and we will allow you as much time as you want when you have finished writing to compose yourself. Examples of each of the three aspects of the event (thoughts, feelings, and sensations) that you must write about, are listed below. You may use this as a rough guideline for how to structure your writing.

Example:
Event: When I was three, my dog ran away.
Feelings: I felt sad, alone, frightened, angry.
Thoughts: I didn't understand why my dog would want to
              leave me.
              It isn't fair.
              I loved my dog very much.
              Would I ever see him again?
Sensations: I had a queasy feeling in my stomach and a
              lump in my throat.

The narrative experimental group were given the following instructions:

> You were recently asked to answer some questions about the most traumatic or stressful event of your life. We would now like you to write briefly about that event. Don't worry about grammar, spelling or sentence structure. The important thing is that you write about your deepest thoughts, feelings, and sensations about the experience. Let yourself go and touch those deepest emotions and thoughts you have. Most importantly, try to form a narrative about the experience. Start by describing the circumstances that led up to the event, then describe what happened during the event. Next, write about the consequences of the event. That is what happened and how it made you think and feel. Finally, try to conclude by describing how the event turned out. That is, how did it resolve, or what did you do to deal with the event? In other words, tell a story about what happened and how it made you feel. Some people find writing thoughts, feelings, and sensations about a stressful event upsetting, and may cry, feel sad or depressed afterwards. This is quite normal, and we will allow you as much time as you want when you have finished writing to compose yourself.

TABLE 1. Means and Standard Deviations of
Essay Characteristics and Changes in Mood by Group

		—Essay Characteristics—			—Mood Change— Positive	Negative
Group	Emotional	Personal	Narrative	Length	Mood	Mood
Control	0.42 (0.92)[a]	0.74 (1.20)[a]	1.53 (1.64)[a]	297 (110)[a]	1.34 (3.94)[a]	−1.14 (4.37)[a]
Fragmented	4.49 (1.67)[b]	4.85 (1.31)[b]	3.71 (1.51)[b]	406 (125)[b]	−3.50 (3.73)[b]	2.45 (5.93)[b]
Narrative	4.92 (1.18)[b]	5.05 (1.15)[b]	5.15 (1.51)[c]	391 (116)[b]	−2.78 (5.04)[b]	2.92 (7.24)[b]

Note: Standard deviations appear in parentheses. Different superscripts represent significant between-group contrasts ($p < .05$).

All participants were contacted by phone each week for 5 weeks after writing to complete the IES and symptom report.

RESULTS

All participants completed the writing task assigned to them without problems and none reported any difficulty with thoughts or emotions raised by the writing task. We first examined if essay characteristics differed by group using analysis of variance (ANOVA). The overall effect of group was significant for how emotional $F(2,112) = 140.7$, $p < .001$; how personal $F(2,113) = 152.4$, $p < .001$; narrative use $F(2,113) = 74.9$, $p < .001$; and essay length $F(2,113) = 9.6$, $p < .001$. Contrasts were performed to determine, more specifically, how the groups differed (see Table 1). Both experimental groups' essays were more emotional and personal than controls' essays and were also significantly longer. No differences were observed between fragmented and narrative essays for the amount of emotion used, how personal the essays were, or the length of the essays. Both experimental groups' essays were rated as containing significantly more narrative than control groups' essays. Narrative essays were rated as containing significantly more narrative than fragmented essays. Group means and contrasts are summarized in Table 1.

The effects of writing on immediate (i.e., pre- to postwriting) mood for each group was examined next. The change in mood was calculated for both positive and negative mood by subtracting prewriting mood from postwriting mood. This change score was used in subsequent analyses.[1] The overall ANOVA test for group was significant for both positive mood, $F(2,113) = 13.4$, $p < .001$ and negative mood, $F(2,113) = 4.9$, $p < .01$). Contrast tests revealed that writing produced significantly greater positive mood reductions and negative mood increases

[1]There is disagreement about the appropriateness of Δ (change) scores (versus a covariance analysis), although support for Δ scores can be found (e.g., Llabre, Spitzer, Sabb, Ironson, & Schneiderman, 1991). We chose to use Δ scores for ease in interpretation and comparison to other work in this area (Lutgendorf & Antoni, 1999; Smyth et al., 1999), although we also conducted the covariance analysis and found that the pattern of results was unchanged.

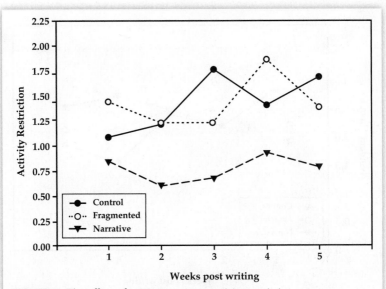

FIGURE 1. The effect of writing group on activity restriction.

in both experimental groups, compared with controls (see Table 1). The short-term effects of writing on mood did not differ between the fragmented and narrative experimental groups (see Table 1). This finding suggests participants are emotionally engaged in the task (i.e., taking the writing seriously). The immediate effect of writing about traumatic experiences on mood has been shown previously to be negative (Smyth, 1998) and may represent a necessary condition for improvement (Smyth & Pennebaker, 1999).

Multilevel random effects models (PROC MIXED in SAS) were used to test effects of group, time, and the interaction of group and time (group*time) on symptoms, activity restriction, intrusive thoughts, and avoidant thoughts. Time was coded as number of weeks postwriting (1 to 5), and baseline scores of each dependent variable were used as covariates. Composite symptom and activity restriction measures were

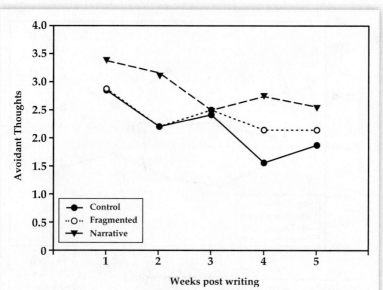

FIGURE 2. The effect of writing group on avoidant thoughts.

computed by summing all reports of symptoms or restriction
at each time point. Group (control, fragmented, and narrative)
was unrelated to symptom report, all $F(2,107) < 1.0$).[2] Individuals asked to form a narrative reported less restriction of
activity because of illness $F(2,107) = 8.17$, $p < .01$ (see Figure 1)
and showed higher avoidant thinking than the other groups
$F(2,107) = 3.70$, $p < .05$; see Figure 2). Group was unrelated
to intrusive thoughts, $F(2,107) < 1.0$, not significant). No
group*time effects were significant, all $F(2,107) < 1.75$, not
significant).

[2]*The symptom checklist has also been used to construct three subscales: upper respiratory
symptoms, musculoskeletal symptoms, and miscellaneous symptoms (Greenberg et al.,
1996). This strategy was evaluated and does not alter the results (no subscale was related
to group) so the simpler method of cumulating symptoms is presented. It also must be
noted that symptom levels were examined both in raw form and adjusted for gender
specific content with no differences in results.*

DISCUSSION

This study examined the role of narrative formation in written disclosure interventions by attempting to experimentally manipulate narrative use in writing. These data are the first demonstration that instructions to form a narrative during written disclosure produce a different response to writing than does fragmented or control writing. Participants were willing and able to follow the instructions given in this study and the experimental manipulation (manipulating narrative use without compromising the expression of thoughts and feelings) appears to have been successful. Participants given the fragmented expression instructions disclosed similar amounts of emotion and personal topics, differing from the narrative group only in the degree of narrative use when writing. Although both experimental groups expressed their deepest thoughts and feelings about the most traumatic experience of their life, the fragmented writing group was not distinguishable from the control group on any measure. In contrast, the narrative writing group showed some indication of health improvements and, albeit in an unexpected fashion, alteration of avoidant thoughts. This preliminary finding suggests that the mere expression of thoughts and feelings surrounding a traumatic experience may not be sufficient for improvement and that narrative formation is necessary.

Our hypothesis that intrusions would be reduced by narrative writing was not supported (Lutgendorf & Antoni, 1999). This may reflect the need for increases or improvements in narrative formation, as suggested by Pennebaker, Mayne, and Francis (1997). One session of writing may not be sufficient to produce such changes. The fact that we found evidence for some health improvement, however, makes this interpretation less likely because alterations in narrative are presumed to underlie both cognitive (i.e., intrusions) and physical (i.e., health) benefits (Pennebaker, Mayne, & Francis, 1997). The persistent elevation of avoidant thinking was unexpected and not consistent with speculation that avoidant thinking increases after writing, then rapidly returns back to or below baseline levels (Smyth & Pennebaker, 1999). It is interesting to note, however, that another study using a single writing session (Greenberg et al., 1996) reported increases in avoidant thinking after writing, although health benefits were observed. It is possible that a single writing session, despite producing health benefits, serves a sensitizing function. In response, participants may actively try to avoid thinking of the traumatic content. Multiple writing sessions may not produce this avoidance response as participants have the opportunity to habituate to the traumatic memory over several days (Smyth et al., 1999). At this point, however, the role of intrusive and avoidant thinking in written disclosure is not clear and needs clarification through additional research.

Although no differences in symptom report existed, this must be interpreted in light of the overall low level of symptoms reported in this sample (i.e., a "floor" effect). Future research needs to replicate these preliminary findings in a sample experiencing higher rates of illness symptoms or clinical illness. An alternative explanation is that participants were unwilling to express physical symptoms over the phone. This study used a minimal intervention (i.e., a single writing session). It is currently unclear if increasing the number of sessions would serve to enhance group differences (e.g., a "dose" effect) or eliminate them since both groups, regardless of instruction, imposed organization or narrative structure. This study did not examine how an experimental group given typical instructions (i.e., no attempt to interfere with or maximize narrative) would respond. Are instructions to form a narrative beneficial while instructions to form a fragmented style detrimental? Overall, this preliminary study suggests that the organization aspects of narrative play a critical role in the health benefits of writing about traumatic events and that written disclosure lacking narrative formation may not be beneficial.

REFERENCES

DeSavino, P., Turk, E., Massie, E., Riggs, D., Penkower, D., Molnar, C., & Foa, E. (1993, November). *The content of traumatic memories: Evaluating treatment efficacy by analysis of verbatim descriptions of the rape scene.* Paper presented at the 27th Annual Meeting of the Association for the Advancement of Behavior Therapy, Atlanta, Georgia.

Diener, R., & Emmons, E. (1985). Personality correlates of subjective well-being. *Personality and Social Psychology Bulletin, 11,* 89–97.

Foa, E., & Riggs, D. (1993). Posttraumatic stress disorder in rape victims. In J. Oldham, H. B. Riba, & A. Tasman (Eds.), *American Psychiatric Press Review of Psychiatry* (Vol. 12, pp. 273–303). Washington, DC: American Psychiatric Press.

Foa, E., Roghbaum, B., & Molnar, C. (1995). Cognitive-behavioral treatment of posttraumatic stress disorder. In M. Friedman, D. S. Charney, & A. Y. Deutch (Eds.), *Neurobiological and Clinical Consequences of Stress: From Normal Adaptation to Posttraumatic Stress Disorder* (pp. 483–494). New York: Lippincott-Raven Publishers.

Greenberg, M. A. (1995). Cognitive processing of traumas: The role of intrusive thoughts and reappraisals. *Journal of Applied Social Psychology, 25,* 1262–1296.

Greenberg, M. A., Wortman, C. B., & Stone, A. A. (1996). Emotional expression and physical health: Revising traumatic memories or fostering self-regulation. *Journal of Personality and Social Psychology, 71,* 588–602.

Horowitz, M., Wilner, N., & Alvarez, W. (1979). Impact of events scale: A measure of subjective stress. *Psychosomatic Medicine, 41,* 209–219.

Janet, P. (1909). *Les névroses.* Paris: Flammarion.

Llabre, M., Spitzer, S., Saab, P., Ironson, G., & Schneiderman, N. (1991). The reliability and specificity of delta versus residualized change as measures of cardiovascular reactivity to behavioral challenge. *Psychophysiology, 28,* 701–711.

Lutgendorf, S., & Antoni, M. (1999). Emotional and cognitive processing in a trauma disclosure paradigm. *Cognitive Therapy and Research, 23,* 423–440.

Pennebaker, J. W. (1993). Putting stress into words: Health, linguistic, and therapeutic implications. *Behavioral Research Therapy, 31,* 539–548.

Pennebaker, J.W., & Beall, S. (1986). Confronting a traumatic event: Toward an understanding of inhibition and disease. *Journal of Abnormal Psychology, 95,* 274–281.

Pennebaker, J., Mayne, T., & Francis, M. (1997). Linguistic predictors of adaptive bereavement. *Journal of Personality and Social Psychology, 72,* 863–871.

Smyth, J. (1998). Written emotional expression: Effect sizes, outcome types, and moderating variables. *Journal of Consulting and Clinical Psychology, 66,* 174–184.

Smyth, J., Hockemeyer, J., Anderson, C., & Stone, A. (2001). Is it safe to write? Does writing about emotionally disturbing events elicit sustained distress in patients with chronic illness? Manuscript submitted for publication.

Smyth, J., Stone, A., Hurewitz, A., & Kaell, A. (1999). Writing about stressful events produces symptom reduction in asthmatics and rheumatoid arthritics: A randomized trial. *Journal of the American Medical Association, 281,* 1304–1309.

Smyth, J., & Pennebaker, J. (1999). Telling one's story: Translating emotional experiences into words as a coping tool. In C. R. Snyder (Ed.), *Coping: The psychology of what works* (pp. 70–89). New York: Oxford University Press.

van der Kolk, B. & van der Hart, O. (1991). The intrusive past: The flexibility of memory and the engraving of trauma. *American Imago, 48,* 425–454.

A Literary and Film Analysis

TITLE. The third article for dissection is titled "Arresting Monstrosity: Polio, *Frankenstein*, and the Horror Film," which was published in *PMLA*, the official journal of the Modern Language Association. (Much of what appears in *PMLA* is quite diverse within the humanities and language study, but focuses strongly on various kinds of literary analysis.) Notice that the title has two parts: a clever opening, followed by some explanatory terms that help to define the article's focus. Readers understand that the article will examine both the text version of *Frankenstein* and the films that it spawned, but that it will also consider the role of polio in images or depictions of the creature that Dr. Frankenstein created. We can expect, then, that the article will discuss literature, film, and medicine, and that it will do so in historical context.

AUTHOR AND AUDIENCE. The article was written by Dwight Codr, whose brief biography appears at the bottom left of the first page. He is an assistant professor in the English Department at the University of Connecticut, a major, state-supported research institution. The biography also mentions a (relevant) course that he teaches and summarizes some of his other publications and a book in progress. Given the prestige of this journal and the author's institutional affiliation, we can expect that the article is well researched and of high quality, even though he is an early-career scholar. The audience for this piece will be readers of, and subscribers to, *PMLA,* especially those who are interested in nineteenth- and early twentieth-century literature and film, and within that, Mary Shelley and *Frankenstein,* her gothic novel, and the film adaptations of it.

PURPOSE. In addition to the clues that we get from the title, the purpose of the article is stated quite openly in the second sentence. The first sentence sets the scene: since the publication of an important "metacritical" book in 1987, scholars have focused on how *Frankenstein* (the novel) has been used to create "cultural hysteria." Then, in the second sentence, the author explains exactly what he will do:

> I wish to argue that given the context of epidemic poliomyelitis, mid-twentieth-century cinematic re-mediations of Shelley's monster were uniquely important in articulating mass fears, perhaps more so than its original depiction (which, for reasons I will discuss, would have been an inappropriate reference point for polio culture).

What we can expect, then, is that the author will support a case that the film adaptations of *Frankenstein* were connected to public concerns or fears about polio. The third sentence refines the purpose a bit more by suggesting not that the films exploited the fear of polio but that they "worked in the service of public health initiatives. . . ."

SKELETON AND MAJOR ORGANS. The skeletal structure of the article is revealed in its subheadings, which appear as follows:

Monstrous Bodies before Karloff

The Karloffian Monster in Context

The Karloffian Monster

The Karloffian Monster and the Crippler

Notes

Works Cited

Although these headings aren't especially helpful in giving us specific information about the contents or direction of the article, they do tell us that much of the focus will be on Boris Karloff's famous film version of *Frankenstein* and its influence on society. There's also a slight hint at a historical progression, with a focus on "monstrous bodies before Karloff" (this section focuses mostly on how *Frankenstein* was depicted in prose and then in images), followed by a much longer section that provides more context and history. The distinctions between the "monster in context" and "the monster" will need to be seen in reading the piece, however. Given the title, we might assume that the fourth section will turn to an analysis of the relationships between polio and the *Frankenstein* films. Notice also the amount of text within each subsection. The first subsection has by far the shortest amount of text; the second subsection has the longest. We can expect, then, that a good deal of background and context are required for the author to then turn to his claim and sufficiently document and support it.

MINOR ORGANS. In addition to the brief biography discussed earlier, the only minor organs in the piece are three quotations before the introduction, none of which really play a role in the article but perhaps pique the reader's interest and show the connection between *Frankenstein* (the first two) and polio (the third). At the end of the article, nineteen notes appear, preceded by some brief acknowledgments. Notice that in this journal, it's appropriate for the author to elaborate on certain details in the numbered notes, a practice sometimes avoided in other disciplines that prefer authors to include all information in the body of the text.

USE OF OUTSIDE SOURCES. All references to outside sources appear in the final section titled "Works Cited" (as opposed to "References" in the social science and mathematics articles). These labels are just a matter of convention. In the body of the text, authors' names appear in parentheses followed by page numbers (not years). However, film titles are associated with their year of release: "James Whale's *Frankenstein* (1931). . . ." When the author quotes something that was quoted in another work, he indicates it as follows:

> ". . . and my steel leg swung forward absurdly" (qtd. in Wilson, "And They" 184).

Because there are two works by Wilson included in the Works Cited, the author has to include part of the title of the work he is quoting from ("And They," which refers to the full title "And They Shall Walk: Ideal versus Reality in Polio Rehabilitation in the United States"). This contrasts with APA style and other formats that differentiate authors by year of publication. (Note how these conventions are also indicative of the citation differences discussed in Chapter 6.)

DOCUMENTATION. Especially because *PMLA* is an official publication of the Modern Language Association, all articles follow the MLA style guide scrupulously. The flag for the source within the text is a parenthetical reference that contains the author and then, if necessary, part of a title if the author has more than one work listed in the "Works Cited," and then the page number(s). In this article, the "Works Cited" list is rather complicated because it includes, among other things, articles, books, films, a memo, YouTube clips, and chapters in edited collections. The schematic for an article in this style looks like this:

> Lastname, Firstname. "Title of Article." *Title of Journal* volume.issue (year): xxx–xxx. Print or online.

Notice that, unlike APA formatting, MLA requires you to say what form you got the work in (print, web, YouTube, DVD, etc.).

It would take this chapter into a lengthy section on MLA reference style to show how each of the other kinds of reference is formatted; obviously, the best solution is for you to consult the *MLA Handbook for Writers of Research Papers*.

GRAPHICS. Because this article focuses strongly on film depictions, there are eight black-and-white images from films, all labeled as "Figures," with descriptions and, for some, a source acknowledgment, which is usually required as a condition of obtaining permission to reprint an image. (Some of the images in the article had to be deleted from this version precisely because of such permissions issues; they are indicated in the article with the words "image deleted" in brackets.)" In addition to these eight images from films, early in the article there appears an illustration of *Frankenstein* that was part of the frontispiece of a play adaptation by Richard Brinsley Peake, an early nineteenth-century dramatist.

COLORATION. The article is written in a style that is common to literary, artistic, and historical interpretation. The following passage shows how the author synthesizes various film depictions as part of his interpretation—something that the films add up to or signify.

> Most of the films listed above feature villains who experience some kind of personal trauma and, in attempting to cure, become killers. Although Dr. Frankenstein and other madmen of horror are "scientists," the polio epidemic provided a medical frame of reference for their science. For instance, in *Night Monster* (1942) three doctors visit the estate of a wealthy former patient of theirs, Curt Ingston, who is now a quadriplegic; in a series of dialogues, each doctor reveals his careerist motivations and mercenary interests, indicating an unethical blurring of care and research.

The prose here is clear and appealing, with an emphasis on illustration as support. A quick reading of the entire article shows a deft movement between historical information and literary and film interpretation that cumulatively supports and documents the main argument the author makes up front. As is common in this and related disciplines, a high price is not placed on concision, even though the journal imposes a page limit on submissions: it's possible to "roam around" the subject, adding details and side points, and even minutiae that are relegated to the footnotes at the end. Unlike the social science article and very unlike the mathematics proof, the writing here feels loose and exploratory even while heavily drawing on examples and historical information.

JARGON. This piece relies very little on the specialized terminology of some literary criticism. Words that are common to film and literary criticism do appear, such as "genre" and "allusion," but these are also generally understood by the educated public. A few scattered specialized terms show up, such as "nondiegetic," but on the whole, this article signals its "membership" in the field through the detail and thoroughness of its analysis.

Although we're considering only this one article in the humanities, it's important to realize that the role of jargon varies considerably across publications (as it does in all fields). Compare this highly overwritten and jargon-filled excerpt from *The Johns Hopkins Guide to Literary Theory and Criticism*, edited by Michael Groden and Martin Kreiswirth (Johns Hopkins University Press, 1994):

> Previous exercises in influence study depended upon a topographical model of reallocatable poetic images, distributed more or less equally within "canonical" poems, each part of which expressively totalized the entelechy of the entire tradition. But Bloom now understood this cognitive map of interchangeable organic wholes to be criticism's repression of poetry's will to overcome time's anteriority.

Arresting Monstrosity: Polio, *Frankenstein*, and the Horror Film

Dwight Codr

He was paralyzed with fright!

—Dr. Phipps in *Night Monster* (1942)

It wasn't my imagination. It was a giant, and when I got up he had ahold of my arm.

—Peter von Frankenstein in *The Son of Frankenstein* (1939)

Old broken bodies made new!

—Frederick Bradman, on therapy for poliomyelitis (1933)[1]

EVER SINCE THE publication of Chris Baldick's metacritical approach to the history of *Frankenstein*, in 1987, scholars have focused on the ways in which Mary Shelley's 1818 novel has

DWIGHT CODR, assistant professor in the Department of English at the University of Connecticut, Storrs, teaches a semester-length course on Mary Shelley's Frankenstein. The author of published essays on Daniel Defoe, John Law, and Elizabeth Inchbald, he is working on a book on finance and the ethics of uncertainty in the long eighteenth century.

been deployed, often to "articulate cultural hysteria" (O'Flinn 208). I wish to argue that given the context of epidemic polio-myelitis, mid-twentieth-century cinematic re-mediations of Shelley's monster were uniquely important in articulating mass fears, perhaps more so than its original depiction (which, for reasons I will discuss, would have been an inappropriate reference point for polio culture). In exploring the ways in which polio is encoded in cinema, I aim to show how the *Frankenstein* franchise and other horror films of the polio era worked in the service of public health initiatives and that if, as critics sometimes suggest, the first golden age of horror began with James Whale's *Frankenstein* (1931), it was because it pro-vided a cinematic grammar exceptionally appropriate to the age of polio.

This is largely unexplored territory.[2] As Marc Shell puts the problem, "Recent books about disability and the cinema suffer from a failure to consider the simultaneous advent of popular cinema (with its focus on kinesis) on the one hand and the epidemic of polio (with its forced stasis) on the other" (134–35). Part of the reason for this, Shell argues, is that Holly-wood acknowledged polio's importance but went to great lengths to avoid its explicit presentation, as his adroit reading of Hitchcock's *Rear Window* illustrates. Polio, therefore, often appeared to audiences as a coded and oblique network of ref-erences and allusions rather than as the overt subject matter of cinema. Adding to Shell's analysis a consideration of horror films from the same period suggests a further dimension to polio culture: in horror, films traded less on stories of struggle and sought instead to exploit and reproduce the "spine-chill-ing" fears activated by the threat of disease. This essay shares Shell's interest in a culture that was terrified of poliomyelitis— a term coined to describe swelling of the gray matter of the spinal cord. The same culture was also increasingly consuming terrifying films routinely described, as Whale's *Frankenstein* was, as capable of sending "cold chills up and down the good old spinal cord" (Williams). In horror films, paralytic, deformed, and otherwise "abnormal" bodies do not typically represent the individual in a state of transition to "normalcy" but instead depend on and revel in the vast difference between the normal and the abnormal.

To underscore the impact of the convergence of cinema and polio on Shelley's monster, the first section of this essay briefly surveys its embodiment before Boris Karloff; the second section demonstrates the coded—at times, barely so—presence of polio in the golden age of horror; in this light, the third section analyzes relevant moments and motifs in the *Frankenstein* film series. The last section evaluates a 1947 film produced by the National Foundation for Infantile Paralysis in relation to the horror films previously discussed and closes with a consideration of the social implications of "the Karloffian monster." This phrase here describes not only Karloff's screen performances but also later cinematic horrors that drew on the aspects of Karloff's monster—his body, gait, experiences, associates, and habitations—that coincided with and helped to define polio culture. I aim to isolate and study a strand of cultural hysteria as it manifested itself in the genre of the horror film; my goal is to show the symptoms and results of this cross-contamination between the spheres of cinema and public health, specifically the impact of polio culture on the horror film and the role of the horror film in the fight against polio.

MONSTROUS BODIES BEFORE KARLOFF

So ingrained in our cultural consciousness is Karloff's monster that it is easy to forget how substantially it deviates from the monster described in Shelley's novel and portrayed in early theatrical and cinematic productions. Shelley's monster, for instance, suits the hostile physical expanses to which he is paradoxically confined: "I [Victor] suddenly beheld the figure of a man, at some distance, advancing towards me with superhuman speed. He bounded over the crevices in the ice, among which I had walked with caution." Espying the monster outside Geneva, Victor remarks, "I thought of pursuing the devil, but it would have been in vain, for another flash discovered him to me hanging among the rocks of the nearly perpendicular ascent of Mont Salêve. . . . He soon reached the summit and disappeared." Victor further wonders, "Who could arrest a creature capable of scaling the overhanging side of Mont Salêve?" After Victor's deposition, the magistrate replies, "I would willingly afford you every aid in your pursuit, but the creature of whom you speak appears to have powers which would put all my exertions to defiance. Who can follow an animal which can traverse the sea of ice and inhabit caves and dens, where no man would venture to intrude?" Elsewhere Victor observes that he "saw him descend the mountain with greater speed than the flight of an eagle" and move "with more than mortal speed" (65, 48, 49, 139, 100, 141). Combining these testaments to the monster's abilities with the reminders of his hideousness—too numerous and obvious to require listing—reveals an author and era comfortable pairing ostracizing physical deformity with superior physical competency.

Nineteenth-century graphic artists emphasized this competency, not his ugliness or unholy creation. The monster appearing on the cover of Richard Brinsley Peake's adaptation as it was printed in Dicks' Standard Plays is European in appearance and handsome as well (fig. 1). Lithe and flexible, reclining with the confidence of an unthreatened man, he towers over the diminutive Victor, whose off-balance pose and slender, downwardly pointed sword symbolizes his physical impotency. For contrast, a strategically drawn baluster, intimating the monster's colossal genitalia, registers his manliness and impossible virility. The monster's handsomeness in this and other images suggests that his monstrosity consists in something other than ugliness, that ugliness is an accident whose removal does not compromise the character's fundamental monstrosity.[3] The monster's monstrousness is not

FIG.1 Frontispiece of Richard Brinsley Peake's *Frankenstein*. Courtesy of Ruth Lilly Special Collections and Archives, IUPUI University Library.

necessarily his ugliness, at least not in the nineteenth century or at least not for everyone.

The earliest cinematic incarnations of the monster explore ugliness but do not abandon the physicality of the theatrical adaptations. In J. Searle Dawley's *Frankenstein* (1910), Charles Ogle's sinister and bestial monster moves fluidly, his gestures confident and organic. In *Life without Soul* (1915), Percy Standing's monster involved "none of the grotesque trappings of Charles Ogle" and "wore no distinguishing make-up" (Glut 63). Though these early films deviate from Shelley's novel in obvious ways, their monsters continue the tradition of presenting the creature as virile, lithe, strong, agile, and even, at times, handsome.[4] These early bodies are manifestly capable of the physical feats described by Shelley, and they evidence a general consistency with the monster's physical potentiality. So how do we go from a character capable of descending mountains with eagle-like speed, of bounding across seas of ice, to the more limited Karloffian monster?

THE KARLOFFIAN MONSTER IN CONTEXT

A widely recognized source for Karloff's performance was Paul Wegener's unsteady and stiff Golem (1920 [*Der Golem*]). This, however, does not explain why audiences, actors, and filmmakers kept evoking his Golemesque attributes in the ensuing decades. Establishing the polio context helps to do so. Karloff's monster appeared in the years between the first two major polio outbreaks and attained iconic status in the next two decades, as the polio fear approached its climax. A complex and multiform disease, polio causes, among other symptoms, muscle tightening, stiffness of the legs or arms or both, slackening of facial muscles, labored or abnormal respiration, and slow, unsteady movement, all of which feature in the performances of Karloff and his successors. The kinetic similarities have been noted by polio survivors but not by historians of polio or by readers of Whale's film. Charles Mee writes of a childhood experience when his doctor and "three of her strong-armed assistants sat me up on a cot and swung my steel-clad leg over the side. Like Frankenstein. . . . Then they tilted me forward and lifted me up at the waist on my left side only so that the foot came off the floor, and my steel leg swung forward absurdly" (qtd. in Wilson, "And They" 184). Similarly, Michael Perrault writes of his childhood, "Eventually, I did [walk again]. But it wasn't without cold hard metal inserts under my arches in ankle-height orthopedic shoes attached to heavy chrome braces that clunked and gave me Frankenstein-like movements." Whereas braces and orthopedic shoes had helped Perrault and others walk, Jack Pierce, the makeup artist for Whale's film, "gave Karloff a five-pound brace to wear on his spine to keep his movements impaired and stiff, and a pair of raised boots that further hampered his walking, weighing an uncomfortable twelve and one-half pounds each" (Glut 103). Under such conditions, "any conception of the Monster as fleet . . . disappeared" (Lavalley 263). Whether the underlying body needed support or impediment, the impact of these technologies on viewers—of the cinematic monster or the polio victim—was the same. Seeing Karloff in Whale's film was to see a version of polio; for survivors, experiencing polio therapy was to experience being Karloff.

But limiting our attention to Karloff's 1931 performance would be a mistake, for later screen monsters—within and without the Frankenstein canon—made his canonical through repetition, allusion, and citation. In other words, Karloff was undoubtedly influential, but his performance was made meaningful by later screen monsters, portrayed by an array of actors who grafted parts of his monster onto their own. So by "the Karloffian monster" I mean a set of performances that were as responsible for Karloff's iconicity as Karloff was for the performances. Hence, analyzing his 1931 monster requires us to consider as well Karloff's traces in monsters of the later 1930s and the 1940s, which legitimated his original performance. Much is to be gleaned from an evaluation of *Frankenstein*'s precursors—including *Der Golem* and F. W. Murnau's *Nosferatu* (1922), where vampirism translates as plague—but because what is at stake here is Karloff's canonization in and his long reach into the golden age of horror, I focus on later films.

The Karloffian monster emerged, then, out of a series of films from Universal Studios that began with Whale's 1931 *Frankenstein;* Karloff reprised the role for *The Bride of Frankenstein* (1935) and *Son of Frankenstein* (1939). Lon Chaney, Jr., presented the same basic figure in *The Ghost of Frankenstein* (1942); Bela Lugosi, having acted the part of Ygor for *Son,* played the monster in *Frankenstein Meets the Wolf Man* (1943). Glenn Strange exploited the comic potential of an awkwardly mobile monster for *Bud Abbott and Lou Costello Meet Frankenstein* (1948), but Strange had appeared as the monster in two "serious" films before this: *House of Frankenstein* (1944) and *House of Dracula* (1945). Lugosi's and Chaney's monsters were exaggerations of Karloff's, Strange's the most hyperbolic. In 1957, when Hammer Film Productions took over the franchise, Christopher Lee's monster, in *The Curse of Frankenstein,* bore no resemblance to Karloff's: gone were the electrodes, the stiffness, the unbalanced stride. Lee's break with the tradition was nowhere more apparent than in the scene where audiences first saw his visage. Where in close-up the camera had lingered on Karloff's slackened face and sunken eyes, Lee violently dashes away his bandages. Why Hammer went in a new direction is less important than the fact that Karloff's monster, not Lee's, persists in our cultural memory.[5] Polio provided an organizing frame of reference for consumption of the Karloffian monster, and while the end of the polio scare in 1955—the year of Jonas Salk's polio vaccine—corresponds to the end of the Karloffian monster on-screen, its endurance as icon bespeaks the presence of an unresolved cultural remainder, a point to which I will return at the end of this essay.

Beginning in 1916, polio inserted itself into the American imaginary, for two reasons.[6] First, many people were infected or personally knew someone that had been infected by it. Because of reporting discrepancies, mortality and infection statistics vary, but, to provide some perspective, there were 27,000 cases and 6,000 deaths the year of the first polio outbreak (1916). That year 9,000 New Yorkers alone contracted polio. Infections rose and fell over the years. In 1952, a particularly bad year, there were 58,000 cases. Second, the public campaign against polio made it a matter of concern for all citizens, regardless of actual infection. Less than a week after the New York epidemic of 1916 was publicly announced and acknowledged, children, infected or not, were officially barred from entering movie houses (Gould 5), which was part of a larger process of turning a medical matter into one of public policy. Officials stressed hygiene and discouraged attendance at public places of resort, especially swimming pools; doctors became celebrities; March of Dimes' logos appeared in advertisements for films, clothing, financial services, and other products. If one did not suffer from polio, one was enlisted in the fight against it.[7] The president of the United States for much of this era had polio, and, notwithstanding some attempt at concealment, polio made its way into public consciousness through his presence in newspapers, broadcasts, and conversation.

If we intend to read Karloff in a polio context, what accounts for the fifteen-year gap separating the first epidemic, in 1916, from the distribution of Whale's 1931 film? Neither imagery of children suffering from polio nor the technology to circulate it was available until somewhat later. The first publicized acknowledgment of the disease as an American problem did not take place until 1926–27, when FDR established the whites-only Warm Springs Foundation. The invention of the iron lung (1927) further enhanced polio's profile; it assisted sufferers with breathing and saved many lives, but in immobilizing the body and looking rather like a coffin, it "became the most terrifying symbol of polio's destructive power" (Oshinsky, following 150). The National Foundation for Infantile Paralysis (NFIP), designed to heighten awareness and sponsor research, was not founded until 1937 and only came into its own the following year when Eddie Cantor publicly styled its fundraising arm as "the March of Dimes" (MOD). As a result, the images of polio multiplied rapidly in the late 1920 s, were increasingly distributed in the 1930s, around the time of the first *Frankenstein* films, and were universal by the 1940s. In 1941 the Tuskegee Infantile Paralysis Center (TIPC), for African American victims, supplemented the Warm Springs Foundation, NFIP, and MOD; its establishment was "marked by a ceremony broadcast nationally on the radio," featuring an address by FDR (Rogers 784). Although TIPC was an out-growth of Jim Crow, the center's institutional ties to NFIP began the work of communicating that polio was an equal-opportunity disease and that the effort to combat it therefore had to include all racial identities.

The outing of polio was further delayed by the fact that sufferers had been and would continue to be kept out of sight by their families because of stigma. The antipolio campaigns only gradually brought into the public eye what had been kept as family secrets (Wilson, "Crippling Fear" 486–87 and "And They" 176–77).[8] The publicity campaign gained momentum when, in 1934, three years after Whale's first film, another major outbreak of polio occurred, this time in Los Angeles, where *Frankenstein* had been filmed and where its sequel, *Bride,* was being filmed. Reports of "50 new cases a day" induced panic (Paul 221). Perhaps because the outbreak occurred in a city tied to film production, that industry took a keen interest in the polio problem. In the early 1940s the largest source of donations to MOD was the collection boxes circu-lated in movie theaters: "In 1938 annual contributions to the March of Dimes amounted to $1.8 million. By 1945 that figure had reached $19 million, the most ever raised by a charity other than the American Red Cross. Forty percent—almost $8 million—came from local movie houses" (Shell 69). For reasons aside from their professional ties with New York and Los Angeles, theater owners were surely aware, while closures and attendance restrictions continued, that their venues needed to be seen as part of the solution rather than a source of the problem.[9] Just as TIPC had implicitly increased polio's relevance to racial minorities, the theaters' practices incorpo-rated an erstwhile private concern into an expanding public network of information and research.

What did Hollywood have to offer in its films? In *The Healer* (1935), a Warm Springs doctor treats the polio-stricken Jimmy while trying to sort out his own love life during a vacation. *Never Fear* (1949) tells the story of a dancer tragically stricken by polio and her fight against it. A few films had minor characters suffering from polio or subplots pertaining to it—*Leave Her to Heaven* (1945), *Roughly Speaking* (1945)—but even as newspaper readers during this period "may have felt as if there was nowhere to run from the endless train of bad news related to polio" (Foertsch 153), what surprises is how few films directly confronted the epidemic.[10] In those that did, polio often serves as a convenient backdrop for the unfolding of a human drama and has little to do with the historical realities of the disease. *The Healer,* perhaps the most sustained cinematic treatment of polio before Salk's vaccine, simply translated the terms of a 1911 novel about cancer (Herrick). As Shell observes, "a movie or stage play that says it is about polio may not be essentially about polio" (151).

While only a handful of films explicitly confront polio, allusions to it abound in the horror genre. What appears to mark the territory of the horrific in cinema of this period is the frequent citation of polio in forms other than itself: blood, body parts, injections, serums, experiments on simians, laboratories, prosthetics, restraints, therapy, and doctors.[11] Establishing this context for the rise of the horror genre makes it easier to appreciate and understand the fears and anxieties that attended the viewing of many films of the period. To list a few before moving on to a more sustained consideration of others: *The Black Room* (1935) features Boris Karloff as Anton, whose paralyzed arm plays a key role in the plot; in *The Man Who Lived Again* (1936), Dr. Laurence (Karloff) undertakes his diabolical plan with a surgical assistant who requires a wheelchair; the plot of *The Return of Dr. X* (1939) concerns the use of synthetic blood in reanimating the dead. Full of details concerning doctors who seek cures, inject patients with mysterious serums, experiment with animal parts, and immobilize bodies by strapping them down to gurneys or into machines in confusing laboratory spaces, these films recall stories about vaccination programs in the 1930s, about the arrival of

Elizabeth Kenny and her unauthorized therapies focusing on "reintroducing" stiffened limbs to the brain, and about research into and development of respiration devices, braces, restraints, and dietary and hygiene regimens recommended by research centers from Minnesota to Georgia, Tuskegee to New York. Thematically speaking, horror's interest in reanimation also echoed the increasingly unstable boundary between life and death exemplified by the liminality of life in a coffin-like iron lung, as well as the somewhat confusing notion of "live" but "attenuated" vaccines.

During this time, Karloff routinely played the role of patient or doctor wrestling with issues of life, death, body parts, disease, and cure. In *The Man They Could Not Hang* (1939), he plays both. In *Before I Hang* (1940), he is a doctor researching a cure for aging; in *Black Friday* (1940), he reanimates his dead friend by using the brain of a deceased gangster; in *The Devil Commands* (1941), Dr. Blair (Karloff) attempts to make contact with his dead wife. Even when he was not cast, Karloff's presence could be felt in films dealing with such themes. In *The Monster Maker* (1944), the villain, played by J. Carrol Naish, bears a name, Dr. Igor Markoff, that could not more obviously evoke Ygor of the *Frankenstein* franchise and Karloff. While attempting to find a cure for the disease that killed his wife, Markoff cultivates a live form of the disease from "a concentrate of pituitary [gland]," which, when injected into the patient, impairs movement by producing severe physical deformity. This story capitalized on widely publicized experimentation with simian tissue in polio research; scolding his assistant for requesting the removal of a gorilla that is caged in his office, he remarks that the ape is "essential to my work."[12] As Markoff's diabolical plan unfolds, his increasingly deformed victim, the pianist Anthony Lawrence, chastises him: "Markoff! You have set yourself up as a Frankenstein and created a monster! I am that monster; but, if you remember, the monster destroyed the man who created him! That is what I'm going to do to you, Markoff!" At such a moment, in the mid-1940s, Karloff is Markoff, Markoff is Frankenstein, Lawrence is the monster, the monster is Karloffian; the film is thickly huddled and unstably allied with *Frankenstein* in an atmosphere of polio, disability, and experiment.

It is customary to see the mad doctor as interchangeable with the mad scientist, no doubt in part because Karloff was cast in both roles, but this fails to appreciate an important dimension of horror in the golden age, when polio presented true horror stories in the form of the widely publicized 1935 inoculation catastrophes associated with the researchers Maurice Brodie and John Kolmer. Much of the horror of these films consists in the threat that doctors might *become* scientists. Most of the films listed above feature villains who experience some kind of personal trauma and, in attempting to cure, become killers. Although Dr. Frankenstein and other madmen of horror are "scientists," the polio epidemic provided a medical frame of reference for their science. For instance, in *Night Monster* (1942) three doctors visit the estate of a wealthy former patient of theirs, Curt Ingston, who is now a quadriplegic; in a series of dialogues, each doctor reveals his careerist motivations and mercenary interests, indicating an unethical blurring of care and research. As the doctors are murdered in succession, everyone suspects the wheelchair-bound Ingston, believing that he may be faking paralysis. This suspicion subsides when it is discovered that he is a quadruple amputee. But the plot turns again, and Ingston is revealed to be the killer: we learn that he has acquired the ability to psychokinetically materialize arms and legs to carry out his revenge on the doctors who treated him as a research project. Audiences are not told what this research was exactly, but they would not have had to reach far to infer that the doctors were treating arms and legs rendered inoperative by polio to advance their own selfish, shadowy agendas. Although Ingston's paralysis is not explicitly ascribed to polio, one should consider Shell's insight regarding the constitutive ambiguities of polio culture: "How could one tell for sure what was the cause of a person's being in a wheelchair? . . . Captain Ahab . . . in *The Sea Beast* (1926) has lost his lower leg, so we might figure that his situation is that of an amputee. But what if he is tricking us? Or what if amputation were a treatment for polio? How would we know for sure?" (150–51). Ingston represents the polio victim not because he is so described but because the audience is forced to ask, What if he is tricking us? The film takes us to the heart of polio culture not because it places a quadruple amputee at the center of its narrative but precisely because it refuses its audience an explanation for this central fact of the narrative.

To audiences in the theaters Shell discusses, who had likely just been asked to donate to MOD, Ingston's psychokinetically generated legs and arms would have been richly meaningful. They may have provided wish fulfillment for some victims, a psycho-cinematic kinesis that fantastically solved what Shell describes as the "forced stasis" of polio, but they also reminded audiences that a scientific solution to paralysis was, in 1942, as tragically unlikely as a psychokinetic one. In addition, they recall the mysterious movement of polio from victim to victim. How could a disease that impeded its victims' mobility be so easily transmitted? Although this is not hard to grasp, since many polio victims retained or regained mobility and since bodily intimacy was not, in any case, necessary for transmission, such realities do little to ameliorate anxieties about disease (as similarly irrational anxieties about HIV transmission in the 1980s and 1990s demonstrate). Much of the highly publicized medical research leading up to the vaccine was concerned with questions of transmission: did the disease require physical contact? did it spread through the air? could it be spread through objects, such as pencils? was it transmitted along a nasal-oral or fecal-oral route? "Polio fears were exacerbated by the lack of solid medical knowledge regarding the disease" (Wilson, "Crippling Fear" 469). A variation of the transmission question serves as *Night Monster*'s central mystery: how can a man confined to a wheelchair hunt down his victims? Ingston's homicidal mobility serves as a trope for this line of inquiry, and, like the disease he figures, it was frightening to the extent that it was inexplicable. Psychokinesis enters the film's reality through the magical kinetics of film, suggesting that the palpable threat of immobility provides an exigency, authority, and market for films whose frights and mysteries derived from editing trickery.

The Ape (1940) weaves together aspects of *The Monster Maker* and *Night Monster:* Dr. Bernard Adrian (Karloff) attempts to cure the wheelchair-bound paraplegic Frances, the victim of a "paralysis epidemic" that recently hit the town (extras in the film use crutches). Adrian discovers that human spinal fluid cures paralysis; when an ape escapes from a local circus, he kills it, dresses himself in its skin, and goes out to collect fluid from members of the community until authorities shoot him dead. Mad as Adrian may have appeared, his motivation for killing was to cure Frances, and he did just that: the film closes with an image of her walking in the sunshine with her boyfriend. Nevertheless, the townspeople rightly feared Adrian, believing that he would treat them as "guinea pigs." The film refers only to a "paralysis epidemic," and although unmistakably dealing with polio—its symptoms, its victims, the race for a cure, medical technologies, simians, epidemic disease—the film never mentions it by name. But, again, few films in any genre did so. Here polio reveals itself only in the paralysis plot and the otherwise baffling ape appearance.

More broadly speaking, *The Ape, Night Monster,* and *The Monster Maker* all work to unsettle markers of difference. Playing on fears that doctors have ulterior scientific agendas, each film makes the doctor out to be criminally insane, displacing the more rational fear of what was happening with real-world doctors working on polio. Presenting their victims as male and female, criminal and official, young and old, rich and poor, collectively these films asked audiences to see past differences and to recognize a shared vulnerability vis-à-vis a complexly figured nemesis/disease (which are occasionally, as in *The Monster Maker*, the same thing). Many such films present carnally threatening simians that, on the one hand, exploit white audiences' racist fears of black male sexuality but, on the other, resolve the ape into a scientific prop, at least provisionally bracketing the issue of race by suggesting that apes are not always black men; sometimes they are research experiments.[13] These films show bad doctors and the disease as menaces to a citizenry defined by its common need for a cure.

THE KARLOFFIAN MONSTER

Important as the kinesiologic similarities of the Karloffian monster and the polio sufferer are to this reading, the intersections of polio culture and *Frankenstein* are not confined to the monster's walk, posture, and appearance.[14] For instance, the immobility that should have rendered the disease less contagious made it all the more terrifying, just as the monster's plodding deliberateness of movement instilled in audiences nervousness rather than a sense of security. Correspondingly, the physical limitations imposed by polio contributed to rather than detracted from the perceived and real lethality of contagion. Scenes in *Frankenstein* and its sequels wherein the slow-moving monster is suddenly at the point of attack dramatize the anxious anticipation of viewers regarding the nature of polio contraction. Viewers at the time did not establish this connection, but a reviewer of *Son of Frankenstein* seemed to sense that the monster's gait, somewhere between humorous and horrifying, had something to do with the film's effect on audiences: "Once more Karloff appears as The Monster, an amazing creature that stalks about in wooden soldier manner, and weeps because he isn't as handsome as Mr. Rathbone. The plot leads to shrieks and nervous paroxysms of laughter" ("New Films"). Shelley had paired the monster's brute strength with the locomotive swiftness of an athlete, thereby enabling the illustrator of Peake's adaptation to render the monster as an Achilles; Karloff paired brute strength with the locomotive impairment of disease, creating a being who was unconquerable and destructive but also "wooden," immobile.

Did Karloff merely bring a dose of realism to the performance, suggesting that such a monster would logically be a little unsteady at first? Certainly, another way of reading Karloff's character is to see in his awkward steps the instability and uncertainty of a child's first steps. As a newborn, the cinematic monster can be read as infantile and incipient rather than adult and "finished." Why, however, were audiences inclined to keep revisiting the spectacle of a giant walking like a child? Polio threatened to impose paralysis on the child, to turn an immobility natural to infancy (the inability to walk or to walk well) into a permanent and thus unnatural condition of life (limping, paralysis).[15] The monster therefore evokes complex fears associated with the idea of a mature mind with an infant's legs, an adult trapped in a child's body.[16] In this way, the Karloffian monster stoked fears about polio by embodying the polio victim as a sort of death-bringing man child, who, enabled by technology just enough to move about, is best kept at a distance.

The importance of children in the *Frankenstein* films is hard to overstate, for they feature prominently in *Frankenstein*, *Bride*, and the significantly titled *Son of Frankenstein*. The scene where the monster kills Maria in the first of these films piqued the ire of the Motion Picture Directors Association of America (MPDAA), leading to the scene's excision. The MPDAA's censure of the scene may have intensified the horror of what remained in the film, however. Now there was a gap between the monster's approach to the child and the bearing of her corpse through the street by her grieving father, a gap that audiences were made to fill in with speculative details of her demise.[17] While it was the philistinism of the MPDAA that had produced this vagary in the plot of *Frankenstein*, provocative indeterminacy is exploited in *Son of Frankenstein*. Repudiating Baron Wolf von Frankenstein's claims that townspeople must be overstating the monster's past villainies, Inspector Krogh informs Wolf that he himself lost his arm to the monster—we see that it has been replaced with a prosthesis—when he was a child.[18] Krogh's account of losing his arm is later echoed when Wolf's son Peter informs his father that he was awoken from his nap by a "giant" who grabbed hold of his arm (see the second epigraph). Krogh starts at this, grabs his prosthesis, and facially communicates the trauma of recollection as well as his determination to kill the monster. Wolf continues to interrogate Peter about this moment of contact, which occurred offscreen, like the monster's encounters with Maria in *Franken-stein* and Frida in *Bride*. To help his father (and the audience) understand what happened, Peter says that he was visited by "a great big man, and he walked like this," giving an imitation indistinguishable from that of a child in leg braces using crutches (fig. 2). [Fig. 2 has been deleted.] Peter's stiffened gait is sup-posed to be an imitation, but it encodes the contraction of polio (fig. 3). Maria and Frida die after a menacing and uncertain pres-ence is allowed to invade a space that should be under parental supervision; the same convention is invoked but also trans-formed when Peter is assaulted while napping in the comfort of his own, erstwhile safe home.

There are multiple overlaps between the films in the *Fran-kenstein* series and polio culture. *Son of Frankenstein* presents several in addition to that involving Peter. Wolf, for instance, subjects the monster to a barrage of medical tests to determine the nature of the affliction that has incapacitated him, and it turns out that the monster suffers from symptoms that charac-terize polio: high blood pressure, rapid heartbeat, enlarged heart. Listing the symptoms in the film at all anticipates the use of increasingly recondite medical language in horror films as audiences grew accustomed to such things as blood

FIG. 3 Frame from *In Daily Battle* (1947). Courtesy of the March of Dimes Archives, White Plains, New York.

pressure and acromegaly and found them to be interesting narrative material. Wolf then puts the monster on a kind of respirator and gives him a chest X-ray (fig. 4). Just after this scene, in which the monster has been fully medicalized, his differently disabled kindred spirit Ygor, exiting a meeting with local officials, is upbraided for coughing all over them and throughout the room ("Hey! You spit on me!" complains one official). The officials here, representative of the public health establishment, come into threatening contact with Ygor through effluvia that is implicitly tainted by its metonymic connection to the film's monster, Ygor's "friend." Further, when the inspector later asks the baron why he works in a dilapidated laboratory adjacent to the main house, given the potent fumes emanating from below, Wolf replies, "The structure was built by the Romans over a natural sulfur pit and was used by them as mineral baths," evoking the Warm Springs property to which FDR retreated for its therapeutic waters.

Though the question of the monster's relation to technology is significant to the novel and its many adaptations, it

FIG. 4 Frame from *Son of Frankenstein*.

takes on unique relevance for the Karloffian monster. The introduction of electrodes on the monster's neck makes explicit a fusion of organic and inorganic material that no earlier performances and few post-Universal films emphasize.[19] The electrodes suggest the monster's machinic nature, illustrated through comparisons of the *Frankenstein* monster with other cinematic cyborgs and robots (see, e.g., Goldman 279–80). The electrodes became (and remain) synecdoches for the monster, much as braces would be for the polio victim. This is more than visionary reading; in explaining the reason for the electrodes in a 1939 interview, Jack Pierce, the makeup artist responsible for Karloff's stylization, revealed that "Karloff has not only spent 864 shooting hours in three pictures with those big bolts plugged into his neck but he carries a five-pound steel spine—that you can't see—to represent the rod which conveys the current up to the monster's brain" ("Oh, You"). The electrodes were imagined as the visible sign of a metallic brace that constrained and defined Karloff's motions. Furthering this tendency to interweave flesh with metal, the films regularly feature the monster in a laboratory space, strapped to a chair (Bride) or to a table (Frankenstein Meets the Wolf Man), limbs restricted by bands (a routine treatment for polio sufferers), and surrounded by electronics. Perhaps the most obvious nod to polio culture along these lines comes in a pair of scenes featuring the monster on a respirator. In *Son* the distraught Ygor looks on as the doctor tests the monster's breathing (fig. 5); in *House of Frankenstein* the monster breathes thanks to a respirator inside a pressurized, body-length chamber (fig. 6). [These figures have been deleted.] The moment surely looks back to a similar scene in *Metropolis*, but it just as surely looks laterally, at terrifying and tragic images of bodies encased in iron lungs.

THE KARLOFFIAN MONSTER AND THE CRIPPLER

Polio is an important context for understanding the *Frankenstein* film series—as well as horror films more generally during the period—not merely because the disease offered frightening images and themes that could be incorporated into films already deemed horrific but also because golden-age horror organizes itself according to the logic of a polio culture, one that gave it a ready and real set of terms, images, and fears to employ and exploit. But polio culture is not all that is at stake here; this final section looks at the impact that organizing public health initiatives around the figure of the monster had on polio's victims. Representing disease as a kind of monster naturally led public health officials to the shadowy figures of horror film, but whereas the horror film could always cut ties with its coded significations and send its monsters to the grave with impunity, the polio-era public health film was forced to explicitly equate the monster with the "crippled" polio victim. One effect was to make the victims of the disease into monsters.

It is impossible to say with precision what is the nature of a culture's diffusive fears and how the overlaps described in the preceding sections affected ordinary viewers in movie houses (though, as I have indicated, polio survivors have noticed similarities). However, the evidence plainly suggests exchanges between the two discursive, symbolic, and icono-graphic registers, and if NFIP was not exactly sponsoring new *Frankenstein* films, it was nevertheless looking to horror to help articulate its mission and mobilize supporters. In 1947 MOD, NFIP's fund-raising arm, released a promotional film officially entitled *In Daily Battle*; unofficially, the film took the name that polio had popularly assumed: *The Crippler*. It begins with a pre-lude spoken by the United States surgeon general, Thomas Par-ran, who observes that polio's "treacherous attacks" are adding more names each year to the list of its victims; Parran encour-ages the audience to watch "this motion picture" to understand polio and the campaign against it. The film proper then opens with an ominous musical note, a shot of an eerily illuminated sky, and a disembodied voice: "My name is Virus Poliomyelitis. I cause a disease which you call infantile paralysis." Materializing in the clouds is an obscure shadow of a human-looking body bearing a crutch in its arm, emphasizing that polio and the polio victim are the same menacing presence. The child on crutches is the victim *and* embodiment of the terrifying Virus Poliomyelitis. The voice continues: "I consider myself quite an artist, sort of a sculptor. I specialize in grotesques, twisting and deforming human bodies. That's why I'm called the Crippler. You've never seen me, but I'm sure you've seen my shadow." The film thus aligns the audience's fears of the disease with the people who have been broken by it, running the risk of turning the campaign against polio into a campaign against polio's victims.

As the shadow moves from sky to earth, the narrative takes shape. The camera settles on an adolescent country boy leading a horse through a farmyard; as he approaches a barn, the crutch-bearing shadow enters the screen from the right (fig. 7), growing larger as the voice continues: "I'm never invited, but I've been an invisible guest in practically every kind of home." By the time the sentence ends, the shadow has overtaken the

FIG. 7 Frame from *In Daily Battle*. Courtesy of the March of Dimes Archives, White Plains, New York.

boy, blotting him out as the boy increasingly shows signs of illness. "This is what I've been looking for!" enthusiastically reports the shadow. This scenario is repeated twice: next the shadow overtakes a natty college-age man, and finally it descends on a blond girl leaving her house for school (fig. 8). As the shadow moves from country to city, the voice of the Crippler resumes, his speech occasionally punctuated with melodramatically evil laughter: "It's easy to scare city folks, and I seem to get better results when people are afraid of me. I have many disguises that I use to fool people; you could call them symptoms. . . . As you probably know, I'm very fond of children, especially little children." The camera sweeps past a group of African American children: "I have no prejudices; I'm quite impartial. . . . I feel very active today; I may even start an epidemic." The use of ominous shadow in horror films extends back to German expressionist cinema, but in its proximity to the child it visually echoes a scene in *The Ghost of Frankenstein* in which the monster looms above a sleeping girl (fig. 9). [This figure has been deleted.]

FIG. 8 Frame from *In Daily Battle*. Courtesy of the March of Dimes Archives, White Plains, New York.

Eventually, the film drops the Crippler conceit and explains how doctors relay messages to NFIP and how local agencies work in this coordinated effort to help families address their needs. A triumphal march commences after the recovery of the three victims—which is gradually revealed in a lengthy montage featuring doctors, nurses, public officials, switchboard operators, and the system of diagnosis, treatment, and care that NFIP helped put into place. A different nondiegetic voice, sounding confident and optimistic, closes the film to images of happy children running: "And with your help, your National Foundation carries on its relentless crusade for the ultimate extinction of the shadow that creeps through the land, seeking whom it may destroy. Your continued support will hasten the day when all our children, *free of the Crippler's terror,* may enjoy their heritage in happiness and health" (my emphasis). NFIP successfully reintegrates polio's

victims into family and society following their "cure" and
allows them to live out a harmonious, multicultural, distinc-
tively American "heritage." What was to be done about those
who would not regain full mobility is a matter that lurks on
the dark side of the film, in the space of a monster, one
imported from a series of films that had made it possible for
the menacing Virus Poliomyelitis to appear in an educational
film as the "crippled" shadow body of the polio victim.

Just as horror had been trading on the terrifying imagery
of polio for its effects, NFIP's use of the Crippler figure suggests that cinematic terror was seen as useful in mobilizing the
public. However, NFIP received multiple complaints that *In
Daily Battle* was too "gruesome." One viewer "remarked that
the beginning of the film was more like a film intended for a
spook show on Halloween night rather than one intended to
educate the public about a disease" (Belknap). Responding to
complaints about the film's effect on young viewers, Hart Van
Riper, director of NFIP's medical department, apologetically
wrote in an internal memo (Jan. 1948) that "[w]hen the script
of this film was approved by the Medical Department . . . it
was my distinct understanding that the purpose of the film
was for stimulating Chapters to better organization and hence
better service, and for stimulating interest on the part of organized groups in the community to become part [of MOD]."
The film was apparently pulled shortly thereafter from the
libraries of local MOD chapters. In concealing their indebted-
ness to polio culture, horror films flourished; public health
officials, conversely, encountered problems incorporating horror's conventions into their productions. Where filmgoers
appeared to have been stimulated into buying ever more tick-
ets for access to a steady stream of terrifying reminders of
polio, NFIP discovered that it had material enough to work
with already, that polio carried horror enough for audiences,
and that it did not need to borrow that which it had already
lent to Hollywood.

NOTES

I am deeply grateful to David Rose, at the March of Dimes Archives, for his assistance with the research for this paper and to Meghan Freeman, Gregory Colón Semenza, and Cathy Schlund-Vials for providing feedback on earlier drafts.

1. "By means of surgery . . . muscles can be transplanted and found of much more value in their new functions than they previously were. Old broken bodies made new!" (897).

2. Clark discusses other medical issues at stake in classic horror films.

3. Notwithstanding the frontispiece in Dicks' Standard Plays, the monster was "hideous in aspect" and "tremendously appalling" in the performances of Peake's adaptation, according to one account ("First Reviews").

4. Summarizing Lavalley, Nestrick writes that "several stage versions [before Whale's film] introduced speechlessness but kept the rapidity of movement attributed to him in the novel" (295).

5. Glut and others have detailed the material history of Hammer's changes. All Frankenstein monsters must nevertheless engage with Karloff's, "a definitive screen version that every subsequent retelling has had to confront in one way or another" (Worland 157).

6. For reasons of space, I must restrict my focus to the American experience of *Frankenstein* during 1916–55.

7. The history of polio recounted here comes from Oshinsky; Gould; Shell; and Paul.

8. Shell observes that the imperative to secrecy pervades accounts of polio written by survivors (esp. 52–53, 57–58, and 73–74).

9. Closures of places of public resort due to polio were common at this time. In Trenton, New Jersey, for instance, theaters, Sunday schools, stores, playgrounds, parks, and churches were closed, and "gatherings of any kind" were prohibited ("Trenton").

10. Shell discusses additional polio films, including *Sister Kenny* (1946), but most films that explicitly address polio were released after Salk's vaccine.

11. See Tudor. I follow Tudor in arguing that the genre of horror exists only in relation to the specific historical conditions of horror films' release.

12. The film is not clear about certain details. Markoff injects his victims with acromegaly, which is a pituitary disorder, not a substance. Essentially, Markoff uses simian glandular tissue to formulate a cure for the deforming disease but weaponizes it in the process.

13. This raises significant questions about horror, primates, race, and disease research that I do not have space to explore here. In horror, apes are at once racialized identities and deracinated experimental matter.

14. Cox describes Karloff's monster as characterized by a "gentle and tragic . . . awkwardness," a phrase that captures the sentimental affect that scholars of polio associate with later attitudes toward those impaired by it (223).

15. Related to the monster's posture is the cinematographer Arthur Edeson's German-expressionist-influenced framing of Karloff in ostentatiously geometrical structures, near intersecting support beams or, more famously, in a doorway, his hands lightly touching the door frame (for balance?). At once underscoring his physical instability (needing support) and metaphorizing his own inhuman geometricity, these shots align the monster with the unstable polio victim as well as with the mechanical apparatuses involving braces and crutches designed to produce provisional motional stability. For more on the debt to expressionism, see Cox, esp. 223–27.

16. Glut writes that for him, Karloff "was in effect just a newborn baby in a giant body" (xvii). Nestrick similarly senses that the inability to speak and walk has the effect of "mak[ing] an adult a monstrous child" (296) and that

"[s]eeing this grotesque adult [the monster] without these skills is somehow a terrifying reminder that our adulthood depends on our acquiring them." I share Nestrick's sense of the childishness of the monster's walk and would add that in the polio era adulthood was no guarantee of able-bodiedness.

17. Glut too finds the gap more terrifying than the elided scene, proposing that the audience's imaginative bridge-work results in a "suspicion that she was raped by the Monster" (114).

18. Although the more popular image of the polio victim is one of a child with paralyzed legs, polio was responsible for paralysis of the arms as well.

19. An example of a post-Universal monster with this characteristic is the one portrayed by Nick Brimble in Roger Corman's *Frankenstein Unbound*.

WORKS CITED

The Ape. Dir. William Nigh. Perf. Boris Karloff. 1940. Mill Creek, 2009. DVD.

Baldick, Chris. *In Frankenstein's Shadow: Myth, Monstrosity, and Nineteenth-Century Writing*. Oxford: Clarendon, 1990. Print.

Before I Hang. Dir. Nick Grinde. Columbia, 1940. *YouTube*. Web.

Belknap, Clinton. Memo. 30 Jan. 1948. TS. "Radio, Television, Film." March of Dimes Media and Publications Records. Box 3, ser. 8.

Black Friday. Dir. Arthur Lubin. Universal, 1940. *IMDb*. Web. 7 Jan. 2014.

The Black Room. Dir. Roy William Neill. Columbia, 1935. *YouTube*. Web.

Bradman, Frederick. "Salvage." *Hygeia: The Health Magazine* Oct. 1933: 896–97. Print.

Bride of Frankenstein. Dir. James Whale. Perf. Boris Karloff. 1935. Universal, 2004. DVD. Frankenstein: The Legacy Collection.

Bud Abbott and Lou Costello Meet Frankenstein. Dir. Charles Barton. Perf. Glenn Strange. 1948. Universal, 2000. DVD.

Clark, Stephanie Brown. "Frankenflicks: Medical Monsters in Classic Horror Films." *Cultural Sutures: Medicine and Media.* Ed. Lester D. Friedman. Durham: Duke UP, 2004. 129–48. Print.

Cox, Tracy. *"Frankenstein* and Its Cinematic Translations." *Critical Essays on Mary Wollstonecraft Shelley.* Ed. Mary Lowe-Evans. New York: Hall, 1998. 214–29. Print.

The Curse of Frankenstein. Dir. Terence Fisher. Perf. Christopher Lee. 1957. Warner Home Video, 2002. DVD.

The Devil Commands. Dir. Edward Dmytryk. Columbia, 1941. *YouTube.* Web.

"The First Reviews of *Presumption.*" 29 July 1823. *Romantic Circles.* U of Maryland, Aug. 2001. Web. 7 Jan. 2014.

Foertsch, Jacqueline. *Bracing Accounts: The Literature and Culture of Polio in Postwar America.* Madison: Fairleigh Dickinson UP, 2008. Print.

Frankenstein. Dir. J. Searle Dawley. Perf. Charles Stanton Ogle. Edison, 1910. *YouTube.* Web.

Frankenstein. Dir. James Whale. Perf. Boris Karloff. 1931. Universal, 2004. DVD. Frankenstein: The Legacy Collection.

Frankenstein Meets the Wolf Man. Dir. Roy William Neill. Perf. Bela Lugosi. 1943. Universal, 2004. DVD. The Wolf Man: The Legacy Collection.

Frankenstein Unbound. Dir. Roger Corman. 1990. Twentieth Century-Fox, 2006. DVD.

The Ghost of Frankenstein. Dir. Earle C. Kenton. Perf. Lon Chaney, Jr. 1942. Universal, 2004. DVD. Frankenstein: The Legacy Collection.

Glut, Donald. *The Frankenstein Legend: A Tribute to Boris Karloff and Mary Shelley.* Metuchen: Scarecrow, 1973. Print.

Goldman, Steven L. "Images of Technology in Popular Films: Discussion and Filmography." *Science, Technology, and Human Values* 14.3 (1989): 275–301. Print.

Der Golem, wie er in die Welt kam. Dir. Paul Wegener. UFA, 1920. *YouTube.* Web.

Gould, Tony. *A Summer Plague: Polio and Its Survivors.* New Haven: Yale UP, 1995. Print.

The Healer. Dir. Reginald Baker. Monogram, 1935. *YouTube.* Web.

Herrick, Robert. *The Healer.* New York: Macmillan, 1911. *Google Books.*
    Web. 7 Jan. 2014.

House of Dracula. Dir. Earle C. Kenton. Perf. Glenn Strange. 1945.
    Universal, 2004. DVD. Dracula: The Legacy Collection.

House of Frankenstein. Dir. Earle C. Kenton. Perf. Glenn Strange and
    Boris Karloff. 1944. Universal, 2004. DVD. Frankenstein: The
    Legacy Collection.

In Daily Battle. March of Dimes, 1947. DVD. March of Dimes Media
    and Publications Records.

Lavalley, Albert J. "The Stage and Film Children of *Frankenstein:* A
    Survey." *The Endurance of* Frankenstein: *Essays on Mary Shelley's
    Novel.* Ed. George Levine and U. C. Knoepflmacher. Berkeley:
    U of California P, 1979. 243–89. Print.

Leave Her to Heaven. Dir. John M. Stahl. Twentieth Century-Fox, 1945.
    YouTube. Web.

The Man They Could Not Hang. Dir. Nick Grinde. Columbia, 1939.
    YouTube. Web.

The Man Who Lived Again. Dir. Robert Stevenson. Gainsborough, 1936.
    YouTube. Web.

The Monster Maker. Dir. Sam Newfield. 1944. Mill Creek, 2009. DVD.

Nestrick, William. "Coming to Life: *Frankenstein* and the Nature of
    Film Narrative." *The Endurance of* Frankenstein: *Essays on Mary
    Shelley's Novel.* Ed. George Levine and U. C. Knoepflmacher.
    Berkeley: U of California P, 1979. 290–315. Print.

Never Fear. Dir. Ida Lupino. Filmakers, 1949. *YouTube.* Web.

"New Films." *Daily Boston Globe* 14 Jan. 1939: 2. Print.

Night Monster. Dir. Ford Beebe. Universal, 1942. *Viozz.* Web.

Nosferatu. Dir. F. W. Murnau. 1922. Mill Creek, 2009. DVD.

O'Flinn, Paul. "Production Replaces Creation: The Case of *Franken-
    stein." Literature and History* 9.2 (1983): 194–213. Print.

"Oh, You Beautiful Monster." *New York Times* 29 Jan. 1939: X4. Print.

Oshinsky, David M. *Polio: An American Story.* Oxford: Oxford UP, 2005.
    Print.

Paul, John Rodman. *A History of Poliomyelitis.* New Haven: Yale UP, 1971.
    Print.

Peake, Richard Brinsley. *Frankenstein: A Romantic Drama, in Three Acts.*
　　[London], n.d. Print. Dicks' Standard Plays 431.
Perrault, Michael. "Standard Issue." *Bent: A Journal of CripGay Voices.*
　　N.p., Nov. 2002. Web. 14 July 2012.
The Return of Dr. X. Dir. Vincent Sherman. Warner Bros., 1939. *YouTube.*
　　Web.
Rogers, Naomi. "Race and the Politics of Polio: Warm Springs, Tuskegee, and
　　the March of Dimes." *American Journal of Public Health* 97.5 (2007):
　　784–95. Print.
Roughly Speaking. Dir. Michael Curtiz. 1945. Warner Bros., 2009. DVD.
　　Archive Collection.
Shell, Marc. *Polio and Its Aftermath: The Paralysis of Culture. Cambridge:*
　　Harvard UP, 2005. Print.
Shelley, Mary. *Frankenstein; or, The Modern Prometheus.* 1818. Ed. J. Paul
　　Hunter. New York: Norton, 1996. Print.
Son of Frankenstein. Dir. Rowland V. Lee. Perf. Boris Karloff. 1939. Universal,
　　2004. DVD. Frankenstein: The Legacy Collection.
"Trenton Enforces 'Polio' Quarantine." *New York Times* 6 Aug. 1945: 17. Print.
Tudor, Andrew. "Why Horror? The Peculiar Pleasures of a Popular Genre."
　　Horror: The Film Reader. Ed. Mark Jancovich. London: Routledge,
　　2002. 47–56. Print.
Van Riper, Hart. Memo. 29 Jan. 1948. TS. "Radio, Television, Film." March of
　　Dimes Media and Publications Records. Box 3, ser. 8.
Williams, Whitney. "'*Frankenstein* Grewsome Entertainment." *Los Angeles*
　　Times 29 Nov. 1931: I3. Print.
Wilson, Daniel J. "And They Shall Walk: Ideal versus Reality in Polio Rehabil-
　　itation in the United States." *Asclepio: Revista de historia de la medicina*
　　y de la ciencia 61.1 (2009): 175–92. Print.
–––––––. "A Crippling Fear: Experiencing Polio in the Era of FDR." *Bulletin*
　　of the History of Medicine 72.3 (1998): 464–95. Print.
Worland, Rick. *The Horror Film: An Introduction.* Malden: Blackwell,
　　2007. Print.

A Note about Disciplinary Representation

The three brief dissections of articles in the sciences, social sciences, and humanities show clear differences in the ways these generalized disciplines write to convey their knowledge. This exercise, though, ignores some further (important) principles that it's worth understanding as you navigate your way through your different courses and into your major.

- *Disciplines Themselves Are Highly Diverse.* Although you might be mostly interested in scholarly articles based on research in a specific field, it's important to remember that the kinds of texts that field produces are varied. Keep your eyes open for that variety—look at the different *sections* of journals to see what else they publish in addition to scholarly articles. Look around in the discipline for other kinds of journals; for example, most fields have journals that focus on their subjects and journals that focus on the teaching of their subjects.

- *Writing Isn't All the Same in Quality.* Just as we can find excellent, clear, well-researched and argued material in any field, we can also find sloppy, jargon-filled, awkwardly written, badly researched, or poorly documented material. The journal and its reviewers and editorial boards usually create a "gate" to keep out the latter. Much depends on the nature of the publication and its prestige.

- *Anatomy Ignores Behavior.* We've been taking apart articles as though they are cadavers, looking at their parts and how those parts work together. But we haven't explored the content—the *conversation* going on around evidence for a mathematical assumption, a relationship between writing and health, or the depiction of Frankenstein in movies during a time of heightened concern about polio. In other words, we haven't seen how these articles really behave within their disciplines. Who ended up citing them? How important were they to their conversation? Did people take issue with them? Who built on what they presented? As you move more fully into your field(s) of interest, remember that anatomizing texts is extremely helpful to begin to understand how knowledge is created and negotiated there, but it's insufficient. The *knowledge* comes next.

Putting It into Practice

This chapter has provided a guide for conducting an anatomy of a text: a detailed description of the text's use of discipline-based conventions, including how it contributes to the advancement of knowledge through the way it organizes and conveys information. It led you through those processes by asking you to choose an article in a specific discipline-based area and then follow along, applying the strategies and perspectives to that selection. It then conducted three additional dissections to demonstrate how writing varies across different generalized domains of knowledge: the sciences, the social sciences, and the humanities.

You can put everything you learned in this chapter to good use through the following activities:

- Continue to research the forms and genres of writing in your field and in other fields.

- If you're enrolled in general-education courses that will not be part of your major, don't neglect to understand how writing works in those courses. Pairing the strategies here with respect to professional publications in the field with the strategies offered in earlier chapters focusing on assignments, you can begin to understand how your classroom work is related to the ways that people create and convey knowledge in the field.

- Recognize that a single article or other text may not represent the field fully or accurately; keep "looking around" to see whether the patterns you notice occur elsewhere or not, or if they do, with what variations.

Key Concepts Glossary

Throughout this book, key concepts appear as sidebars with brief definitions. These key concepts, or key terms, represent "threshold concepts" in writing—concepts that apply to writing across all contexts and situations. Understanding these key concepts and being able to use the language that represents them is an important step to becoming a versatile writer who can adapt quickly to different writing genres and situations. Although that process is never easy or automatic, knowing what to look for—how to "read" and understand the context and the way it uses writing to communicate ideas—can speed up the adaptation and help you succeed as a writer. Being familiar with all the key concepts is an important outcome of reading and studying this book.

Most of the key concepts in the sidebars are explained and demonstrated in the sections where they appear. This glossary offers further information about the concepts, outside the context of the chapters, so that you can explore and understand them more fully.

An **addressed audience** is a predefined audience you write to directly, such as a senator, a character in a scenario, or a member of your small-group forum in your class. The knowledge you have about your addressed audience will vary from a lot (e.g., a family member or a close friend) to some (e.g., a teacher, someone in your class) to a little (e.g., a senator, the manager of a company, or the admissions director at a university). Your corresponding knowledge will come from various sources of information: in the case of a family member, from many years of personal experience; in the case of a senator, perhaps just from what you've read and seen on TV; in the case of an anonymous but addressed person, such as the owner of a company, from just stereotypes about what company owners are like and what their interests are.

An **annotated bibliography** is a bibliography in which each entry includes not only the reference to a work but also a description of and/or commentary on that work, like a mini-abstract. Some instructors like to assign annotated bibliographies either as independent papers (that demonstrate your knowledge of a topic) or as part of a larger research project (sometimes due along the way, to compel you to collect sufficient resources before you write your paper). If you're writing a research paper, look for existing annotated bibliographies on your topic or question because they'll refer you to many relevant works. You can read the annotations and decide which works will be the most useful to you, saving you time when you are conducting searches. Look carefully at the date of the bibliography to be sure you're not ignoring recently published material. Remember that an annotated bibliography is already obsolete the day that it's published. Online bibliographies that are continuously updated avoid this problem.

Community of practice is a term that is often used to describe a group of people who use language (and writing) in a particular way based on their needs and interests. Unless you know how knowledge is created and conveyed in that community of practice, you may feel and behave like an outsider. Over time, communities of practice develop many ways of working and communicating together as they try to achieve common goals. A community of practice could be a student committee you serve on; a social group organized around a particular activity, such as canning, knitting, gaming, or golf; an academic group, such as people working together on a grant proposal; or a professional group, such as people who work in a nonprofit organization. Large organizations might involve broad communities of practice (e.g., your college or university is one) and consist of subgroups, such as departments or support units, clubs, or sports teams. Learn to study and understand the conventions and norms that the community of practice has established, especially for writing. How does the writing work? Who does it? Why? How are documents produced—what cycles of work are involved? What do documents look like?

Conditional rhetorical space refers to the kind of writing "space" you're in when you write for a teacher but also try to adhere to the conventions of writing in the profession beyond your institution. It requires you to be aware of what your teacher expects *and* what is expected in the field. The rhetorical space of the classroom is a hybrid of sorts, bringing together the goals of teaching and learning with the requirements of nonacademic or professional settings (e.g., disciplines, workplaces, etc.). The writing you do in school is often designed to prepare you for those settings, but you're not in them yet, so your instructor will gauge the success of your writing on the basis of its professional potential *and* the specific classroom requirements of the task. In some cases (as described in Chapters 2 and 3), your writing may be entirely classroom based. The "conditional" part of the concept, then, is a matter of degree: if you're working on a capstone project as part of an internship in a local company, your writing will be far more "located" in the professional space than if you're writing a microtheme in a course in order to learn the material.

A **content footnote** is a remark or an aside that clarifies or elaborates on something in the main part of the text but that would otherwise interrupt the flow of its ideas; it usually appears at the bottom of the page but sometimes in a series of notes at the end of the text. As described in Chapter 6, a content footnote offers an opportunity to add something to your paper, such as an elaboration of a point or some very specific additional information that would take readers too far afield in the main body of the text. Use content footnotes very sparingly. Some publication styles eschew them and prefer that you either incorporate the material into the text or eliminate the footnote. Content footnotes can also appear as endnotes (which can be frustrating for readers, who must flip to the end of the chapter or article to read them and then go back to where they were).

Critical source work refers to a process of analyzing the nature, quality, contents, and genres of sources during your search process, before you actually use the sources. The effectiveness of your paper or writing project will depend crucially on whatever sources you refer to in it. Imagine a paper filled with sources that have no credibility, plucked from the Internet at random, written by people without expertise, and biased or misleading in their content. When you engage in critical source work, you study where each source comes from. Where did you find it? How reputable is the publisher or journal? How do you know? Who is the author? What sort of credentials and expertise does the author have? What does the author do, and where does he or she work? Has anyone commented on the book or article you've found? Are there reviews, or, if it's an article, can you find data about how many other people have cited the article? (Some search engines or sites list works that have also cited the source, which, incidentally, is a good way to find more sources that are relevant to your synthesis of scholarship on your topic.) If you can say without any doubt that your source and author(s) are credible, then you'll feel much more confident that the contents of the source can be trusted and woven into your paper as you see fit.

Critical thinking is an all-purpose term that refers to the careful and thoughtful analysis of information or phenomena. It requires a kind of positive skepticism that doesn't take everything at face value but tries to weigh it, reflect on it, and reach a fuller understanding of it and its implications. According to the National Council for Excellence in Critical Thinking, critical thinking is

> the intellectually disciplined process of actively and skillfully con-ceptualizing, applying, analyzing, synthesizing, and/or evaluating information gathered from, or generated by, observation, experience, reflection, reasoning, or communication, as a guide to belief and action. In its exemplary form, it is based on universal intellectual values that transcend subject matter divisions: clarity, accuracy, pre-cision, consistency, relevance, sound evidence, good reasons, depth, breadth, and fairness.

See also *Engaged thinking* and *Reflection*.

Decentering refers to the process of getting out of yourself and think-ing about the needs and interests of your potential readers. What do they want to know? Why? How do the purpose and context of your writing help to determine that? Research has shown that, as children mature, they become less egocentric—that is, they begin to see the world less through only their own minds, needs, desires, and con-sciousness. For example, in explaining to others how to play a card game, children eventually become more attuned to thinking about what a new player needs to know and how to explain it so that the new player understands the game. Egocentrism in writing, though, follows many students right up to college. Inexperienced writers and thinkers may see an issue only through their own opinions and perspectives, and appear to be unable to "decenter," that is, to move outside themselves to see the issue through other lenses. Decentering requires thinking about something from multiple perspectives, but it doesn't mean "giving up" your own beliefs. On the contrary, anticipating what others are thinking will prepare you to make a more convincing case for your own views, but those views may be tempered, or better informed, or more complex, or even changed, as a result of your decentering.

Documentation is the process of showing the exact source of each reference (however included) for information you bring into your paper from elsewhere. Documentation can include information about books and articles, speeches, interviews, films, ideas, and a number of other materials. There are two reasons why documentation is important when you're working with sources. First, you want to be sure that you give credit to the sources you consult. You can't just insert other people's ideas and words into your writing without saying where those ideas and words came from and acknowledging the effort people put into creating them. Second, your readers may want to consult the sources themselves, and without your documenting them, there's no way your readers can do that.

Drafting refers to the processes—plural—of generating and organizing original ideas and information, sometimes along with others' ideas and information, into textual or multimodal form. Writers use many forms of drafting, some of which are quite unique and idiosyncratic based on different times of the day, locations, surrounding context, and processes. The emphasis is decidedly on creating something preliminary—even a sketch—that can be successively refined over time, with appropriate self-evaluation or feedback from others. When a teacher wants you to create a *draft*, he or she means that it will be imperfect—a first attempt and not a finished piece.

Enculturation refers to the process of becoming a member of a group (e.g., a discipline, a laboratory, a church, etc.) and learning how its members communicate with other members and with others outside the group. In the context of writing, enculturation requires understanding the *community of practice* (see Key Concept entry) where the writing and other forms of communication take place. It means using the community's language and following the conventions that it has established for writing (both the form of the writing and the processes used to produce it). For example, if you're hired to work in a nonprofit organization, even if you've practiced some professional writing in college and learned about some of the managerial and business practices that a nonprofit will use, you still need to become a "member" of the organization. This will take time. You'll be seen (and you'll see yourself) as an apprentice for a while—as someone who will need the counsel of the other employees (and preferably a mentor who can devote some time to helping you "learn the ropes"). This book is designed to give you the *metaknowledge* (see Key Concept entry) to help you to be an inquisitive explorer of your new setting, trying to adapt to its forms of communication as quickly and as successfully as possible.

Engaged thinking is a kind of thinking that fully explores an idea, concept, phenomenon, or other material, by turning it around and examining it from different perspectives. For this reason, engaged thinking takes some time; it can't be done quickly or haphazardly. Teachers in all disciplines highly favor engaged thinking and look for evidence of it in what you say and write about the course material. It typically requires more than just a description of an event or a phenomenon. It requires "going deeper," seeing connections, relationships, and patterns among different ideas or concepts. See also *Reflection*.

Formative evaluation is a kind of evaluative commentary or feedback that is designed mainly to improve, not to judge, a final product or performance. Let's say you're rehearsing for a play or musical or an important speech. Either expert coaches or groups of people who play the role of the final audience can provide you with feedback that's designed to help you improve your performance so that when it's "for real," the actual audience will find it to be successful. Because it's not a final evaluation, formative evaluation is advisory and low-stakes. In writing, formative evaluation can come from responses from your teacher, your peers, or others to the drafts of your papers and projects. You can use those responses to improve the paper so that its final (high-stakes) evaluation is stronger.

Genre refers to a specific *type* of writing that can be recognized by a combination of its characteristics and the uses to which it is put. Like genres of music (e.g., country, metal, ska, zydeco, blues, reggae, etc.), there are hundreds, even thousands, of written genres. For the most part, genres represent stable sets of characteristics. A regular front-page news story, for example, will have the characteristics of a factual report: it will try to capture the most essential details about an event in as objective a way as possible. Organizationally, it begins at a relatively high level of generality and then it provides more and more specific details (sometimes even in smaller print). Similarly, the college lab report is a genre; it has a specific goal, structure, style, and so on. However, genres are also *socially constructed*. In other words, the "rules" are decided by the people who create and use the genre. For this reason, genres are often in a state of evolution. The genre of a post to social media, such as Facebook, has emerged and has changed relatively quickly. The genre of the novel has also changed, but more slowly, over hundreds of years. Genres also vary according to specific contexts in which they're used. The instructor in your Heat-Transfer course might expect a certain level of detail and elaboration in your lab report that the instructor in your Chemistry course might not expect.

As you learn to write in a new genre, it's helpful first to understand the general conventions of that genre, such as its usual style, structure, purpose, readership, and so on, and then to see how the genre is used in the specific setting in which you're working. A patient report in nursing has general characteristics of objectivity, brevity, and clarity, but it can follow more specific conventions in a particular hospital or clinic.

An **implied** or **invoked audience** is an audience that you construct from the way you write. If you imagine an audience made up of people who are completely opposed to an argument you're making, they aren't actual people, but your writing is invoking them as if they were. Writing for an implied or invoked audience can be tricky, because eventually you'll have actual readers. If you generalize too much about them, an individual reader may think, "Hey, I'm not like the reader that the writer seems to be addressing." If you invoke too specific a reader, other readers may feel similarly excluded. For this reason, your text needs to include a range of perspectives, which sometimes requires a delicate approach as you make and support your points.

Incubation refers to the time between deliberate work on a writing project when you're consciously focusing on other things but your unconscious mind may still be working on ideas for the project.

Research suggests that people subconsciously may "mull over" or think about projects while their mind is engaged in other thinking and activities. Theories of incubation suggest that, although you aren't aware of this subconscious or semiconscious work, it may be going on in the background. Trying to churn out a final draft of a large project all at once gives your mind no time for this kind of subconscious rumination. A good practice, especially after you've worked intensively on a writing project, is to put it aside for a while and focus on other things. You may be surprised to find that new ideas emerge before you return to it or when you do so, and that you can also look at it through new eyes and see problems and possibilities that weren't there before.

Interdisciplinarity refers to the joining together of different disciplines, or specific approaches, theories, or research from different disciplines, in order to enrich a particular inquiry or to form a new path of investigation. In some cases, disciplines that historically have remained separated—each producing knowledge independently of the other—come together because they are developing mutual goals, research agendas, or questions for inquiry. A good example is what happened when computer science came together with medicine to create the human genome project. The idea of mapping the human genome emerged from medical research, but the prospects of creating a complete map by human means was virtually impossible. Once the massive computational abilities of computers merged together with this goal, it became possible. In other cases, disciplines begin to borrow from other disciplines in order to pose specific questions. A good example of this process happened in the field of writing studies. Writing experts knew something about what happens when people write, but they needed expertise from cognitive psychology, a field in which a great deal is known about information processing, the effects of memory, and so on. Within the field of psychology, the subfield of psycholinguistics offered much new research and scholarship.

Invention is a term used in rhetoric to refer to the process of generating ideas and considering them along the way for a speech or written text. It has a very long history, stretching back to the classical rhetoric of the ancient Greeks, and has become a metaterm for all strategies that are designed to explore a subject. Over the years, writers and writing scholars have developed dozens of invention techniques, some of which are described in Chapter 4. Many of them involve a visual dimension, such as mind-mapping diagrams (e.g., trees, clusters, loops, cells, boxes, and the like). This kind of invention typically generates kernels of ideas in categories, using higher-level terms. Other kinds of invention are more textual, such as freewriting. The idea behind freewriting is to write freely and fluently, without stopping, and without concern for formal features, in order to generate ideas. Some forms of invention rely on speech, such as recording yourself as you think out loud about a project. Invention can also be practiced collaboratively, either face-to-face or by using digital tools like Padlet, which allows a group of people to post ideas quickly from their laptops or devices that then appear on a single screen. As a writer, you should practice different kinds of invention until you find ones that work consistently well for you. Also, be aware that some kinds of invention work better for some kinds of texts and situations than others.

A **keyword** is a common term used to catalog or index resources (e.g., books, articles, reports, etc.). Using keywords in this way allows people to retrieve the works using search systems. For example, if you're trying to find information about new apps that provide outsourced health care to consumers (such as the ability to send a picture of your child's ear canal to a doctor or a clinician in order to get a diagnosis from your home), you might use the keywords *app, outsource, health care,* and *health* in different combinations. Remember that individually, keywords will take you to massive amounts of information, but when they are brought together, those keywords begin limiting the search and zeroing in on your interests. A search on Google for "do it yourself," "health care," and "apps" yields thousands of sites, but more important, it also provides further keywords relating to this topic, such as "mobile health," which you may not have known or thought about before you started your search. Obviously, it helps to keep a list of the keywords as you refine your search.

A **learning (b)log or academic journal** is a paper notebook, a file on your computer, or a space online where you write about course material very informally in order to learn the material better and to prepare for exams and formal papers. The purpose of such a (b)log is to create a space for you to write informally about what you are learning. Some research shows that, when you write about complex material, you learn it more fully through the explorations that your writing affords. Writing allows you to test what you know by compelling you to articulate it on-screen or on a page, revealing gaps in your knowledge; by rehearsing what you've heard, read, or seen; or by allowing you to extend and apply information to your own life or to other contexts. See *Self-sponsored writing*.

Low-stakes writing is writing that is informal, is done quickly (without much, if any, revision), is worth a small percentage of a grade (or none at all), and is not concerned about refined style, perfect grammar, or other characteristics of polished writing that is directed to an audience. Some low-stakes writing is self-sponsored, meaning that you do it for your own purposes, such as reflecting on your learning, keeping a journal or diary, or freewriting your way to ideas about an upcoming paper or writing project. Other kinds of low-stakes writing may be assigned by a teacher in order to foster your learning of course material by creating a context for thinking. Very low-stakes assignments can include journal writing, a "reading log," or other kinds of reflections on the course material. Other low-stakes writing assignments may require you to respond to a prompt, such as a minicase or a scenario, in order to apply material you're learning to a specific context so that you learn it more fully.

Metaknowledge refers to knowledge about knowledge—what knowledge is and how it's created. It's a way of standing back from what you're doing and thinking consciously about it. For example, when you're engaged in a process or activity, you may be simply *doing it*, usually because it takes up a lot of your intellectual and/or physical resources. When you think more consciously about that activity or process, though, you are applying some level of metaconsciousness, or metaawareness, or metacognition in order to reach a higher-level understanding of your actions. You can practice meta-analysis by taking an ordinary activity, such as tying a shoelace, and explaining how it's actually done. What you normally do unconsciously now requires you to stand back from the activity and think about it at a higher level. Now imagine a much more complex activity, such as playing a difficult video game. When you're immersed in the game, you just *play* it. But later, when you reflect on what you did well or not well, you're applying a metalevel analysis to your actions. If you gain a lot of experience, you'll have accumulated *metaknowledge*, a set of strategies, understandings, and perspectives that help you to continuously improve performing the activity. So it is with writing: various lenses or perspectives help you not only *to* write but also to think *about* your writing.

A **microtheme** is a short writing assignment that is usually done in one draft, but it requires certain kinds of analysis or problem solving, or focused preparation for a class session, such as rereading through a particular analytical lens. Along a continuum, from the most informal (low-stakes) writing to the most formal (high-stakes) writing, microthemes stand a little left of center. They're still brief, designed to get you thinking about or applying the course material; they're less the "outcome" of your learning than its "input." Typically, your instructor will use the results of microtheme assignments in class, as you further learn the material, and the instructor will assess them informally, sometimes just jotting a few comments in the margins or using a simple set of evaluation criteria. You may be assigned a number of microthemes in a course, perhaps one per week.

Modeling is a process of looking at the behaviors and products of writers in a specific context in order to acquire knowledge and produce texts that adhere to the conventions that define the community's expectations. For example, if you've never taken minutes at a meeting, it will help you a lot to see what a set of meeting minutes looks like and how someone writes them. The behaviors and artifacts (such as pieces of writing) that you might examine are called *models*. Sometimes you'll be given models that represent "excellent" examples of the texts produced in a specific context. At other times, you may be given very poor examples to show you what not to do. In educational settings it's more common to get models that have both strengths and weaknesses, and you'll be asked to analyze the models (sometimes using a set of evaluation criteria or a *rubric*—see Key Concept entry) so that you can begin to internalize or understand what makes a test successful or unsuccessful according to local standards. When you use models, be careful not to assume that you should imitate what you see. Models are meant to be examples for specific occasions and not universal exemplars.

Objective shape refers to a conscious mapping of the structure or organization of your or another writer's draft. Now you shift gears and ask yourself consciously how the draft hangs together. Can you describe, name, or label the parts? How would you describe the way they transition from one to the next? What topics or focus can you describe in each paragraph, section, or part? See *Subjective flow.*

Paraphrase refers to a restatement of an idea or a piece of text in new words (not those of the original). It's sometimes used to "translate" a difficult text into an easier one or to clarify some aspects of the original. When you paraphrase a source, it's very easy to stick too closely to the words of the original. Paraphrasing is not quoting. If you want to quote, then don't use any words that aren't your own; reproduce the original exactly, and place it within quotation marks to show that the words are taken directly from the source. If you decide to paraphrase, perhaps for stylistic reasons or to make the original words fit in better with your own text, then be sure that you're describing the original in new words. A good strategy is to put the original away and then try writing what the original said without looking at it.

Peer response, or **peer review,** refers to a process of getting and giving feedback on the work in progress from people in a peer group, usually other members of your class. Remember that peer response can be worthless if you don't prepare for your interactions with the peer group, think about the broader aspects of your peers' papers and not just the small details, and offer your responses diplomatically and with attention to detail. When you're on the receiving end of feedback, you can urge your peers to provide you with the most useful peer response by asking them questions about your draft whose answers will improve it. Chapter 5 offers lots of guidance for how to give and receive peer response.

A **peer-reviewed journal** is a professional or academic journal whose articles have been reviewed, usually anonymously, by "peer" experts who serve on the journal's editorial board or are on a panel of designated reviewers. This process ensures that articles published in the journal are of high quality and integrity. Typically, when a scholar submits an article for publication, the article is sent to two or three other scholars (without the author knowing their identities). These other scholars read and critique the article, bringing all their expertise to the task. This ensures that what's published in the journal meets the rigorous scholarly standards of the expert community that it is usually addressing. Your instructors like you to consult peer-reviewed journals because they maintain a high level of intellectual integrity and can therefore be trusted.

Persona   refers to the sense of self that you project through your choices of language (e.g., words, sentence structures, etc.) or, more generally, your writing *style*. It is related to the concept of *ethos* described in Chapter 4. When you choose who to "be" in your text, you're projecting a particular persona. For example, if you're writing an e-mail to a landlord, requesting that your security deposit be returned even though there was some minor staining on the carpet in your apartment, you can choose a threatening persona ("If you don't send me back my deposit, I will take legal action against you!") or a conciliatory persona ("I understand how difficult it is to maintain property, but the stains were so insignificant and we took good care of the apartment overall. Could you please consider sending us back our deposit?"). The effect of your e-mail will be quite different depending on your choice of persona—and so it will be in anything you write.

Primary research   refers to original research that you conduct yourself, such as a survey or set of interviews, a controlled experiment, a search for historical documents surrounding an important event, or observations or measurements of some phenomenon, such as animal behavior or the erosion of a riverbank. **Secondary research**   refers to the gathering of what scholars and researchers have done and said about the object under study—that is, what *they* have found in their own primary research. In your college courses, you will be assigned projects that require a mix of primary and secondary research. In general-education courses, courses with larger enrollments, and introductory courses, you're likely to be assigned projects that require secondary research. Your task is to find out what researchers have learned about specific questions, phenomena, processes, or objects. You then pull all of that information together to create a synthesis of the current state of knowledge. Usually, as you move forward in the curriculum and then into your major, you'll be asked to conduct your own research (using methodologies such as observation, timed trials, surveys, or experimental treatments) or to create your own artifacts (e.g., in music, a composition; in architecture, the design of a building or a landscape; in materials engineering, a new holder for smartphones). Chapter 6 provides more information about these two kinds of research.

Prior knowledge refers to what you already know or have experienced and can use in a new situation. Every bit of knowledge in your mind is in a sense "prior"; it's the sum total of all your learning. In the context of writing, prior knowledge can be either very helpful or a hindrance. For example, if you were taught over and over not to use the personal pronoun *I* in your writing, you might find yourself in a situation where *I* is not only useful but also required. Your prior knowledge—what you learned before—won't stand you in good stead. But let's say that you've been given an assignment to write a thesis-driven paper, and that you've learned about theses and have practiced writing them many times before. Your prior knowledge will be activated when you see the assignment, and you'll have a clear sense of how to proceed and what criteria to use to judge the success of your thesis statement as it develops.

Proofreading refers to the most minute kind of rereading to prepare a manuscript for submission or publication. It requires searching for very small flaws on the surface of the text, such as missing apostrophes on possessive nouns, spelling errors, dropped letters, and the like. It's a fine-tooth-comb kind of reading that takes place at the very end of the writing process. For example, its the kind of process that will identify the missing apostrophe in the *it's* at the start of this sentence and, will take out the comma that appears after "and" a few words back from here. Because you may become re-immersed in your ideas when you proofread, which can stop you from doing a meticulous search for small errors, try reading your writing backward when you are proofreading.

Quotation, in the context of source work, refers to the exact copying of a piece of text from a source into your own paper, with an acknowledgement of where the piece of text came from. Quotation is often used because the language of the original is important for readers to see in its exact form. As explained in Chapter 6, the use of quotation varies across different disciplines and fields of thought. In the humanities, quotation is used more heavily to reflect the specific choice of words that an author uses to describe an idea or a phenomenon; the words often matter as much as what they describe. In the hard sciences, the conclusions of research are often more important than the exact words used to describe those conclusions. For example, in a civil engineering article on soil distortion around a particular type of tunnel, the following quotation shows the importance of the *source* (indicated by the numbers 8 and 9, which refer to numbered references in the reference list) rather than the specific *words* of the authors.

> The existing researches indicate that the important influence factors of the double-hole tunnel evacuation stress and distortion include gap and burying depth of the double-hole tunnel [8, 9].

In contrast, articles in philosophy, history, literature, and other humanities will be more likely to quote exact words instead of providing broad findings.

Recursivity refers to a common phenomenon in drafting in which the writer continues to discover ideas, put language on the screen or page, and revise in cycles, rather than as a linear process. Although the writing process is often described linearly (first you come up with ideas, then you draft, then you revise and edit, and then you present your final product), rarely does writing move in such a lockstep way. You may begin writing and then move back into a stage of thinking through your ideas again, especially because the drafting has made your ideas visible. While revising, you may realize that you need to cut out an entire section of your draft and rewrite, and that propels you back into coming up with new ideas. Computers now make these processes invisible, because all of your changes disappear as you make them. But research on writers shows that they move around in the process. Imagine a circle with different stages in the process located on different parts of the circle. Recursiveness means moving around, forwards and backwards, to different positions on the circle as you write.

Reflection refers to a kind of thinking that considers ideas, phenomena, and experience from multiple perspectives, generating new learning. Reflection can focus on your personal response to your learning or to your growth and development as a learner, or it can focus more externally on something beyond yourself. The term *reflection* implies that what you're considering "bends back" into your consciousness, where you think about it more fully. It can require you to take different perspectives, even though you don't at first agree or sympathize with those perspectives. For example, if you're opposed to gun control, reflecting on that complex issue will require you to see the issue through the eyes of someone who is in favor of gun control. Why would they think this way? What reasons might they give? Are any of those reasons valid? What other complexities can you imagine that relate to tighter restrictions on gun ownership? Are there compromise positions? Who is most affected? And so on. See also *Engaged thinking*.

A **response guide,** or *revision guide*, is a set of questions, usually created by an instructor, that guide your responses to the drafts of your own and/or your peers' papers. The questions call your attention to the most important aspects of your writing as they relate to the learning goals of the assignment. When you receive a response guide, be sure to consider each question carefully, whether it's directed toward your own draft or the drafts of others in preparation for a peer-group revision conference. Read the question as a guide to analyzing your draft, and work through the entire text, considering it through the lens of the question. Take notes on your impressions, and use those notes as you move toward revision.

Revision means, literally, "re-seeing." It requires you to pay attention to the major elements of a piece of writing, such as its structure, voice, and presentation of ideas. It is not *editing*, and it is not *proofreading*, and it lies at the heart of improving not only your own drafts but also your knowledge and abilities as a writer. In order to revise your draft effectively, you need to stand back from your writing and read it as if you hadn't written it. What would the reading experience be like for a reader? Does the text make sense? Does it follow a clear organizational pattern based on its genre? Is it written in an appealing, readable style? What's the voice, and is the voice appropriate for the genre and context? (For example, a police officer wouldn't write a police report in a subjective, meandering voice: "The driver emerged from the car, and I could see that he was wearing frayed khakis and old sneakers that looked like they'd trudged through many a muddy field. The day was crisp and bright. I moved to the right side of the car, my right shoulder hurting from the tennis injury I'd suffered two weeks before.")

Revision can be prompted through self-evaluation (when you apply various criteria or perspectives to your own draft, identifying weaknesses). Revision can also be prompted through the formative responses of other readers, including an instructor or peers in your class. These responses are designed to give you information about *other* people's reading experiences that you can then use to improve your text.

In contrast to revision, *editing* means attending to more local concerns, such as your choice of words, the style and balance of your sentences, and the consistency with which you apply certain rules and conventions. Most publishing houses and journals have professional editors who work through manuscripts in order to bring them up to the standards of the press or journal. When you edit your own writing or your peers' writing, you look for inconsistencies, wrong or inappropriate word choices, awkward style, odd or incorrect syntax, and similar problems. The goal is to make the writing more readable and consistent.

Rhetorical appeals refer to three strategies in the art of persuasion: appealing to logic (logos), emotion (pathos), or the writer's credibility (ethos). Deriving from classical rhetoric, these appeals are the staple of many introductory writing courses. When you appeal to logos, you appeal to the reader's sense of logic; you argue using facts, evidence, and strategies such as deductive reasoning. When you appeal to pathos, you appeal to the reader's emotions and empathy, using strategies such as specific cases and examples or language that evokes emotions. When you appeal to ethos, you use strategies that convince the reader of your own credibility, expertise, or trust. See Chapter 4 for a detailed description of each appeal and its manifestations.

A **rubric** is set of criteria or expectations for a product—in this case, a piece of writing. It's designed to help guide the evaluation of the product, but it's also a very useful device for the creator of the product, who can use it to gauge success throughout the process. Rubrics usually take two forms. One form is called an *analytical rubric*, which consists of a set of features or characteristics that are scaled (e.g., with values such as "excellent," "good," "average," "poor," and "unacceptable," or "strong," "OK," and "needs work."). Characteristics can include organization, sophistication of ideas or content, quality of thesis, style, and grammar and mechanics. Figure 1 shows a simple analytical rubric for a literacy narrative (an assignment calling for an autobiographical account of one or more experiences developing the ability to read and write).

Criteria	Strong	OK	Needs Work
Sophistication in representing themes of literacy			
Focus			
Innovativeness in structure, style, or representation of content			
Evidence, but not forced, of a connection to ideas and concepts in the course so far			
Overall textual effectiveness (writing quality and style, description, dialogue, lack of error, and elements specific to this genre: authenticity, detail, story-like, open-endedness, showing and not telling)			

FIGURE 1 Sample Analytical Rubric for a Literacy Narrative

The second form of rubric is called *descriptive* or *holistic*. This kind of rubric describes the qualities associated with a piece of writing along a scale, from "most effective" on one end to "least effective" on the other end. Typical scales include "strong," "average," and "weak," or grading categories (A, B, C, D, F), or numbers. Figure 2 shows a descriptive rubric for a case study assignment in a Theology course.

A *strong paper* (90–100 points) will demonstrate clear understanding of the case by reporting it accurately and summarizing the essentials of the case. It will directly identify the main issue of the conflict. It will sort out the relevant from the irrelevant facts. It will take into account the context of the case and comment on its importance and implications, if applicable. It will identify what is not known and suggest areas where more information is needed and why. It will identify the major parties involved and attempt to offer sympathetic perspectives from their points of view while clearly stating why these views are important for a proper understanding of the case. It will offer a clear position of what the writer would do if she or he were in a similar leadership position. It will defend this position. If needed, it will consult outside sources in gathering that information (if possible). It will offer a revised third-level analysis that clearly articulates what was changed after class discussion and why. It will have little to no spelling, grammar, and/or syntax errors.

An *adequate paper* (70–89 points) will demonstrate a basic understanding of the case by reporting the majority of it accurately and summarizing many essentials of the case. It will make an attempt to address the main issue of the conflict. It will sort out most of the relevant facts but may include one or two irrelevant facts. It will address the context of the case but may not comment on its importance and implications, if applicable. It will identify at least one unknown item and will suggest an area where more information is needed but will not say why. It will identify some of the major parties involved and will attempt to offer sympathetic perspectives from their points of view but may not state why these views are important for a proper understanding of the case. It will offer a clear position of what the writer would do if she or he were in a similar leadership position but may not offer a defense of this. If needed, it may consult outside sources in gathering that information (if possible). It will offer a revised third-level analysis but may not articulate what was changed after class discussion and why. It may have only a few spelling, grammar, and/or syntax errors, but they will not distract the reader from the main content.

FIGURE 2 Sample Descriptive Rubric for a Case Study Assignment in a Theology Course

(*continued*)

A *weak paper* (0–69 points) will demonstrate a misunderstanding of the case, evidenced by an inaccurate summary of the majority of the case essentials. Little to no attempt will be made to address the main issue of the conflict. It will not sort out relevant facts, as evidenced by including many (more than two) irrelevant facts. There will be little to no mention of the context of the case or its importance and implications. It will identify little to no unknown information and will not suggest areas where more information is needed. It will identify very few, if any, of the major parties involved and will show no attempt to offer sympathetic perspectives from their points of view. It will offer a very vague personal position, if any, of what the writer would do if she or he were in a similar leadership position. It will give a vague defense, if any, of this position. It consults no outside sources in an attempt to gather missing information. It will not include a revised third-level analysis or an explanation of any or lack thereof. It may have several, grammar, and/or syntax errors to the point of distracting the reader from the main content.

FIGURE 2

A **search strategy** refers to a detailed plan for locating the best and most relevant sources for a research project, whether it involves primary or secondary research. When you begin a high-stakes research project and you're not sure yet what you want to study, it's fine for you to roam around a little in the literature before you decide on your focus. Sometimes the results can surprise you as you learn about new discoveries or perspectives relating to the general topic areas you're exploring. Eventually, though, when you've decided exactly what to study, you need to develop a strategy to find the best, most reliable, and most relevant resources for your project. Such a strategy will include a list of the indexes, search engines, and other tools that are best suited to the task. You should also create a plan to collect your information and work it into your schedule. Many students' projects suffer when the students wait too long to begin their search and have to desperately rush through the stacks in the library or pluck material at random from the Internet. The result is a paper that's weakly informed and sometimes includes barely relevant resources that are forced to fit into a paper that loses its coherence in proportion to the ill-fitting material. After creating a schedule and a plan to collect material, use the strategies outlined in Chapter 6 to read and annotate each source so that you can use it most effectively in your text.

Secondary research refers to the gathering of what scholars and researchers have done and said about the object under study—that is, what *they* have found in their own primary research. When you engage in secondary research, you synthesize existing scholarship instead of providing your own investigations of the object under study. See *Primary research*.

Self-evaluation refers to a process of standing back from your writing, often seeing it through the eyes of your intended or imagined readers, and then critically assessing its readability, structure, logic, style, clarity, coverage of information, and other features that are important to the genre and purpose of the writing. Make no mistake: this is often very difficult. First, your writing reflects the expression of *ideas*, and your mind wants to jump back into them without considering other people's experience reading your prose. That's fine—especially because you *do* want to get the ideas directly from your own perspective. But, eventually, force yourself to get outside yourself and begin thinking evaluatively about your draft. How does it hang together? How well does it read? How is it structured? A good way to self-evaluate is to look at the criteria that will be used to evaluate your writing and turn them into questions that you can ask of your own draft. Becoming a critical reader of your own writing, especially after you've generated a full draft and can consider it objectively, is a highly useful skill.

Self-sponsored writing is writing that you're motivated to do on your own, rather than as an assignment or work-related task. Most writing done in social media is self-sponsored—no one is forcing you to write, and you can decide when and how much to write, and for what purposes. Some people do a lot of self-sponsored writing, in a diary or journal, for example, or because they participate avidly in online discussions through various general or specialized forums, or because they like to write creatively, either alone or in the context of social media, such as fan fiction. In academic coursework, self-sponsored writing can take the form of a learning (b)log in which you write about your course material in order to explore it and learn it more thoroughly.

Semidrafting is the process of writing draft material that leaves gaps and/or instructions to yourself to work on in a future drafting episode when you have more time or information. When you semidraft, you write what you already know or can express at the time of your writing. You know that you need to stop and put energy into other things before you can move on (such as finding a reference, looking up a word, or remembering some specific detail that's not right at hand). But stopping also interrupts the flow of your writing—other ideas are stacked up waiting to be expressed, and if you go hunting for a specific quote in your notes somewhere, those ideas won't wait around for you. One common technique in semidrafting is to use brackets to indicate the bits and pieces you need to find and fill in (later), when you're done moving your text forward as much as you can. Here's an example:

> Dialects are mutually comprehensible varieties of a given language that represent regional/geographic or ethnic/cultural sets of features that differ from the normative, or standard, form of the language in systematic ways by the participants who speak them. [check on source and accuracy] An idiolect [continue here with description of personal varieties that are not shared by other members of a group—W. C. Fields?]

Structure of activity refers to the specific processes that an assignment requires and includes both mental processes, such as comparing two phenomena, and physical processes, such as taking notes. If your instructor doesn't explain the structure of activity that an assignment involves or doesn't lead you through that structure by engaging you in the activities, then you should try to map it out for yourself. Ask yourself what's required for each stage of the assignment. What do you need to do first? What knowledge do you need? How should you prepare for the first step? Do the same for each step or stage of the project. If terms like *analyze* are used, pull them apart. What does it mean to "analyze" in this context? How should you go about doing it?

Subjective flow refers to the effect of a draft's structure or organization on you or another reader from a purely impressionistic perspective. You allow yourself to experience the draft without bringing a lot of analysis to bear on it—you just *read* it, and then share your impressions of what happened in terms of its organization. What did you get first, second, and third from the draft? What sort of journey did the draft take you on, from scene to scene or from part to part?

A **summary** is a piece of text that condenses key information from a source—or sometimes the entire source—in the writer's own words, without replicating parts of the original text. When you work on a research paper or project, summary can be an effective way to incorporate other people's ideas and writing into your paper or project. You need to write about the work in your own words, capturing its main ideas or gist without a lot of excessive detail. It helps to read the work, such as an article, thoroughly beforehand. Then put it aside and ask yourself: What is this work about? What is its main point or conclusion? If you're writing a review of the research on a specific topic or question, what does the work you've consulted say about that topic or question?

Summative evaluation measures a final product or performance against some criteria, as a theater critic will do for the opening performance of the same play or musical that you received formative evaluation on during its earlier stages of rehearsal. In the context of writing, summative evaluation assigns a judgment—that is, a score, a grade, a thumbs-up or thumbs-down in a contest, or some other ranking that measures your paper or project against a set of criteria or against other papers and projects.

Support in writing refers to the evidence (facts, experience, data), logical reasoning, or other appeals you can use to convince readers that your thesis or other assertions are valid and that readers should accept them. Without support, your writing becomes mere opinion. Opinions alone are fine in a casual conversation, but they won't work well in an academic setting, where people expect you to back up your opinions with evidence and sound reasoning—that is, to *support* your assertions. Support comes in many forms, as described in Chapter 4, but some of the best and most powerful support resides in irrefutable facts and evidence. If you claim that using tax dollars to install fences along hundreds of miles of interstate highway will not only save the lives of many animals but also save the lives of many humans (who die in high-speed crashes into deer, for example), then having statistics showing this will go a long way toward convincing people of your claim. (Convincing them that it's worth the cost of the fencing—which itself needs a very reliable estimate—to save one or two lives a year from crashes into errant deer is another matter. How much is one life worth? Who is willing to pay for it?)

A **thesis** is the central organizing idea or argument in a piece of writing. In much academic writing, the thesis is clearly identifiable, usually appearing somewhere early in the text (at the end of the first paragraph of a shorter essay or the introduction of a longer essay or article). However, as explained in Chapter 4, theses can appear in different places in a text; some kinds of writing, for example, "lead up" to the thesis, which is really a conclusion about what's been discussed or discovered.

Many teachers are attracted to thesis statements because they want to know, in short order and at the start of your paper, just what it is that you intend to demonstrate, argue, or document. Unless the genre of your writing doesn't call for a thesis statement (such as a dialogue between two theorists, as described in Chapter 3), it won't hurt you to include a carefully written thesis somewhere at the start of your paper.

Transfer in writing theory refers to the deployment of existing knowledge and skills (for writing) to a new situation—for example, when a student uses the knowledge gained in a General Composition course to write a thesis statement for a paper in a Psychology course. But writing in the new setting may be unfamiliar. It's rarely the case that you can just effortlessly adapt your skills to a new setting; you need to consciously and intentionally think about and analyze the requirements of the new setting and see what you already know—what prior knowledge you bring—that can apply there. If the writing is very unfamiliar, you'll need to analyze how it works (as shown in Chapter 7) and then, through at least some trial and error, learn how to write effectively in the new setting. The term *transfer* is itself somewhat problematic, although it's used here because it's so common and familiar; a more accurate term might be *adaptation or transition*.

A **working bibliography** is a list of all the sources to be used in a research project. It can be organized alphabetically, categorically, or by the sections of a paper. It may not represent the final bibliography because some works maybe deleted or added. Think of it as a constantly evolving document that represents your search at particular stages. As you add references to your bibliography, look for ways to organize them into subcategories or headings, or include notes that tell you where each work will fit best in the project. Annotating (writing summaries) of each work will also help to jog your memory as you're putting together a literature review or deciding how and where to incorporate the work into your paper.

A **zero draft,** or **writer-based draft,** is a draft of a high-stakes writing project that you write mainly to yourself as audience in order to reduce, for the time being, some of the pressure of getting everything "right" for a demanding audience. Sometimes thinking too much about your audience can be paralyzing, stopping the flow of your writing at each turn. Writing to and for yourself first can free you from the constraints of your (demanding) audience, and many writers report that doing so leads to better writing because from the start it's less preoccupied with "sounding smart" or appealing to all the needs and dispositions of readers. If you suffer from writer's block or worry all the time about how your reader will respond to each sentence you write, try writing as if you were the only reader. Entertain, enlighten, and inform yourself first, and your writing may flourish in unexpected ways.

Credits

p. 9, Fig. 1.1: Werner, Robert, "A Section of the Online Syllabus from Global Migrations." University of St. Thomas. Used with permission.

p. 14: "Quantitative Chemical Analysis." Reprinted with permission from Encyclopædia Britannica, © 2015 by Encyclopædia Britannica, Inc.

p. 14: The Writing Center at The University of North Carolina Chapel Hill, http://writingcenter.unc.edu/handouts/art-history/

p. 14: The Writing Center at The University of North Carolina Chapel Hill, http://writingcenter.unc.edu/handouts/political-science/

p. 14: The Writing Center at The University of North Carolina Chapel Hill, http://writingcenter.unc.edu/handouts/sociology/

p. 20: Keil, Christian. Newcomb's Problem and Expected Utility, University of Michigan, From Econ/Phil 408, http://www.lsa.umich.edu/sweetland/undergraduate/writingprizes/2011prizes

p. 20: Soderborg, Seth. The Effects of Conditional Cash Transfer Payments on Voter Support for the Partido dos Trabalhadores, University of Michigan, PolSci 381, http://www.lsa.umich.edu/sweetland/undergraduate/writingprizes/2011prizes

p. 23: Hedberg, Patricia R. Personal correspondence. Used with permission.

p. 24: Getman-Eraso, Jordi, Two assignments from the handbook created for the Writing Across the Curriculum Program at CUNY — Bronx Community College. Used with permission.

p. 24: Getman-Eraso, Jordi, Two assignments from the handbook created for the Writing Across the Curriculum Program at CUNY — Bronx Community College. Used with permission.

p. 27: Saavedra, Luz, Rubric. Used with permission.

p. 31: Connery, Brian A. Using Journals in the Cross-Curricular Course: Restoring Process, *Journal of Advanced Composition*, Vol. 8, 2014.

p. 48: Ray, Sarah. Academic Forum. Used with permission.

p. 49: Lutfy, Christine, Academic Forum. Used with permission.

p. 52: Hatton, N., Smith, D. (1995). Reflection in Teacher Education: Towards Definition and Implementation. The University of Sydney: School of Teaching and Curriculum Studies.

p. 64: Scott, Professor Britain. Course on Gender and Psychology. University of St. Thomas. Used with permission.

p. 65: Cavert, William, Microtheme assignment from a course in World History. University of St. Thomas. Used with permission.

p. 68: Bean, John. *Engaging Ideas*, 2e, p. 16. Jossey-Bass; 2nd Edition. September 6, 2011.

p. 72: Lane, K., Maria D. Writing assignment from "Geography of New Mexico and the Southwest." University of New Mexico, Department of Geography and Environmental Studies. January 2010. Used with permission.

p. 74: Cohen, Charles L. "The Fifty-Word Assignment," University of Wisconsin Writing Across the Curriculum, http://writing.wisc.edu/wac/node/64

p. 81: Summers, Gerald. Excerpt from invertebrate zoology class assignment. Used with permission.

p. 98: Lawrence, Todd, Assignment from ENGL 202 — Folklore and Literature. Used with permission.

p. 109, Fig 4.7: Zoe, Charmaine, "A Mindmap About the Brain." Reprinted with permission.

p. 143, Fig. 5.1: Fried, Jason. "Copyediting: Man vs. Machine" August 27, 2009. Reprinted with permission. https://signalvnoise.com/posts/1879-copyediting-man-vs-machine

p. 149, Fig. 5.2: Hendrickx-Solberg, Melissa, "Evaluation Criteria for an Anthropology Interview Paper." Used with permission.

p. 164, Fig. 5.3: Lamb, Melissa. Courtesy of Dr. Melissa Lamb, Professor, Interim Environmental Science Director, Geology Department, University of St. Thomas.

p. 179: The American Political Science Association, http://www.apsanet.org/ABOUT/About-APSA. Reprinted with permission.

p. 179: The Entomological Society of America, http://www.entsoc.org/about_esa. Reprinted with permission.

p. 216: Miller, Merle. *Plain Speaking: An Oral Biography of Harry S. Truman,* Random House, 2005.

p. 217: Miller, Baila, Stephanie McFall, and Richard T. Campbell. "Changes in Sources of Community Long-Term Care Among African American and White Frail Older Persons." *Journal of Gerontology*: 1994, Vol. 49, No. 1, S14-S24.

p. 218: Mossman, Mark. "Representations of the Abnormal Body" in "The Moonstone" [in *Victorial Literature and Culture,* Vol. 37, No. 2 (2009), pp. 483-500].

p. 242: University of Toronto Press Journals, http://www.utpjournals.com/Ultimate-Reality-and-Meaning.html Reprinted with permission.

p. 254, Fig. 7.2: Hall, Andrew B, "What Happens when Extremists Win Primaries" in *American Political Science Review,* Vol 109, No. 1, Feb 1, 2015. Copyright © 2015 American Political Science Association. Reprinted with permission of Cambridge University Press.

p. 255, Fig. 7.3: Younson, Justine et al. "A Human Domain Antibody and Lewis[b] Glycoconjugate That Inhibit Binding of *Helicobacter pylori* to Lewis[b] Receptor and Adhesion to Human Gastric Epithelium," *Journal of Infectious Diseases* (2009) 200 (10): 1574-1582. p.1581. By permission of Oxford University Press.

p. 258: Drum, Kevin, "America's Real Criminal Element: Lead" in *Mother Jones,* January/February 2013. Reprinted with permission.

p. 258: Haberman, Cory P. and Jerry H. Ratcliffe, "Testing for Temporally Differentiated Relationships Among Potentially Criminogenetic Places and Census Block Street Robbery Counts" in *Criminology,* Aug 2015, Vol 53, No. 3, Wiley-Blackwell.

p. 259: Thomas, Lewis. *Lives of a Cell: Notes of a Biology Watcher,* Penquin Books, 1978.

p. 264: Veklych, Bogdan, "A One-Formula Proof of the Nonvanishing of L-Functions of Real Characters at 1," *Amer. Math. Monthly,* 122, #5 (May 2015), 484–485. Copyright 2015 Mathematical Association of America. All Rights Reserved. Reprinted with permission.

p. 274: Smyth, Joshua; True, Nicole; Souto, Joy. Effects of Writing About Traumatic Experiences: The Necessity for Narrative Structuring. *Journal of Social and Clinical Psychology:* Vol. 20, No. 2, pp. 161–172. doi: 10.1521/jscp.20.2.161.22266. (2001). Reprinted with permission.

p. 293: Codr, Dwight, "Arresting Monstrosity: Polio, Frankenstein, and the Other Horror Film." Reprinted by permission of copyright owner, the Modern Language Association of America, from "Arresting Monstrosity: Polio, Frankenstein, and the Other Horror Film." *PMLA* (2014): 171–87.

p. 293: *The Johns Hopkins Guide to Literary Theory and Criticism,* ed. Michael Groden and Martin Kreiswirth. Johns Hopkins University Press; 2nd Edition, November 3, 2004.

Photo Credits

p. 94: Williams, Stuart, Markup. Photo by Tim Bray. Handwritten annotations by Stuart Williams.

p. 297: Courtesy of Ruth Lilly Special Collections and Archives, IUPUI University Library.

p. 311: Frame from "In Daily Battle" (1947). Courtesy of the March of Dimes Foundation, White Plains, New York.

p. 312: AF archive/Alamy

p. 315: Frame from "In Daily Battle" (1947). Courtesy of the March of Dimes Foundation, White Plains, New York.

p. 316: Frame from "In Daily Battle" (1947). Courtesy of the March of Dimes Foundation, White Plains, New York.

Index

lore, use of, 117
Lorenz, Konrad, 88
low-stakes writing
  academic journal, example of, 35–37
  academic journal, tips for writing,
    45–46
  academic journal, uses for, 38–45
  defined, 32, 336
  example of, 31
  forums and dialogues, 46–50
  functions of, 23–26, 32
  learning blogs, example of,
    35–37
  learning blogs, tips for writing,
    45–46
  learning blogs, uses for, 38–45
  as preparation for formal writing,
    44–45
  Putting It into Practice, 56
  reflection, value of, 51–56
  writing to learn, 33–35

M

mathematical proof, text example,
  262–267
Meister, 108
metaknowledge, 16–18, 336–337
microthemes
  analysis, 77–79
  audience decisions, 67–68
  critical thinking and, 74–89
  defined, 57, 337
  evaluation (informed judgment),
    81–87
  fact-finding, 75–77
  formality, level of, 65–66
  form of, 61–63
  interpretation and, 87–89
  overview of, 56–60
  purpose or goal of, 63–65
  Putting It into Practice, 90
  structure of activity, 68–74
  synthesis, 80–81
mind mapping, 107–109

minicases, 59
MLA. *See* Modern Language
    Association (MLA) citation style
modeling, 17–18, 337
Modern Language Association (MLA)
    citation style, 226–231, 291
multimedia web projects, drafting
    process, 137

N

near-transfer, 97
Newton, Sir Isaac, 80
note-taking, academic journaling
    and, 40–43

O

objective shape, 151, 152–153,
    338
observations, use of, 116
open-ended thesis, 112
opinion, 86, 117
organization of text
  communities of practice, 19–22
  comparison of texts, 246–248
  draft revisions, structure, 151–154
  example text, literary and film
    analysis, 289–290
  example text, mathematical proof,
    262
  example text, social-psychological
    study, 269–270
  IMRAD formula, 132
  objective shape, 151, 152–153, 338
  organizational patterns, 122–123
  organizational trees, 124–127
  outlines, 127–133
  subjective flow, 151, 152
outlines, 127–133

P

paraphrasing, 206–210, 215, 338
parenthetical documentation,
    224–225